LIVING OFF THE GOVERNMENT?

Living Off the Government?

Race, Gender, and the Politics of Welfare

Anne M. Whitesell

NEW YORK UNIVERSITY PRESS

New York

NEW YORK UNIVERSITY PRESS
New York
www.nyupress.org

© 2024 by New York University
Please contact the Library of Congress for Cataloging-in-Publication data.

ISBN: 9781479828562 (hardback)

ISBN: 9781479828586 (paperback)

ISBN: 9781479828609 (library ebook)

ISBN: 9781479828593 (consumer ebook)

This book is printed on acid-free paper, and its binding materials are chosen for strength and durability. We strive to use environmentally responsible suppliers and materials to the greatest extent possible in publishing our books.

Manufactured in the United States of America

10 9 8 7 6 5 4 3 2 1

Also available as an ebook

CONTENTS

1

The Undeserving Poor

A Brief History of Government Assistance

On March 25, 2020, the 116th US Congress passed the Coronavirus Aid, Relief, and Economic Security (CARES) Act, a $2.2 trillion economic stimulus package that was designed to address the economic fallout of the COVID-19 pandemic. This historic bill, which was passed with remarkable speed and bipartisan support, distributed direct relief payments to American families, providing up to $1,200 per adult and $500 per child, among several other provisions.

"Under the CARES Act, we're sending direct payments to millions of American workers," President Trump announced in April 2020, speaking at a Coronavirus Task Force briefing. "That's great. And you deserve it." Emphasizing this notion of deservingness, he added that these payments would let "each American know that we are getting through this challenge together as one . . . family."[1]

Across three aid packages, under two presidential administrations, Americans would ultimately receive more than $900 billion in government assistance. However, the scale of government aid provided to Americans during the COVID-19 pandemic, and the broad political support it received, was more the exception than the norm, representing an aberration in our social safety net. First, the sheer amount of money spent dwarfed previous stimulus plans. Part of this was due to the size of the payments, but also to their broad terms of eligibility. Individuals making less than $75,000 a year, and households making less than $150,000 were eligible for the full payment; payments were gradually phased out for those whose incomes were higher than the thresholds.[2] The economic impact payments, while technically "means tested," had income thresholds high enough to encompass much of the middle class. The widespread support for the payments among both elites and the public was also unfamiliar. The last time Americans had received stimulus payments from the federal government, in 2009, public opinion was split on whether they were a good idea. In contrast, in April 2020 nearly nine in ten Americans believed the payments were the right thing to do, and a majority thought more than one payment would be necessary.[3]

Temporary Assistance for Needy Families

The size of the COVID economic relief packages and the support behind them stand in stark contrast to the federal government's traditional position toward welfare reform, which began as a bipartisan effort in the 1990s. Bill Clinton, accepting the Democratic presidential nomination in July 1992, declared that those on welfare needed to liberate themselves "because welfare should be a second chance, not a way of life."[4] The Clinton administration released its welfare reform plan, the Work and Responsibility Act, in June 1994.[5] Just a few months later, Republican congressional candidates pledged their support for a "Contract with America," which promised to bring to a vote legislation that would cut welfare spending, limit receipt of welfare to two years, and include work requirements.[6] The Contract with America proposal, complete with a lifetime limit on welfare benefits and activity requirement, was introduced at the beginning of the 104th Congress in January 1995 as HR 4.

It would take until November 1995 for the first attempt at welfare reform to pass, as HR 4 was combined with the budget reconciliation package. President Clinton vetoed the legislation because of budget cuts made to Medicare, Medicaid, and the Earned Income Tax Credit (EITC). Clinton also vetoed a second version of the bill in January 1996, but signaled he was open to the Senate's version of the bill.[7] As with the first veto, Clinton was opposed to spending cuts to other safety net programs. Notably, Clinton's concerns were never about whether welfare reform provided enough assistance to struggling families, or whether the program's requirements represented government overreach into the lives of low-income women. In fact, his original proposal would have barred unwed minor parents from receiving benefits, and his administration permitted waivers that allowed many states to experiment with what would eventually become national policy.[8]

Republican leadership introduced HR 3734, the Personal Responsibility and Work Opportunity Reconciliation Act (PRWORA), in June 1996. The greatest pushback to the legislation came from Congresswomen of color, but they largely felt ignored. Representative Patsy Mink, who served on the Democratic taskforce on welfare reform, said she tried to represent the interests of "poor women who have no representation in Congress . . . and who are left out in much of this debate" but was constantly butting heads with the administration.[9] Similarly, Representative Barbara Rose Collins spoke from her experience knowing people who received welfare, but felt "nobody was interested in listening."[10] Meanwhile, prominent feminists in Congress, including Nita Lowey and Barbara Kennelly, voted in favor of the final bill. Gwendolyn Mink argues feminist support for welfare reform comes from white, middle-class feminists' inability to separate their own fight for access to the workplace with poor mothers' obligation to do so.[11] This tension, between women of color in Congress who often spoke from personal experience and their white women colleagues, reflected a decades-long disagreement over the priorities of the women's movement.

Clinton announced in July that he would support PRWORA, giving Democrats political cover to vote for the legislation. Ultimately, Democrats in Congress were split on the legislation that ended welfare as an entitlement. Many of those who voted in favor were up for reelection, and those who voted in opposition were some of the more progressive members of the Democratic caucus.[12] PRWORA was signed into law on August 22, 1996, replacing Aid to Families with Dependent Children (AFDC) with Temporary Assistance for Needy Family (TANF).

Among the many changes related to federal cash assistance programs was a change in the funding structure. Prior to PRWORA, each state received a matching grant to cover the costs of providing assistance to AFDC families; as the caseload for a state increased or decreased, so did the amount of aid from the federal government. In replacing AFDC with TANF, though, Congress established a block grant, in which states would receive a set amount of funding, regardless of the number of cases enrolled in a given year. As of 2021, the annual spending available through the TANF block grant was $16.5 billion; that level has remained flat since TANF was enacted in 1996.[13] This funding structure is one of several ways that states are incentivized to reduce the number of people receiving aid.

In the years immediately following the passage of welfare reform, states spent the majority of their TANF block grants on cash assistance for needy families. Over time though, the percentage of funding going directly to recipients in the form of cash aid has decreased; in 2021, states spent on average only 23 percent of their grants on basic assistance.[14] Large portions of the block grants are instead allocated toward other programs that meet one of TANF's four purposes: provide assistance to needy families, encourage self-sufficiency through work, reduce out-of-wedlock pregnancies, and promote two-parent families.[15] Moreover, states often use their funding to provide the supports necessary for TANF recipients to meet work requirements. As a result, low monthly payments have been a characteristic of TANF since its inception. The median monthly payment for a TANF family of three in 2021 was $498, or $5,976 annually.[16]

Just months before President Trump would tell Americans that they "deserved" an economic impact payment, the Trump administration touted the seven hundred thousand Americans removed from the TANF rolls since the 2016 election as evidence of "increasing self-reliance through economic activity while decreasing reliance on government programs."[17] The administration's support for shrinking cash assistance programs reflected the broader view of the Republican Party establishment and its voters. The 2016 Republican Party platform offered a fond reflection on welfare reform: "By making welfare a benefit instead of an entitlement, it put millions of recipients on a transition from dependence to independence." At the same time, the party expressed fear that President Obama had "made TANF a mockery" by encouraging people to remain dependent on the government.[18] That same year, 64 percent of Republicans surveyed by the General Social Survey (GSS) said the United States spends too much on welfare.[19]

Deservingness throughout American History

For decades, politicians have decried the abuse of government programs by those who do not truly need help. Speaking before a joint session of Congress shortly after taking office in 1981, President Ronald Reagan reassured lawmakers that "those who, through no fault of their own, must depend on the rest of us—the poverty stricken, the disabled, the elderly, all those with true need" would not see any cuts made to their social safety net programs. The food stamp program and welfare needed reform, however, to remove "from eligibility those who are not in *real need* or are abusing the program" (emphasis added).[20] In laying out his economic plan, Reagan drew a sharp distinction between those citizens who are deemed deserving of government assistance and those who are seen as undeserving. Reagan was not the first president to make such a distinction; in fact, separating the deserving from the undeserving has a long history in the United States.

The American political system has been plagued by inequalities since its beginning. While the common narrative is that the United States has a government "of the people, by the people, for the people," historically this has not been true. The country has made progress in the nearly 250 years since declaring independence from the British, ending slavery and expanding the franchise. The fact remains that those who are marginalized because of their race, ethnicity, gender identity, socioeconomic status, and a host of other characteristics have less of a voice in the American political system. Those whose identities lie at the intersection of multiple axes of marginalization have even less of a voice. The government is not of them, by them, or for them.

This discrepancy is evident in the provision of government assistance. The United States has never been a welfare state like some of its Western European counterparts. The strong belief in individualism and a "pull yourself up by your bootstraps" mentality means that as other countries developed more comprehensive social safety nets the United States lagged behind. As explained in further detail below, there are some exceptions to this—policymakers created programs to provide assistance to populations perceived as being "deserving" of government help. Who is deemed deserving, however, is shaped by the same biases that create an unequal American political system.

The recipients of government assistance, from military veterans to low-income families with children, can be placed along a continuum of deservingness (see figure 1.1). Some of these groups are inherently seen as deserving of aid, and as a result, there is both less need for advocates to fight for their benefits and more people willing to express their support. In contrast, TANF recipients are seen as some of the least

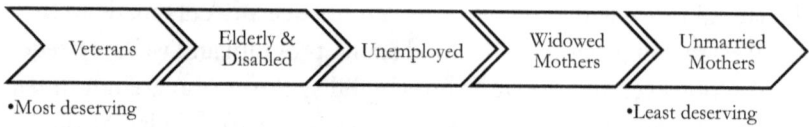

•Most deserving   •Least deserving

Figure 1.1. Continuum of Deservingness

deserving of government aid. This has serious implications for their political representation and the policies that target them.

Scholars writing on the notion of what qualifies certain populations as "deserving" of assistance have noted its roots in the American value of individualism, as well as compliance with the "family ethic" and acquiescence to the patriarchy.[21] The underlying assumption of American individualism is that individuals are responsible for themselves and prosperity awaits anyone willing to use their talents and energy; nothing is owed to them by society.[22] Surveys from the 1980s show that the vast majority of respondents believe that people, rather than the government, are responsible for their own well-being.[23] This is certainly not a new phenomenon; "Calvinist ideas about the virtues of hard work and the sin of idleness" prevailed in the Massachusetts Bay Company.[24] Colonial poor laws drew on these ideas through an emphasis on a strong work ethic and self-discipline. The importance of self-reliance continued after independence; Alexis de Tocqueville wrote in *Democracy in America* that Americans "form the habit of thinking of themselves in isolation and imagine that their whole destiny is in their own hands."[25] As the country became more industrialized, prominent figures such as Thomas Edison stressed the importance of hard work.[26] The inability to support oneself through hard work, and the acceptance of public assistance, "became a sign of individual failure."[27]

Exceptions to the principle of individualism are made for those who have a history of being responsible for themselves, but can no longer be expected to do so. This most prominently includes military veterans and the aged. Military veterans are seen as deserving of government aid because of their prior service to the country. In her book *Protecting Soldiers and Mothers*, Theda Skocpol writes that pensions paid out to Civil War veterans in the late nineteenth century were some of the "politically most successful social policies ever devised in the United States."[28] The program benefited families across class and racial lines because soldiers

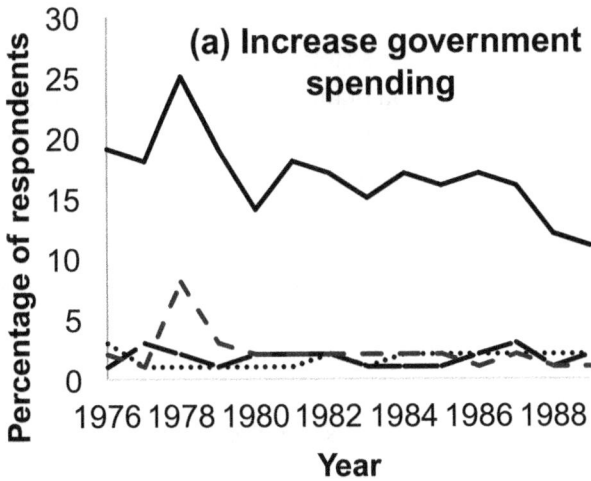

(a) Increase government spending

Percentage of respondents

1976 1978 1980 1982 1984 1986 1988

Year

— · — Aid to Veterans ——— Aid to Elderly

········· Welfare — — — Aid to Disabled

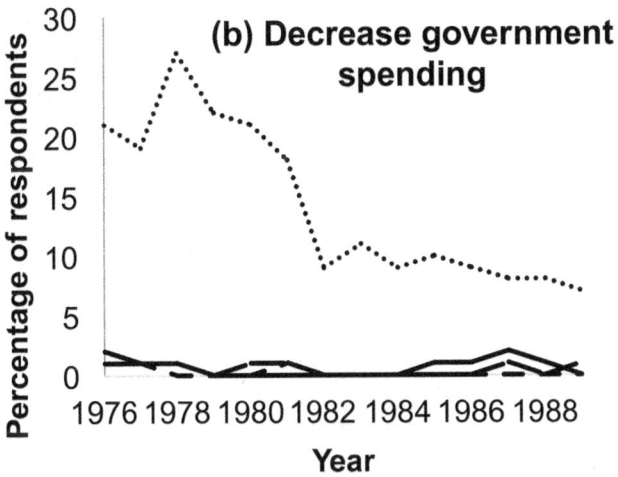

(b) Decrease government spending

Percentage of respondents

1976 1978 1980 1982 1984 1986 1988

Year

— · — Aid to Veterans ——— Aid to Elderly

········· Welfare — — — Aid to Disabled

Figures 1.2a–b. "In which area would you like to increase/decrease government spending?"
Source: Cambridge Reports/National Omnibus Survey, 1976–1989.

had "earned" their benefits; distribution of Civil War pensions did not have the negative connotation of involving "charity" or "welfare."[29] Providing support for veterans remained popular; in a 1937 Gallup poll, over 70 percent of respondents favored providing pensions for World War veterans.[30] Even when American military interventions are unpopular, the public broadly supports those who serve in the military. Americans' rhetoric around "supporting the troops" appears to extend to providing financial support. In a 2019 Pew survey, over 70 percent of both Democrats and Republicans said they would increase spending for veterans' benefits.[31]

Figures 1.2a–b show the results of public opinion polls that ask respondents to identify in which areas they would like to increase government spending.[32] As is clear from the graph, Americans look at aid to the elderly favorably; the history of old age insurance in the United States suggests that the elderly are generally seen as deserving of government aid as well. The American Federation of Labor (AFL) endorsed national, need-based old age pensions by 1909, and endorsed the principle of state-level old age pensions in the 1920s.[33] In one of the first resolutions to address the topic, a delegate to the AFL Convention wrote: "When a man gets old and worn out [. . .] he finds it hard and often impossible to get work, which failure tends sometimes to reduce him to pauperism, to an object of charity and to the poorhouse." Therefore, he argued, the AFL should endorse "an old-age pension law that will do for the aged who have given so much to the industrial struggle what the soldier's pension is designed to do for the old soldier."[34] Notably, however, the old age programs run by the states in the 1920s and 1930s often denied aid to individuals deemed "undeserving" for a variety of reasons, from failing to support their families to having been convicted of a crime. Furthermore, applicants with children or relatives who could provide financial support were also disqualified from receiving aid.[35]

Social Security is the program that most strongly reflects the types of pension plans the AFL endorsed in the early twentieth century. The program, established in 1935, provides benefits for those who lose income due to retirement, disability, or the death of a family member, and is funded by a payroll tax paid by employees and employers. Even when the Social Security Act was passed during the Great Depression, politicians stressed that the public aid programs created under the act would not change the economic status quo. One sponsor of the bill stated that the law "does not alter at all the fundamentals of our capitalistic and individualistic economy" and it would not "relieve the individual of primary responsibility for his [sic] own support and that of his dependents."[36] Today, Social Security is the most expensive and most generous safety net program in the United States.[37] Despite its large price tag, the American people continue to support Social Security; since 1998, more than 50 percent of GSS survey respondents have consistently said that the country spends too little on the program.[38] Social Security recipients, in addition to being elderly, are also retired workers. Because they have "paid into the system," they are generally regarded as deserving of these benefits upon retirement.

Veterans are seen as deserving because of their service to the country, and the elderly and disabled are generally considered deserving because their circumstances make it difficult for them to support themselves financially. What about the unemployed, though, who theoretically should be able to find a job? There is a range of deservingness among those who need financial assistance because they are unemployed, with those who have recent connections to the labor market seen as the most deserving of aid. For instance, unemployment insurance recipients can be seen as more deserving than adults receiving General Assistance because the former have a more immediate connection to the labor market. General Assistance is seen as a "program of last resort" for poor adults without dependent children.[39] As Patricia Ventura writes, unemployment insurance remains crucial for the survival of many Americans during hard economic times, but "welfare holds a symbolic significance because it is general cash assistance and not funds to be spent in very circumscribed ways or over intensely short periods."[40] Veterans, retired workers, and the unemployed benefit from participating in a "social insurance" program, but those receiving cash assistance are relegated to social policies that many view as serving only the dependent.[41]

Gender and the (Un)deserving Poor

Feminist scholars argue that America's social welfare system, in addition to placing a strong emphasis on individualism, relies on assumptions about a patriarchal system.[42] Mimi Abramovitz describes deservingness as being in alignment with traditional family values, or the "family ethic," which draws from the "gender-based division of society into public and private spheres."[43] Both capitalism, in the public sphere, and patriarchy, in the private sphere, have put women at the bottom of the hierarchy. Miller extends upon Abramovitz's argument, stating that women who do not conform with the family ethic—such as lesbians, unmarried mothers, and divorced women—are punished for their manlessness, while women who follow the family ethic are able to sustain a comfortable life.[44] Mettler argues that gender bias became institutionalized during the New Deal era as policymakers created two tracks of social policy: one set of policies regulated at the national level and applicable to "independent citizens" and a second set of policies implemented at the state level for "dependents."[45]

This bias stretches back hundreds of years—women with an established family were offered aid by colonial governments, while undeserving women were forced to work in exchange for aid.[46] Women's economic self-sufficiency was limited because of protective labor legislation and pay discrimination.[47] The bias in favor of the traditional familial structure and against those who do not meet the norm continues to play out today in the distribution of social welfare benefits. Social Security presents a bias against single adults, for instance, because their dependents are not covered as family members.[48] In the following section, I review which women have been eligible for public assistance and explain how views on their deservingness have shifted over time, thus changing the ways they are represented politically.

Mothers' Pensions

Prior to the passage of the Social Security Act of 1935 that established Aid to Dependent Children, the only programs specifically designated for poor women and their children were mothers' pensions distributed by state and local governments.[49] The first statewide mothers' pension law was passed in Illinois in 1911, and within two years seventeen more states had adopted similar legislation.[50] Mothers' pensions were designed to keep the mother in the home, performing domestic duties, and out of the labor force.[51] Reformers during the Progressive Era were concerned that women working outside the home would have an adverse effect on their children and lead to the disintegration of the family unit.[52] All mothers, poor women included, were to have the means to "provide each newborn soul with an environment which will foster its highest development."[53] Moreover, given the choice, children should be kept with their mothers rather than turned over to the state; even a "very poor home" offered a better opportunity for a child than "an excellent institution."[54]

At the 1909 White House Conference on Children, policymakers stated that mothers' aid would be distributed only to the children of "worthy" parents.[55] In a report on the progress of mothers' pensions, the Children's Bureau of the US Department of Labor reported that in a number of states a family wishing to receive aid must prove that "the home will be a satisfactory place for the rearing of children."[56] In practical terms, this meant that widows were generally seen as more deserving of aid than mothers who had children out of wedlock. Recipients of mothers' pensions were also overwhelmingly white, with only 4 percent of recipients belonging to racial or ethnic minority groups.[57]

While widows were the primary recipients of mothers' pensions (over 80 percent of the caseload in 1931), aid was extended to women in other circumstances. Ten states granted aid to all kinds of needy mothers, including divorced women, deserted wives, and women whose husbands were mentally or physically incapacitated or incarcerated. Implicit in these policies was the belief that it was tolerable for women not to have a husband if it was due to death, but divorce or desertion was less acceptable.[58] As of 1931, only three states explicitly allowed unmarried women to receive aid—Michigan allowed unmarried mothers to receive aid beginning in 1913, while Nebraska and Tennessee extended eligibility later.[59] Even when they could receive aid, women who were not widows were often subjected to household visits by welfare officials to ensure that they were raising their children in a "suitable home."[60]

Mothers' pensions received support from a variety of organized interests. The AFL endorsed a mothers' pension resolution in 1911, and it began playing an active role in promoting legislation in the 1920s.[61] Women's organizations, comprised of middle-class and elite women, were the driving force behind mothers' aid legislation. Such organizations included the National Consumers' League, General Federation of Women's Clubs (GFWC), and National Congress of Mothers, sometimes working independently and at other times working in coalitions to advocate for mothers' pension legislation.[62] State-level groups instrumental in passing reforms included the Women's Suffrage League of Virginia and the Women's Christian Temperance Union in Tennessee.[63] Speaking at the Second International Congress on Child Welfare, Mrs. G. Harris Robertson, representing the Tennessee Congress of Mothers, argued that the mother should be honored "wherever found—if she has given a citizen to the nation, then the nation owes something to her."[64] Between 1911 and 1920, forty states enacted mothers' pension laws, in no small part due to the activism of these organizations.[65] As I will describe in more detail in chapter 2, this is just the first example of organizations advocating on behalf of aid recipients for policies that will materially affect them.

Aid to (Families with) Dependent Children

Created under the Social Security Act, Aid to Dependent Children (later renamed Aid to Families with Dependent Children, or AFDC) provided the first federal support for low-income families.[66] Similar to mothers' pensions, policymakers in the Children's Bureau believed that state and local government should bear most of the responsibility for the programs, with the new addition of federal grants.[67] Within a matter of years, however, the ADC caseload differed significantly from the families receiving mothers' pensions. Under the 1939 Social Security amendments, widows and their children were now eligible to receive Survivor's Insurance (SI).[68] These two programs—SI and ADC—created two subsets of poor mothers and their children, in which the former is seen as deserving and the latter is seen as undeserving. The difference in deservingness can be seen in the benefit trends for SI and AFDC recipients. Between 1970 and 1990, the benefits for children covered under SI increased by 53 percent, while the benefits for children in AFDC families decreased by 13 percent.[69]

As widows and their children were diverted from the ADC rolls, divorced and never married women constituted a larger proportion of welfare recipients; from 1938 to 1948, the percentage of children with unmarried mothers on ADC increased from 2 percent to 14 percent.[70] This, in turn, led to the perception that welfare was a program for morally corrupt single mothers. The welfare caseload was also increasing at a quicker rate than the population. From 1960 to 1971, the number of welfare recipients tripled from three to ten million.[71]

Public opinion on the issue of welfare was also changing, with many Americans believing that welfare recipients were "on relief for dishonest reasons."[72] The results of many surveys in the 1970s and 1980s suggested the general public thought the government was spending too much on welfare.[73] As shown in figure 1.2b, in the late 1970s about 20 percent of survey respondents thought the government should decrease spending on welfare, while no more than 2 percent of respondents said spending on other types of assistance should decrease. Even as the percentage of respondents who felt that welfare spending should decrease declined in the 1980s, it was still several times greater than the percentage of respondents who favored decreasing spending for other groups. There was a growing concern that recipients were becoming dependent on government assistance; a 1986 White House report referred to AFDC as "an enabler—a program which enables women to live without a husband or a job."[74]

These stereotypes are epitomized by Ronald Reagan's story about a "welfare queen" in Chicago who drove a Cadillac and financed her lifestyle by collecting welfare payments, as well as nutrition assistance and Social Security payments, under eighty different names.[75] In reality, Reagan's "welfare queen" was a composite character—bringing together all the worst traits from infamous welfare fraud cases—but the image had a lasting effect. The welfare queen was framed as a "grasping woman" who "takes more than her share" and saw herself as exempt from needing a husband or a job.[76] A majority of Americans believed that welfare recipients preferred to live on welfare, or had more children to stay on welfare.[77] Media reinforced this stereotype by tying use of state assistance to laziness and abuse or fraud.[78] In 1988, Congress passed the Family Support Act, which required states to enroll 15 percent of AFDC recipients in job training or basic skills programs.[79] Campaigning for president in 1992, Bill Clinton made welfare reform one of his key issues, and when he took office, he promised to "end welfare as we know it."[80] With politicians from both political parties questioning the motives of welfare recipients, the nation was primed for reform.

Temporary Assistance for Needy Families

The welfare system under AFDC was "designed to perpetuate a system in which women's place is in the nuclear family."[81] These goals continue implicitly in TANF; the program's stated goals include reducing the incidence of out-of-wedlock births and promoting two-parent families.[82] Prior to PRWORA, abortion rates were declining but out-of-wedlock births were increasing. Policymakers were concerned about the promiscuity of welfare recipients and the possibility that women were having children to stay on welfare, thus creating a cycle of poverty. PRWORA provided an "illegitimacy bonus" for the five states that reduced unwed births the most without increasing abortion. The benefits were based on the birth and abortion rates for all women in the state, not just welfare recipients, even though women in the middle and upper classes are more likely to have abortions and give birth out of wedlock than low-income women.[83] Under PRWORA, Congress allocated $250 million for states to develop abstinence-only sex education programs.[84] To promote state programs that encouraged the formation of two-parent families, the Department of Health and Human Services established a $10 million high performance bonus for states that saw the greatest increase in the percentage of children residing in two-parent households.[85] Congress reinforced the importance of two-parent families in the Deficit Reduction Act through increased funding for "responsible fatherhood" programs. Underlying both measures is the assumption that marriage is the best solution to poverty.

Unlike its predecessor though, TANF is not set up to keep mothers inside the home as full-time caregivers. The program, as Scott Allard describes it, "provides most assistance through social service programs supporting work activity" rather than delivering welfare checks.[86] Recipients are required to engage in work activities, typically for thirty hours a week, although states have the option to increase this requirement. Recipients that fail to meet these requirements are sanctioned; depending on the state, sanctions can range from a temporary decrease in benefits to a permanent case closure. Furthermore, recipients are limited to five years of federal assistance. Once again, states are granted discretion to either shorten the time limit or to use their own funds to provide benefits beyond the federal five-year limit. The new work requirements and time limits placed upon recipients reflected the belief that welfare recipients perpetuated a culture of dependency. Sparks writes that poor minority women were portrayed by legislators and congressional witnesses as "abusers of the system, immoral, and badly in need of discipline."[87]

Race and the (Un)deserving Poor

The history of the American welfare state is as racialized as it is gendered. The institution of slavery had a long-lasting impact on wealth inequality in the United States, as enslaved people lacked economic rights and could not accumulate wealth. Wealth inequality along racial lines continued after the end of slavery, as Jim Crow kept Black Americans "at the bottom of the economic hierarchy."[88] Explicit discrimination, tight credit markets, and predatory practices such as subprime lending prevent Black Americans from becoming homeowners, which serves as a significant source of wealth for many Americans.[89] Americans have been opposed to public policy that corrects that inequality, either implicitly or explicitly.

Social welfare programs were designed to reinforce this economic inequality. In many areas of the country, recipients of mothers' pensions were overwhelming white.[90] Agricultural and domestic workers were excluded from old-age and unemployment insurance in the Social Security Act of 1935; not coincidentally, a large percentage of these workers were Black Americans in Southern states.[91] Black workers who were not categorically excluded from receiving Social Security had, on average, lower payments than white workers, because benefit levels are tied to previous earnings.[92] Those Black workers were also paying a larger percentage of their incomes into the program than white workers; Black families had median incomes below the Social Security tax wage base, so 100 percent of their income was taxed. White families had median incomes above that wage base, which meant not all of their income was subject to the Social Security tax.[93] Thus, even in federal, universal programs designed to benefit the most "deserving" recipients, Black Americans were put at a disadvantage.

Under AFDC, states had discretion to determine eligibility criteria and benefit levels; it is not surprising, then, that states with a history of slavery and Jim Crow had the strictest eligibility criteria and the lowest benefit levels. Piven and Cloward argue this local variation served the ultimate purpose of adjusting policy "day by day to meet labor needs"—in essence, cutting Black Americans off from AFDC could force them back into low-wage agricultural or domestic work.[94] Federal policies that would have increased the wages of Black workers, such as Nixon's Family Assistance Plan, were defeated in Congress.[95] Decades after the passage of federal civil rights legislation, Black Southerners living in states with a stronger historical racial regime are more likely to live in poverty.[96]

TANF is no different from its predecessors. Race has been shown, time and again, to be a critical factor in determining welfare eligibility rules as well as the generosity of state welfare programs. In states that have a larger Black population, state spending on welfare decreases, even after considering other variables such as state economic conditions.[97] Cash benefits are also lower in these states.[98] In states where Black Americans represent a larger proportion of the TANF caseload, sanctions are more stringent and time limits are shorter.[99] These restrictions maintain the racialized economic inequality that has existed in the United States for centuries.

Deservingness and the Intersection of Race and Gender

Black women were not the intended recipients of mothers' pensions; policymakers were not concerned about keeping Black mothers at home with their children. Due to demographic changes, the introduction of survivors' benefits, and legal challenges to discriminatory practices, however, Black women made up an increasingly large percentage of the AFDC caseload. Between 1939 and 1961, the share of the ADC caseload composed of Black families increased from 14 to 40 percent.[100] As the public image of welfare recipients gradually shifted to poor Black mothers and their children, Black mothers were blamed for the circumstances of their families. Researchers, such as anthropologist Oscar Lewis, promoted the idea of a culture of poverty characterized by "feeling of marginality or helplessness, or dependence, and of inferiority" and driven in part by maternalism.[101] This line of thinking was common among policymakers as well. Writing in 1965, senior US Department of Labor official Daniel Patrick Moynihan blamed the poverty prevalent in

African American communities on the "deterioration of the Negro family," caused in no small part by the "Black matriarchy."[102]

Collins argues that the image of the welfare mother is simply an updated version of the "breeder woman" stereotype of the slavery era, in which slave owners claimed that Black women were able to reproduce more easily than white women.[103] This essentially lowered Black women to the status of animals and was used to rationalize exercising control of the Black woman's reproductive life.[104] After slavery was abolished and replaced with Jim Crow laws, welfare administrators regularly checked in on women to make sure children were being raised in a "suitable home" and conducted midnight raids to catch evidence of a man in the house.[105] Until the Supreme Court's decision in *King v. Smith* (1968) ruled Alabama's policy unconstitutional, women could even be denied assistance based on their "alleged immorality."[106] Women were supervised to ensure that they were acceptable homemakers and required to prove their frugality by keeping to household budgets.[107]

Beginning in the 1960s, poor Black women began meeting in their local communities to share their experiences navigating the welfare system. Gradually these women formed local community organizations, and in 1966 the National Welfare Rights Organization (NWRO) was founded. As an organization led by welfare recipients, the NWRO was involved in practical, day-to-day activities such as helping recipients appeal grant denials. The organization also pushed for bigger changes to welfare policies, such as a guaranteed annual income and national eligibility standards.[108] In this way, the NWRO targeted both the relief law and relief practice that discriminated against Black women. It also represents one of the few instances in which the interests of welfare recipients were advanced *by* welfare recipients.

The NWRO worked with other social justice organizations, including the Student Nonviolence Coordinating Committee (SNCC), Southern Christian Leadership Conference (SCLC), and Poor People's Campaign.[109] In his Poor People's Campaign, Martin Luther King, Jr., sought to integrate race and class in the fight for social justice. The NWRO and SCLC worked together to form the People's Lobby and organized mass demonstrations across the United States in April 1971. The effort included a march to Wall Street on April 5, 1971, to "force the nation's attention to the failure of people who worry every day about nourishing their money while millions around them are unable to nourish their children."[110] The attempt to establish a cross-racial coalition for economic justice was hampered by conservatives' use of race as a political cudgel, and "what had been liberal 'programs' when they helped whites became 'welfare' when extended across the colorline."[111]

Although there are a greater number of white welfare recipients than Black recipients, Black Americans make up a disproportionate amount of the caseload.[112] In her essay on Black Americans' access to state resources, Amott notes that, in 1983, 56 percent of Black Americans living in poverty received AFDC, compared to 24.3 percent of poor whites.[113] This trend continues under TANF. The image of a welfare recipient as a lazy, immoral Black welfare queen is still prevalent among many Americans and colors their views on welfare policies.[114] Media coverage of welfare recipients often features Black women and presents their personal characteristics as the explanation for why they need assistance.[115] If policymakers believe that Black women end up on welfare because of their personal deficiencies, then it follows that any assistance needs to not only provide monetary benefits but also solve the root problem by reforming the morality of the "welfare queen." TANF provides that opportunity to states through behavioral requirements ranging from mandatory parenting classes and drug screenings to family caps that punish women for having more children.

Noncitizen women and their children are also seen as less deserving of assistance. The Personal Responsibility and Work Opportunity Reconciliation Act of 1996 took away legal permanent residents' eligibility for federal benefits and provided states with wider discretion in determining which other noncitizens were eligible to receive benefits.[116] Immigrant women had long been seen as undeserving and had to prove their "Americanness" to receive benefits. During the Progressive Era, immigrant women were situated as the other in comparison to the Protestant middle-class reformers conducting welfare evaluations. The recipients could be penalized for speaking a foreign language in the home or for living in an "improper" neighborhood.[117] States can choose to exclude noncitizens from their welfare rolls by direct means (limiting the categories of noncitizens eligible for assistance) or through indirect means (stricter requirements for sponsor and parent income deeming).

And Everyone Else?

Notably absent from the continuum of deservingness presented earlier in this chapter are all American residents who receive aid from the government in a form other than direct monthly payments from the government. Many Americans receive health insurance through the government, whether through Medicaid, Medicare, or the Department of Veterans Affairs. Just as those receiving Social Security or veterans' benefits may be seen as more deserving, receiving health insurance because of one's age or veteran status may confer more deservingness on the program. Medicaid recipients, however, range from children and pregnant women to able-bodied adults. The perceived deservingness of those recipients may be more on par with that of TANF recipients; indeed, the majority of TANF recipients also receive Medicaid.[118] At the same time, polling suggests that some Americans do not realize these programs are funded by the government. One vivid example of this was provided by conservative activists who told members of Congress to "keep your government hands off my Medicare."[119]

A common form of government assistance used by Americans of all backgrounds are tax deductions or credits. For taxpayers who do not receive government-funded health insurance, there are a variety of tax deductions available for employer-based coverage.[120] Homeowners also enjoy tax deductions. The home mortgage interest deduction (HMID), for instance, amounted to $484 billion between 2010 and 2014.[121] While changes brought about by the Tax Cuts and Jobs Act of 2017 decreased the number of taxpayers claiming the deduction, those in higher income brackets remain most likely to benefit from it.[122] Moreover, white Americans and older adults are more likely than other racial and ethnic groups in the United States to own homes, thus increasing the disparity between target populations of a program like the home mortgage tax deduction and TANF.

In contrast, the Earned Income Tax Credit (EITC) benefits low- and middle-income families. The program amounted to nearly $269 billion between 2010 and 2014.[123] The use of the tax code to redistribute resources is more popular than direct government assistance; Ellis and Faricy find that survey respondents view individuals as more deserving when they receive a tax refund than when they benefit from direct payments.[124] Piston finds support for a range of tax deductions, including both the HMID and the EITC, are mediated by voters' knowledge of the policies' distributive effects.[125] That is, Americans are less likely to support the home mortgage interest deduction when they learn that the policy overwhelming benefits those in the middle and upper classes, and are more likely to support EITC when they learn about how it benefits low-income households.

Finally, Americans of all backgrounds benefit from public goods provided with government funding. As Franklin Delano Roosevelt pointed out in a 1938 radio address, however, "The first to turn to Government, the first to receive protection from Government, were not the poor and the lowly—those who had no resources other than their daily earnings—but the rich and the strong."[126] Whether it is a local park or a state university, government-backed goods and services are used by those who are deemed "deserving" as well as those who are deemed "undeserving." This book takes a narrow view of the type of government assistance, that which usually has the most stigma attached to it, but also recognizes that everyone receives some benefit from belonging to civil society.

Plan for the Book

In this book, I examine the relationship between representation and public policy when the citizens being represented are on the margins of society and the policy addressing their needs is often looked at with contempt. Specifically, I analyze how the representation of welfare recipients translates into the Temporary Assistance for Needy Families (TANF) programs adopted by the states and argue that state welfare policy is driven by a variety of organizations whose interests are only tangentially related to the interests of welfare recipients. Previous work on the forces that shape US welfare policy acknowledge the importance of race and gender; I argue that, in the social construction of a welfare recipient who is marginalized along both racial and gendered lines, there is a gap in representation that is filled by organizations who seek to capitalize on the expansiveness of the neoliberal paternalism of the current welfare regime.

In this first chapter, I have provided a brief history of government assistance in the United States. Reliance on the government has been frowned upon throughout United States history, and the social programs that do exist primarily support those who are seen as deserving of that aid. This is supported by political science research that shows people are more willing to extend aid to those who are employed or actively searching for work than to those who are unemployed.[127] The typical welfare mother of today is not viewed as worthy of government assistance, and her poverty is often viewed as a result of her own moral failings. When women began receiving state aid in the form of mothers' pensions, it was seen as a necessary step to keep families together when women had been widowed or abandoned by their husbands. Over time, assistance expanded to women who had never been married or who had gotten divorced and the percentage of women in the workforce increased. Women still receiving welfare were portrayed as taking advantage of the system. While other recipients of government assistance, including veterans, the elderly, and the disabled, are seen as worthy of aid because of their service or their inability to provide for themselves, women receiving welfare are seen as creating their own poverty. The sense of who is deserving of aid in the United States is also conditional on race, with African Americans being perceived as lazier than their white counterparts.[128] These stereotypes provide little incentive for policymakers to advocate for more lenient and generous TANF policies.

In the second chapter, I argue that the unique intersectional identity of welfare recipients prevents their interests from being heard through typical channels of political representation (political participation, political parties, and descriptive representation). The status of welfare recipients leaves them in a precarious situation in which their needs are not fully represented by elected officials or by political parties. At the same time, their limited resources prevent them from mobilizing and exerting the kind of influence seen among more affluent populations. This vacuum in representation provides the opportunity for interest groups to advocate for welfare rules advantageous to their own interests, but that may not represent the best interest of welfare recipients. To quantify the influence of various organized interests, I use two measures from the population ecology literature: interest group density and diversity of interests.

The subsequent empirical chapters build upon previous TANF research. First, unlike some of the early research on TANF, this project covers a longer time period, from 1997 to 2016. Earlier work focused on the first few years following the passage of welfare reform for two reasons: data limitations, and a concern that after the initial transition period from AFDC to TANF few states enacted changes in their welfare policies. Focusing on this short time span does not account for how states responded to later changes in the TANF program, such as the revisions made under the 2005 Deficit Reduction Act. It is also does not capture how states confronted the long-term changes that came about because of PRWORA (for example, how would states respond when recipients reached their time limit?). Second, prior research on welfare policy has aggregated welfare rules into indices as a measure of generosity or flexibility. If, according to my theory, different interest groups are influencing only certain rules within a state's TANF program, then these indices mask those nuances. When the welfare rules are looked at in closer detail, rather than through an index or summary measure, there is significant across-time variation.

In the third chapter, I examine the ways in which welfare recipients must conform to social norms to receive benefits. In addition to a strong welfare-to-work approach, TANF's core goals of actively promoting marriage and two-parent families imply that welfare recipients do not know what is in their best interest. Welfare recipients are often portrayed as promiscuous women and irresponsible parents; as a result, many states have adopted behavioral requirements that require recipients to attend parent-teacher conferences or undergo random drug screenings. Do socially conservative organizations speak in favor of these requirements? Do more liberal organizations speak out against them? This chapter addresses how morality politics became tied to the receipt of government assistance.

In the fourth chapter, I discuss the ways in which welfare reform sought to transition individuals from welfare to work. Welfare reform in the 1990s created strict work participation requirements to encourage economic self-sufficiency among recipients. Policymakers on both sides of the aisle believed these requirements would prove to recipients that it "pays to work." In this chapter, I focus on the extent to which a state's business community affects the work requirements placed on recipients.

Closely related, the fifth chapter analyzes policies meant to address the "culture of dependency." To discourage recipients from relying on benefits and passing on this reliance to their children, the federal government limits adult recipients to sixty months of benefits. States, however, have the option of shortening this limit or using their own funds to provide benefits past the federal limit. States may also grant time limit extensions and exemptions to recipients who need to receive benefits past the time limit. Do interest groups representing these vulnerable populations have an effect on the flexibility of a state's time limit? Together, these two chapters address the policies that work to ensure welfare becomes a temporary option.

In the sixth chapter, I explain how welfare reform changed access to public assistance for noncitizens. As the states sought to decrease their caseload, they limited the types of noncitizens eligible for assistance based on when they entered the country and under what circumstances. Moreover, states restricted eligibility on noncitizens with sponsors. Do states with more generous noncitizen eligibility policies have a more active immigration interest group population? Who is advocating on behalf of poor noncitizens?

Finally, in the seventh chapter, I summarize the conclusions found in the empirical analysis. I review the circumstances under which welfare recipients are represented by interest groups and political parties. I examine how the core principles of TANF—personal responsibility and self-sufficiency—have expanded into other social safety net programs. I conclude with suggestions for ways to expand this research in the future.

2

Representing the Needy

Race, Gender, and the Policy Process

Given their perceived undeservingness, the existence of Temporary Assistance for Needy Families (TANF) seems counterintuitive. Unlike recipients of other forms of public assistance, those receiving benefits through TANF face a number of stereotypes that create the perception that they are the "other" and as such are undeserving of assistance.[1] In a society that encourages citizens to pull themselves up by their bootstraps, there should be no safety net for TANF recipients, the "undeserving poor." Americans, and the politicians representing them, have rationalized giving assistance to soldiers because of the sacrifices they have made to the country. They pitied women during the Progressive Era who were abandoned by their husbands and needed government support so they could stay home to raise their children. Social Security remains a popular program in the United States in part because workers pay into the system so they can receive benefits after a lifetime of work. While American individualism and the country's puritanical roots promote citizens' remaining economically self-sufficient, some populations have been seen as deserving of government aid.

Despite the preference for assisting the deserving poor, TANF exists. How are the interests of TANF recipients being represented in government? In America's representative democracy, citizens can participate in the political process to advocate for their own interests, so in theory, TANF may be the result of low-income families' organizing and voting for politicians who will support cash assistance programs. Decades of research in political participation, however, has demonstrated that those without resources—financial, but also time, skills, and connections—are less likely to vote or form interest groups. It seems unlikely that TANF recipients would be spending significant resources advocating on their own behalf. Constituents may also look to politicians (individually or in groups) who share similar experiences or interests and hope they will take into account their needs when making policy. The demographic makeup of Congress and state legislatures does not resemble the demographics of those on the TANF rolls, though, so recipients do not seem to have the benefits of descriptive representation. Moreover, neither political party has taken an interest in prioritizing the needs of welfare recipients.

Given this vacuum of representation, powerful organized interests who stand to benefit from TANF's far-reaching rules fill the gap. These organized interests have the resources that welfare recipients lack, and given TANF's expansive policy goals, they can use the programs' rules to advance their own political interests. These *tangential interests* advocate for themselves, but there are very few actors left to create policy that benefits the target population of TANF: those receiving cash assistance.

Welfare Recipients as the "Other"

Audre Lorde describes the American norm as "white, thin, male, young, heterosexual, Christian, and financially secure."[2] Those whose identities align with the norm hold power, while those whose identities stray from the norm find themselves oppressed. In *Black Feminist Thought*, Patricia Hill Collins lays out how binary definitions of concepts such as race, gender, and class create a dominant group and an "other."[3] In the race binary, white is dominant, while Black is the marginalized other. In a gender binary, men are dominant, and women serve as the other. With respect to class, the wealthy are dominant, while the poor are the other. In each, the "other" is objectified by the dominant group and the binary is reinforced through institutions. Isabel Wilkerson argues that race does more than create a binary within American society. Race undergirds a caste system, the "fixed and embedded ranking of human value that sets the presumed supremacy of one group against the presumed inferiority of other groups."[4] The gender binary has historically been reinforced by institutions such as heterosexual marriage and the daily performance of gendered norms. Moreover, as bell hooks writes, "male supremacist ideology" tells women they have value only "by relating to or bonding with men."[5] A capitalist system perpetuates the division between the "haves" and the "have nots."

Being classified as the "other" in any one of these categories leads to marginalization. Introducing the concept of intersectionality, Crenshaw argues that we must look past discrimination on a single axis and consider those who are marginalized in more than one dimension. Embracing intersectionality allows us to recognize the diversity within groups and the possibility of being both marginalized and in positions of power. Without considering those who are "multiply burdened," our conceptions of identities "become grounded in experiences that actually represent only a subset" of the group.[6] Lorde, for example, warns of the dangers of white women ignoring "their built-in privilege of whiteness," which then makes "women of Color the 'other,' the outsider whose experience and tradition is too 'alien' to comprehend."[7] In a word of caution, bell hooks warns that modern feminism's assertion that "all women are oppressed" ignores how "factors like class, race, religion, [and] sexual preference" create different lived experiences for women, with varying levels of oppression and the opportunity to exercise autonomy.[8]

This multiplicative marginalization is demonstrated in the "public identity" of the welfare queen, which Hancock argues has been used by elites and groups from across the political spectrum to represent all welfare recipients.[9] Welfare queens symbolize the long-held beliefs about poor, unmarried, African American mothers whose poverty was caused by their laziness and promiscuity.[10] The image of the welfare queen comes from an intersection of class, sex, and racial stereotypes.

Social Construction of Target Populations

Welfare queens are examples of a target population, or "the people who are expected to comply with policy directives and who are offered policy opportunities."[11] Those receiving welfare will be the ones expected to comply with the rules of the program; in exchange for their compliance, they will be offered the benefits. In the case of welfare queens, the target population is also strongly associated with a social construction, or "the attribution of specific, valence-oriented values, symbols, and images to the characteristics" of the population.[12] Writing about social constructions, Schneider and Ingram distinguish between positive and negative constructions. Social constructions of poverty may portray the poor as disadvantaged people who are victims of circumstance or as lazy persons who are responsible for their own poverty. They further divide target populations into those with weak and strong political power. Target populations with political power will see public policies that benefit them, whereas those who are weak politically are more likely to be on the receiving end of punitive policies.[13] As I will explore in greater detail in this and subsequent chapters, the social construction of TANF recipients is often negative and they lack political power.

Building off Schneider and Ingram's work, Soss, Fording, and Schram theorize in their Racial Classification Model (RCM) that three factors explain racial disparities in the policy process. First, "policy actors must rely on salient social classifications" to design effective policies for specific target populations.[14] It is assumed that policymakers want to solve public problems; targeting their policies based on the needs of those on the receiving end would appear to be the most efficient way to solve those problems. Second, "when racial minorities are salient in a policy context," race will be used by policymakers to classify target populations. Notably, racial minorities are salient in all policy contexts. Finally, "racially patterned policy outcomes" will be most likely to occur when there are strong cultural stereotypes of racial groups.[15] The stereotypes of Black women as "welfare queens" are deeply embedded in American culture, leading to racialized welfare policies. Soss, Fording, and Schram find that welfare sanction policies—the penalties welfare recipients face when they do not meet program requirements—are racialized; this research has been confirmed by other scholars.[16] Beyond welfare policy, the Racial Classification Model has been used to explain racialized policy outcomes in school discipline and school choice policies, as well as the provision of local public goods.[17]

When all TANF recipients are stereotyped as undeserving welfare queens, advocating for their interests becomes more difficult because of the implicit bias against this target population. Regardless of the negative social constructions associated with welfare recipients, when it comes to advocating for a welfare recipient's interests, we might expect such advocacy to come from a group sharing one of these identities. Similarly, political officials sharing these identities or a political party traditionally associated with this part of the electorate may feel responsible for representing the interests of welfare recipients. This would surely be the expectation if welfare recipients enjoyed a more positive social

construction. Because welfare recipients occupy the marginalized positions within these identities, though, it is equally likely that groups will
be opposed to more generous welfare policies or that elected officials
and political parties will feel less of a responsibility to welfare recipients
than they do to other, more "deserving" groups. Traditional pathways
to representation are limited for those who exist as the marginalized
"other."

Political Participation

Welfare recipients stand at the margins of society as the "other" with
regard to gender, race, and class. To advance their interests—whether
through descriptive representation, representation through political parties, or through interest groups—welfare recipients must first be active
in politics. Such political participation includes electing policymakers
who will represent their interests, contacting elected officials, donating
money to campaigns and political organizations, and participating in
organized groups.

Political participation, in all its modes, varies by gender, race, and
class. Women tend to turn out to vote at higher rates than men, though
the gender gap in turnout decreases in midterm elections.[18] Moreover,
intersectional analysis shows that the size of the gender gap varies by
ethno-racial groups.[19] Early research into the differences in political participation based on gender asserted that women were less interested and
engaged in politics.[20] Further research has shown, however, that men
and women may have different sets of political knowledge and engage
in different political activities.[21] The success of the welfare rights movement in the late 1960s, for example, proved that low-income women
knew about politics and were interested in getting involved.

Regardless of the differences in political participation based on gender or race, some of the greatest disparities in political participation are
based on income. In general, low-income Americans are less likely than
the affluent to participate politically.[22] In the 1990 Citizen Participation
Survey, 17 percent of those who identified as "inactive" in politics reported receiving means-tested benefits. In contrast, only 6 percent of
voters indicated they had received means-tested benefits.[23]

Voting is the most common form of political participation; about two-thirds of the voting eligible population turned out for the 2020 presidential election. Midterm elections generally have lower turnout than presidential election, though the 2018 and 2022 midterm elections saw high levels of voter turnout, at 49 percent and 46 percent, respectively. Even so, there is a wide disparity in voter turnout based on income levels. In the 2018 midterms, 35 percent of voters were adults living in families with annual incomes less than $50,000; adults living in families with annual incomes less than $50,000 constituted nearly 60 percent of nonvoters, however. Those in the highest income bracket (over $100,000) were overrepresented among voters: 28 percent compared to 13 percent of nonvoters in 2018. The disparities were similar in 2022.[24]

Low-income Americans face restrictions on the resources required for political participation. Even the seemingly simple act of voting can be made more difficult for those without transportation or the necessary voter ID.[25] Welfare recipients have less disposable income than those in the middle and upper classes, and so they are less likely to donate money to candidates or organizations.[26] Only 14 percent of the general population surveyed by the American National Election Studies reported contributing money to politics.[27] In contrast, in a pilot study of interviews with wealthy Americans in Chicago, Page, Bartels, and Seawright found that two-thirds of their sample donated money to political campaigns or organizations.[28]

Many welfare recipients also lack the time for political participation. Writing about recipients of mothers' pensions in the early part of the twentieth century, Skocpol states that these women were "too busy with struggles of daily life" to place demands on policymakers.[29] According to an analysis of the 1984 National Black Election Study, Blacks receiving welfare assistance are significantly less likely to join Black political organizations than their more affluent counterparts.[30] TANF recipients face similar struggles, including caring for their children, looking for work, and completing other activity requirements. Individuals with more free time are more likely to participate in activities such as voting, being an active member of an organization, attending protests, and contacting public officials.[31] According to the American National Election Studies (ANES), only 9 percent of Americans with household income below

$25,000 contacted a member of Congress within the past year; 20 percent of those with household incomes above $175,000 contacted a member of Congress. Similarly, only 14 percent of Americans in the lowest ANES income bracket report having attended a community meeting, compared to 24 percent of those in the highest income bracket.[32]

Finally, groups that are negatively constructed may decide not to participate in politics because "they have been stigmatized and labeled by the policy process itself."[33] Schneider and Ingram write that those who are dependent on the state for support—including those receiving welfare payments—are taught to believe that they are powerless and helpless and unable to solve their own problems.[34] What incentives do they have then to participate in the political process? Mansbridge argues that this is one of the most important contributions of descriptive representation; it provides legitimacy to groups that have traditionally been excluded from politics and demonstrates that they can hold power.[35]

The low political participation of the poor has the effect of removing their voices from the policymaking process and instead places trust in elected officials, political parties, and interest groups to represent their interests. This may not be a concern when the preferences of the poor and the affluent align.[36] The preferences of the poor and the affluent, however, diverge most significantly when it comes to the matter of social welfare programs, which suggests that the policies enacted may not reflect the preferences of those who are most directly affected by them.[37]

Descriptive Representation

One avenue through which welfare recipients may find greater representation is descriptive representation, or the election of representatives who look like the "other" or have similar life experiences. Hannah Pitkin describes descriptive representation as when a person or thing stands for others "by being sufficiently like them."[38] She argues that such representation is most appropriate when the purpose "is to supply information about something not actually present."[39] Similarly, Mansbridge argues that descriptive representation is important in situations that require policymakers to make decisions based on uncrystallized interests.[40] For both scholars, descriptive representation is linked to, yet not synonymous with, substantive representation, in which the representative acts in the interest of the group. Given a group that has not already expressed an opinion on an issue, Mansbridge argues that a descriptive representative is in the best position to represent their interests because of their shared experiences. Voters report higher satisfaction with members of Congress that descriptively represent them, suggesting that their needs are being met.[41] In cases where public opinion is already known, a descriptive representative may not substantively represent the interests of the group any better than a policymaker who does not share experiences or look like a member of the group. In fact, Black constituents with at least a moderate level of political knowledge value the ideology of their member of Congress over the member's race.[42]

The most accurate descriptive representative for a welfare recipient then would be a fellow welfare recipient. This is unlikely given the barriers to political participation for low-income citizens, but the public image of the welfare queen tells us that the typical welfare recipient is a poor Black woman. It is also true that more than 90 percent of the adult TANF caseload is women, so a descriptive representative for a welfare recipient would most likely be female.[43] Dodson finds in her interviews with female members of Congress that most female legislators feel responsible for advocating on behalf of all women and not just those within their districts.[44] Furthermore, female legislators see their presence as important for women's issues to be taken seriously within the legislature.[45] Female legislators may act as descriptive representatives for welfare recipients because of their shared gender, but are they also substantively representing their interests? That is, do they act in ways that are consistent with the preferences of welfare recipients?

Previous research on women's representation in legislative bodies has shown that the presence of female legislators does influence parts of the policymaking process. Generally, female legislators are more likely to sponsor and/or introduce women's issue bills than their male colleagues.[46] Some of this may be due to women's professional backgrounds; legislatures with a greater percentage of women with pink-collar backgrounds spend more on social services.[47] In other instances, issues around poverty intersect with women's issues as it concerns women's roles as mothers and caretakers. Mothers introduce more legislation related to families and children; women with minor children are especially likely to introduce such bills.[48] Specifically, with regard to welfare policy, women sponsor more legislation on welfare policy than their male counterparts.[49] In terms of the policy produced from the proposed bills, average TANF benefits increase in states with higher percentages of women in the legislature.[50] This same study, however, found that greater percentages of female legislators lead to stricter TANF policies with regard to transitional childcare and requiring welfare recipients to work before receiving benefits.[51]

Similar to female legislators, Black legislators view themselves as serving group members outside their geographical constituency.[52] Descriptive representation is not limited to one's partisans—Black Republicans are more likely to sponsor bills representing the material interests of African Americans than non-Black Democrats, though this does not translate into support during roll call voting.[53] At the national level, the Congressional Black Caucus, with the exception of Sanford Bishop, was opposed to the Personal Responsibility and Work Opportunity Reconciliation Act (PRWORA).[54] Prior to the passage of welfare reform, the president of the National Black Caucus of State Legislators, Lois M. DeBerry, argued that recent increases in African American representation would provide a safeguard against an overly conservative policy.[55]

At the agenda-setting stage of the legislative process, Black and female legislators pursue distinctive policies; among Black legislators, this includes introducing significantly more legislation on welfare policy than their white counterparts.[56] With regard to policy outcomes, as the percentage of Black legislators in a state increases, the state's welfare spending increases.[57] Preuhs delves further into substantive representation by examining whether racialized institutions influence welfare generosity, as measured by maximum monthly cash benefit levels under AFDC.[58] His results suggest that Black legislators in Southern states with strong racial cleavages in party identification have less influence on welfare generosity than Black legislators in Northern and Western states without these racial cleavages.

Welfare recipients are neither just women nor just African Americans—they occupy a doubly marginalized space. Reingold and Smith, however, emphasize that welfare policy is not a racial policy or a gendered policy, but an intersectional policy involving both identities simultaneously.[59] Since its inception, welfare in the United States has been designed to provide assistance to poor women and their children;

it is only when the demographics of AFDC recipients began changing in the middle of the twentieth century that welfare became more associated with minority recipients—for most Americans, this seems to translate into "Black welfare recipients."[60] This intersectional identity, occupying the "inferior half" of both the gender and race binaries, calls for more nuanced representation. In this situation, Black female legislators are called on to represent both gender and racial interests. Black female legislators such as Patsy Mink and Gwen Moore provide historic examples of balancing these intersecting interests.[61]

Previous research has shown some support for the contention that Black female legislators are best able to represent the intersectional identity of welfare recipients. Black female state legislators are more likely to sponsor legislation on Black interests and women's interests than other legislators.[62] Reingold and Smith find that increased incorporation of minority women in state legislatures is related to more lenient TANF eligibility requirements and greater flexibility in TANF work requirements.[63] At the same time, however, their results show that states with greater legislative incorporation of minority women are less likely to have domestic violence time limit waivers, and there is no significant effect of minority women's incorporation on family cap adoption.[64] The number of Black female legislators is also relatively low, compared to other groups. In these situations, however, an increased presence of minority men can lead to more attention to issues at the intersection of gender and race.[65] This suggests that the "best" descriptive representation fit does not automatically produce the most favorable policy outcomes.

While Black and female legislators can provide descriptive representation for welfare recipients, who may in turn influence welfare policy, it is not sufficient to argue that the demographic composition of state legislatures alone is responsible for current TANF policy. To suggest that all Black legislators equally represent the interests of all Black citizens ignores the diversity within the African American population. Hajnal and Lee note, for instance, that the increasing economic diversity within the African American population may be creating political divisions; therefore, it would be wrong to presume that the interests of middle-class Black voters are the same as those of low-income voters.[66] Similarly, assuming that all women will favor more generous welfare policy overlooks the importance of political parties and previous research that has shown women legislators act on partisan interests first and gendered interests second.[67] The current research on welfare policy and representation also assumes that all representatives are equally interested in all aspects of TANF policy, even though the program is far-reaching and affects many different interests.

Representation through Political Parties

Representation also occurs through political parties; the Democratic Party has traditionally been the political party associated with the expansion of the welfare state, indicating that party is responsive to the needs of low-income constituents.[68] In fact, in the nationwide 2008 American National Election Studies survey, the percentage of Democrats decreases as the socioeconomic status quintile increases.[69] Moreover, since the civil rights movement, the Democratic Party is associated with representing the interests of women and African Americans, so we might assume greater representation of welfare recipients among Democrats than in the Republican Party. During the welfare reform debate of the mid-1990s, however, even female Democratic legislators favored more restrictive welfare policies.[70]

Historically, Democratic Party control has not always resulted in more favorable policies for African Americans; the South is a prime example of this. In his analysis of the South, Key writes that each state's Democratic Party is factionalized, with a range of approaches to party organization and structure.[71] When parties are factionalized like this, cleavages among voters, and thus voting coalitions among policymakers, change depending on the issues.[72] Such instability prevents politicians from being held accountable; as Key notes, "if the electorate wants to reward the 'ins' by another term or to throw the rascals out . . . it has no way of identifying the 'ins' . . . if one considers some southern state governments as a whole, there is really no feasible way of throwing the rascals out."[73] For welfare recipients seeking representation through factionalized political parties, this lack of accountability prevents the election of a coalition that will institute favorable, long-term policies.

Also delving into the differences within parties, Brown argues that there is substantial variation in party coalitions across the states by considering not only which type of voter is more likely to identify as a Democrat or Republican, but also the relative size of social groups within party coalitions.[74] In Alabama, for instance, over 30 percent of the Democratic Party is Black; he calls this strong cleavage by race the Southern partisan cleavage.[75] In Vermont, however, virtually no Democrats are Black, while party members are heavily Catholic and low-income, displaying what Brown calls the New Deal party cleavage.[76] This cleavage has policy implications—Democratic policymakers in Alabama should be more responsive to their Black constituents than their Vermont counterparts, even though in both states Black voters are more likely to identify as Democratic than Republican.

Frymer argues, though, that African Americans are a "captured" constituency of the Democratic Party.[77] A captured group is one in which the group cannot leave the party with which it traditionally identifies because the opposition party has no incentive to appeal to the captured group. In particular, opposition party leaders fear that appealing to the captured group will lead to electoral losses.[78] This pattern can be clearly seen in the relationship of African American voters with the two major parties. Since the 1964 election, Black voters have overwhelmingly supported Democrats, and Republicans have little incentive to appeal to the group.[79] The underlying salience of race in the United States reinforces the captured nature of African Americans.[80] While the Democratic Party is seen as representing African American interests, African Americans do not have a viable exit option even when the Democrats fail to implement their policy demands. As Tate writes, Black support for the Democratic Party may be driven by the "nonattractiveness of the Republican Party."[81]

In addition to gender and race considerations, political parties may be more receptive to some income levels than to others. The partisan gap between the rich and the poor, after declining to near zero in the 1950s, increased in the 1960s and 1970s and a prominent divide remains today, in which Republicans do about twenty points better among high-income voters.[82] Democrats have traditionally been the party of the working poor, at least when it comes to economic issues.[83] Under AFDC, states whose political parties are based on the New Deal cleavage, in which the Democratic Party has a bias toward low-income voters, have significantly higher levels of welfare spending than states divided on the Southern partisan cleavage based on race.[84]

While Brown's results suggest that the Democratic Party promotes policies that are more favorable to the poor, other work has shown this conclusion must come with qualifications. Rigby and Wright find that low-income citizens' preferences are most likely to be adopted in candidate positions when they align with the interests of the affluent.[85] Rigby and Wright use survey responses from Democratic and Republican candidates for state legislature, governor, and Congress to determine the extent to which issue stances respond to the opinions of the American public. Their results indicate that the economic platforms of Democratic candidates align with the preferences of those in the top income third, while Republican candidates' positions align with the middle- and upper-third income groups.[86] The poor's preferences exert influence only when they agree with the upper income levels. Furthermore, these differences are exacerbated in the Democratic Party when there are higher levels of income inequality in a state.[87]

Parties also adjust their positions based on electoral competition. Democrats in competitive districts need to mobilize the base, including low-income voters who may not usually vote; that mobilization can be achieved by adopting a more liberal policy platform, such as one that promotes greater spending on welfare.[88] In contrast, a candidate with little competition has no electoral incentive to appeal to unlikely voters within the party base. In fact, both Democrats and Republicans are more likely to try to mobilize voters of a higher socioeconomic status, though presumably increasing low-income turnout would benefit Democrats.[89]

What happens once those candidates are in office, though? Parties are most responsive to the affluent's interests throughout the election cycle, while the interests of the lower and middle classes are almost completely ignored during nonelection years.[90] Moreover, responsiveness to moral/religious issues and economic issues appears to be strongest in times of Republican control.[91] Opinions about welfare, and the policies that originate from those opinions, are no longer just a "social welfare" matter. TANF also has a strong moral component, with its emphasis on reducing out-of-wedlock births and promoting marriage, and it promotes neoliberalism through its focus on work. Given the strong neoliberal paternalist influence in TANF, we might expect that TANF policy is consistent with the preferences of low- and middle-income Americans when Republicans are in control. It is not sufficient to argue that one political party can account for all the rules included in the vast area of welfare policy.

Interest Group Representation

Should members of a group find the representation they receive through individual legislators and political parties to be inadequate, they may decide to form interest groups to advocate for their interests. In his theory of interest group formation, Truman argued that interest groups are born from conflict as people join together to address a grievance that cannot be resolved individually.[92] As discussed above, though, the poor are less politically active than the affluent; they have fewer resources and less time to devote to political activities such as being active members of political organizations.

Furthermore, those living in poverty have little incentive to join a group, in part because they share no collective identity.[93] Explaining the incentive to vote, Schuessler argues that individuals are motivated by expressive benefits rather than outcomes.[94] How they act becomes an expression of who they are. Because of the stigma attached to receiving welfare, there is no desire to *be* a welfare recipient. They may also receive benefits for a short period of time and have no intention of organizing or joining a group that they intend to identify with only temporarily. The incentive to participate decreases further if they can benefit from the work of other organized interests.

Olson argued in *The Logic of Collection Action* that such indifference can be overcome if the group provides benefits to its members. In the case of an interest group representing welfare recipients, welfare recipients themselves might be able to overcome the resource barriers to political participation and organization if the benefits are great enough. Those who do not stand to materially benefit from the successes of an organization representing welfare recipients may be convinced to participate because they believe in the goals of the organization—what McCarthy and Zald referred to in the social movement context as "conscience adherents."[95] Viable organizations require a variety of resources, including material, informational, moral, and human. These resources may come from internal or external sources.[96] In the late 1960s, welfare recipients were mobilized to fight for their own interests while also receiving external support, but the interests of welfare recipients are less likely to be addressed in the current interest group community.

Overcoming the Collection Action Problem: The Welfare Rights Movement

The welfare rights movement, and specifically the National Welfare Rights Organization, of the 1960s and 1970s seemed to overcome this collective action problem. The movement has its origins in welfare recipients gathering within their communities—with members of their church, residents in their housing projects, etc.—to discuss problems with caseworkers and how to make ends meet.[97] By 1966 the informal meetings among AFDC recipients had produced the NWRO—the "first national protest of poor women."[98] The NWRO organizers saw their purpose as organizing communities of people who traditionally lacked political influence; through their collective efforts, the poor would be able to compete in politics and the marketplace. At its peak, the NWRO had twenty-two thousand members from more than eight hundred local groups in all fifty states.[99]

The NWRO's success was driven in part by the organization's ability to offer selective incentives to group members. AFDC recipients were eligible for special grants to buy items such as clothing and furniture, but the distribution of these grants was left to the discretion of caseworkers. The NWRO coordinated campaigns around these special grants, helping hundreds of recipients file grants in an attempt to overwhelm local welfare agencies. Coordinated occupation of these welfare agency offices led to millions more dollars of aid being distributed than in previous years.[100] Welfare rights organizations also created a handbook for recipients to help them navigate relationships with hostile caseworkers and informed welfare recipients of their rights.[101] When the group could no longer offer these selective benefits to recipients, its membership plateaued and eventually the movement died out. The NWRO became consumed with budgetary issues, was forced to declare bankruptcy, and closed down in March 1975, effectively ending the welfare rights movement.[102]

Moreover, although the NWRO formally agreed in 1967 that membership and voting privileges would be limited to the poor, the organization worked with Friends of Welfare Rights, a separate organization of wealthy supporters who could provide the financial resources that welfare recipients lacked.[103] Much of the senior-level staff were middle-class men. In fact, the typical staff member of the Massachusetts Welfare Rights Organization (MWRO) was a "white, middle-class, recent college graduate."[104] These are the exact types of conscience adherents and conscience constituents identified by McCarthy and Zald.[105] The welfare rights movement could not be sustained by the support of middle- and upper-class Americans. Their motivations differed from those of welfare recipients because they did not depend on the success of the movement to pay rent or feed their families. As with some of the charity organizations in the Progressive Era before them, these advocates were speaking on behalf of the poor and acting in what they believed was in their best interests, but they could not provide the kind of representation that comes from being a member of the group.

Since the decline of the welfare rights movement, there have been few organized groups composed of welfare recipients. In a sample of more than eleven thousand national interest groups, Schlozman, Verba, and Brady report that no organized group was composed of means-tested recipients.[106] Instead, larger interest groups may include welfare recipients among their constituents, but they remain marginalized.

Welfare Recipients as Disadvantaged Subgroups

Empirically, Strolovitch finds that organizations typically spend their time advocating on issues that affect all members of their constituency equally or that disproportionately affect the advantaged among them.[107] From her survey of social and economic justice organizations, she found that groups are more likely to take actions that have greater perceived impact.[108] The problem is that the issues of the advantaged are perceived as more important because those are the individuals with more resources, even if the issues that concern them do not actually affect a greater number of people. Also, in the case of issues affecting the disadvantaged within the group rather than the advantaged, there are more likely to be assumptions that another organization is already taking on the problem. At the same time, the leaders of interest groups representing marginalized populations "believe in and take seriously" the expectation that they represent the least advantaged among them, even if this expectation is not always met.[109] Among the groups she surveyed, Strolovitch found that most organizations' missions extended beyond helping their dues-paying members or donors.[110]

Activists during the welfare rights movement experienced this same marginalization, as the NWRO worked with African American and women's organizations. For example, while both the NAACP and NWRO represented predominantly Black populations, the NAACP was seen as a moderate, middle-class organization in comparison to the more liberal, even militant NWRO.[111] Hancock describes poor Black mothers as receiving conflicting messages from the civil rights movement: "the power of numbers as a moral force for change, and the force of boundaries drawn to exclude them from the benefits of such changes."[112] Among women's organizations, both the League of Women Voters and the National Organization for Women were active during the 1960s and 1970s in promoting welfare reform.[113] These organizations clashed with the NWRO, though, because of disagreements around guaranteed income plans and whether women should be seeking employment outside the home. Even at the height of their advocacy efforts, welfare recipients were not fully integrated into larger interest groups.

In his study of three areas of social policy, R. Allen Hays finds little evidence of low-income recipients of government aid advocating on their own behalf, but discovers that other types of interest groups— including public and private service providers and intergovernmental groups—provide surrogate representation for the poor.[114] This surrogate representation will never be as true to the preferences of welfare recipients as direct representation, because it is biased by the experiences and backgrounds of the surrogates. In some instances, the surrogate's policy preferences may not align with what is in the best interest of the poor, but regardless of how closely their preferences align, the surrogates do have a voice in policies that affect welfare recipients.[115]

Schlozman, Verba, and Brady find little evidence of surrogate advocacy for women, minorities, or the economically disadvantaged in their study of economic organization websites.[116] They do find, however, that religious groups as well as liberal public interest organizations are more likely to mention these underrepresented populations on their websites.[117] Schlozman and colleagues conclude that "disadvantaged constituencies should not count on organizations representing other groups or interests to advocate on their behalf."[118] While this may certainly be the case for welfare recipients, it is quite possible that these organizations are involved in narrow provisions of welfare policy out of self-interest.

Representation through Tangential Interests

As a result of the marginalized position of welfare recipients, welfare reform is rarely taken up as a cause by organizations with a constituency extending beyond the poor. Moreover, welfare recipients are unlikely to organize on their own because of constraints on time and resources. Welfare policy under TANF is broad in scope, however, touching on issues related to neoliberalism and paternalism. TANF is not solely about providing aid to poor families or about teaching moral values to the poor, but rather about the intersection of these two goals. Consequently, welfare policy groups may be interested in a narrow niche of welfare policy related to neoliberalism or paternalism. The organized interest may have no intention of representing welfare recipients, but welfare recipients are "the other" who is affected by the lobbying of the organized interest.

Interest groups may have more influence when there is a narrower scope of conflict. Smith argues that when public opinion is not fully crystallized or difficult to measure, interest groups are more likely to see favorable policy outcomes.[119] Within welfare policy, for example, there may be general agreement that welfare recipients should be working in order to receive benefits, but it is far less likely that there is strong public opinion on which activities should be counted as work. The specificity of these policies provides an opportunity for interest groups (in this case, business interest groups) to influence state policy.

The limited research on how interest groups influence welfare policy supports this theory. Klarner et al. test the influence of business interest groups on three TANF policies: the length of the state's time limit, the monthly guarantee for a family of four, and the existence of a family cap.[120] Using a measure of interest group influence similar to my own (explained in further detail in the "Independent Variables" section in appendix A), they find that business interest group power is unrelated to a state having a family cap, but states with greater business interest group power have shorter time limits and lower TANF guarantees.[121] Shorter time limits and lower benefits provide an incentive for TANF recipients to enter the workplace, so it makes sense that business interests would be more interested in this policy than in the family cap, which punishes women for having children while receiving benefits.

The extent to which interest groups are involved in state welfare policy is dependent on whom they serve. Some interest groups represent the type of conscious constituents seen in both the Progressive Era and during the height of the welfare rights movement. While these people care about the plight of welfare recipients, they are ultimately not materially affected by changes in welfare policy. Other types of interest groups represent broad populations that may include welfare recipients among them (such as women or people of color). These organizations care about the well-being of the populations they represent, but welfare recipients constitute a small proportion of the overall population. As a consequence, the needs of this disadvantaged subgroup are overlooked. Still other types of interest groups stand to benefit from the labor of welfare recipients or can use welfare rules to promote their organizational mission, especially if they relate to promoting American ideals of economic self-sufficiency and personal responsibility. In all of these cases, organizations have *tangential interests* to those of welfare recipients. On a given policy or rule the preference of an interest group may align with the preference of welfare recipients, but their interests can just as quickly diverge.

Interest Groups and Measuring Their Influence on Welfare Rules

The transition from Aid to Families with Dependent Children (AFDC) to TANF gave states great control over details of their welfare programs. The programs are expansive, covering policies that range from required work activities for adults to mandatory immunizations for children. I anticipate that interest groups, rather than taking an interest in a state's entire TANF program, will concern themselves with only select welfare rules.

The interests involved in one state may vary depending on the state's interest group population. The size and shape of a state's interest group population is the result of the resources available; growth in a particular industry, for example, may increase the number of organizations representing that industry, or a change in the partisan control of the state legislature may provide an opportunity to get an issue on the political agenda. To avoid conflict over limited resources, most of these interest groups carve out a policy niche to call their own. In policies as all-encompassing as welfare, though, groups that are not primarily involved in social policy find their interests overlap in some small ways. It is thus essential to incorporate a large variety of groups into the analysis to fully understand the influence of organized interests in state welfare policy.

The dataset of interest groups is used to create two measures of interest group influence. Both measures come from the population ecology literature, which theorizes that the absolute and relative number of interest groups within a state depend on the environment.[122] The first measure is the number of organizations within a state, or the *interest group density*. I anticipate that the absolute size of a state's interest group population will affect its propensity to adopt more generous (or stringent) welfare rules. The second measure captures "how numbers of organizations are distributed across some relevant typology of interests."[123] This *diversity of interests* is measured by calculating what percentage of the state's interest group community falls into a given category. In the simplest terms, the interest groups within my sample can be broken down into those in favor of changing a state's welfare program and those favoring the status quo; it is that balance between interests that will determine whether a state changes one of several welfare rules. As the percentage of organizations favoring a change in welfare policy increases within a state, there will be increased pressure on policymakers to respond to these interests. Because interest groups representing welfare recipients constitute such a small percentage of interest groups within most states, there is little pressure on policymakers to address their grievances. In contrast, business interests are assumed to have power over policymakers because they make up such a large proportion of the total interest group community.[124]

Measuring the influence of interest groups has long been a challenge for interest group scholars. As Lowery notes, researchers have identified influence in several ways, including focusing on who possesses the resources that should enable the exercise of power, who controls the agenda, who has the reputation for being powerful, and who "wins" on a particular policy decision.[125] Regardless of the approach taken, however, the majority of interest group research captures only "a snapshot of influence."[126]

Lowery writes that one problem in defining influence is that we cannot determine the counterfactual; that is, we do not know what would have happened in the absence of lobbying. Studying state welfare policy provides us with the counterfactual, however, because the federal government set standards that became the default if the states decided not to adjust them. In a state without sufficient lobbying to either make the rules more or less stringent than the federal requirement, we would expect the state's rules to reflect the federal standard. For example, the federal lifetime time limit is sixty months. Some states have chosen to shorten that limit to two or three years, while other states have chosen to provide state funding to households that have reached their federal time limit.[127] For these states, we may assume that some interest was lobbying for a change from the status quo—i.e., the federal requirement.

This brings up another issue, however, with identifying influence. It is completely possible that an interest group is lobbying on behalf of the status quo, in which case a success for that organization—an indicator of their influence—would show up as a lack of change in the data. Federal standards, for instance, limit assistance to sixty months over the course of an adult's life. Some states have chosen to adopt more generous policies. If a state maintains the federal standard, however, this does not necessarily indicate that those in favor of a more generous policy do not have influence. It could indicate that interests in favor of a more punitive policy also have influence in the state and exercise opposite pressure—the countervailing influences thus yielding maintenance of the federal status quo.

There are both advantages and limitations in using density and diversity as a measure of interest group influence. By using measures of density and diversity, there is less emphasis on the role of money in lobbying. There is an underlying assumption that an interest group has enough support to survive in an environment with limited resources; organizations without sufficient funding will simply cease to exist. The funding of a group, however, does not necessarily guarantee its success. Within this model, a number of smaller, grassroots organizations can theoretically place similar amounts of pressure on policymakers as a few well-funded interest groups.

Focusing on the interest group population within a state, though, accounts for neither which items are moved onto the legislative agenda, nor for the anticipated reactions of interest groups to change in public policy. As Lowery notes, organized interests stake their positions in anticipation of the reactions of those being lobbied.[128] Similarly, the actors being influenced—in this case, state policymakers—take initial stances in anticipation of the organized interests' lobbying. As a result, it becomes difficult to parse out the sincere preferences of the actors. There are limitations to this research design, but it also provides for a greater understanding of influence because it utilizes the variation in the fifty states and the foundation of the federal guidelines as a type of counterfactual.

Theoretical Expectations

Table 2.1 shows the predicted relationships between increased density of interest groups and the leniency of one of twelve welfare policies. A plus sign indicates a positive relationship between interest group density and policy leniency; for example, as the number of feminist organizations in a state increases, I expect the leniency of the family cap policy to increase. For the qualitative case studies, the table also serves to represent my expectations when an interest group testifies at a state legislative hearing. For each rule, I expect there to be groups in favor of both more lenient (indicated with a plus sign) and more stringent policies (indicated with a minus sign), as well as organizations that do not have a strong interest in seeing the policy become either more stringent or more lenient (left blank).[129] In the following sections, I walk through my expectations for the various types of groups.

African American and Civil Rights Groups

The relationship between the National Welfare Rights Organization and prominent African American and civil rights groups in the 1960s and

Table 2.1. Expectations for Interest Group Preferences of TANF Policies

	Family cap	Drug screening requirement	School involvement requirement	Parenting class requirement	Immunization requirement	Allowable activities	Work exemptions	Time limits	Time limit exemptions/extensions	Sponsor deeming	Illegal parent deeming	Immigrant eligibility first five years
Feminist organizations	+			+	+	+						
Religious/pro-life organizations	+	−										
Health advocacy organizations					−							
Conservative family organizations	−			−								
Ideologically conservative groups							−	−	−	−	−	−
Service providers										+	+	+
Civil rights organizations												
Labor unions						−						
Business groups:												
Chambers of Commerce						−	−	−				
Food and beverage						−	−	−				
Retail						−	−	−				
Agriculture						−	−	−				+
Construction						−	−	−				+
Identity groups:												
Elderly						+	+	+				
Disabled						+	+	+				
Victims of domestic violence						+	+	+				
African American						+			+			
Hispanic						+				+	+	+
Other ethnic/racial minorities						+				+	+	+

Where + indicates that a group is expected to favor a more lenient policy, − indicates that a group is expected to favor more stringent policies, and blank indicates that there is no expected relationship between the interest group and the policy.

1970s provides some insight into how these groups may tackle welfare policy today. The NWRO served a narrower constituency than groups founded during the civil rights movement, but in many ways their constituencies overlapped. While the NWRO did not limit its constituency to African Americans, its membership was predominantly Black.[130] Many civil rights organizations had focused on issues of poverty, though often these issues were not a top priority.[131]

The NAACP, for instance, has been a leader among civil rights organizations, but the group developed few ties with the NWRO. There were many differences between the organizations that created tensions. For instance, the NAACP was "essentially middle class and moderate" and "the oldest and largest civil rights group in the United States," while the NWRO was a new, liberal organization.[132] Furthermore, the NAACP emphasized litigation as a strategy in contrast to the NWRO's militancy, and most of its funding came from its own members, rather than relying on outside supporters. Essentially, "welfare and welfare rights were not accepted as viable mobilizing issues" by the NAACP, even though the NAACP and NWRO shared the goal of racial justice.[133] It was not until Congress passed the Economic Opportunity Act in 1964 that the NAACP began to pay attention to poverty at the national level.[134]

The Southern Christian Leadership Conference (SCLC) was another group with both similarities to the NWRO and differences that created tensions. The groups were similar in that they supported cooperation between whites and Blacks.[135] Tensions, however, existed around who would mobilize Black protesters and whether the SCLC could adequately represent the interests of Black women.[136] There was also a continual fundraising battle between the organizations over who would receive the financial support of white liberals.[137] It appears that both the NWRO and SCLC were looking toward the same conscience adherents for support.

The Congress for Racial Equality (CORE) was also allied with the NWRO, although primarily in just the first two years of the welfare rights movement.[138] Moreover, CORE's support occurred mostly at the local level. In Newark, for instance, the Scholarship, Educational, and Defense Fund for Racial Equality (SEDFRE), an arm of CORE, helped a welfare rights organization write and distribute a publication entitled Your Welfare Rights. SEDFRE also provided the financial assistance necessary for the welfare rights group to train organizers, open offices, and print newsletters.[139] When CORE withdrew its support, the welfare rights organization in New Jersey fell apart.[140]

Given this history, I anticipate that African American and civil rights organizations will be in favor of more expansive welfare policies, but that support may not always be consistent or significant. I expect that groups representing African Americans will be in favor of more expansive allowable activities, for example, because unemployment is high among minorities and greater flexibility in activities will provide recipients with a better chance of meeting requirements. I also anticipate that African American organizations may be more likely to oppose a family cap because unmarried births, which family caps are designed to limit, are often seen as a "Black" problem.[141]

Paden argues that "advocacy for the poor has never been the top priority of civil rights organizations." In the late 1960s, though, major civil rights organizations, including SNCC, CORE, SLCC, and NAACP, supported the plan to fight poverty outlined in the Freedom Budget—a plan that called for $100 billion to fight poverty by providing decent wages, expanded access to healthcare and housing, and a guaranteed annual income.[142] I expect that civil rights organizations will become involved in welfare policy when such policies' requirements infringe upon the rights of recipients. Even welfare recipients without criminal backgrounds are subject to levels of surveillance and regulation usually reserved for parolees and probationers because of states' aggressive investigation of welfare fraud.[143] For example, in some states recipients are required to undergo random drug screenings; policymakers justify these policies by citing the high rates of drug abuse and addiction among those who receive cash assistance.[144] It is in these situations that I expect civil rights groups to become active and advocate for the removal of such requirements.

Domestic Violence Groups

Under welfare reform beginning in the 1990s, states could adopt the Family Violence Option (FVO), which exempted survivors of domestic violence from time limits, work requirements, and child support enforcement. On the national level, interest groups ranging from the NOW Legal Defense and Education Fund to the National Immigration Forum advocated for the federal law to accommodate victims of domestic violence.[145] Advocates argued that survivors of domestic violence may be unemployed because of the abuse they have experienced.[146] They may also be at risk of continued harassment if their abuser knows where they work, thus necessitating exemptions from work requirements. Furthermore, women who have been in abusive relationships may choose to not seek out child support from their child's father because they do not want to disclose their location or they fear retribution.[147]

While an alarming number of women experience domestic violence at some point in their lives, research suggests that low-income women may be more likely to experience violence.[148] Advocacy organizations likely serve survivors who qualify for TANF. After PRWORA was passed, many local organizations found themselves working with states to screen recipients for domestic violence.[149] Domestic violence organizations may find themselves continuing to represent the needs of welfare recipients even after the state has passed all the provisions of the FVO. These advocacy organizations may also be overwhelmed with demand for their services, in which case they may choose to devote their limited resources to seeking state funding.[150]

Disability Rights and Senior Groups

Identity groups should be against welfare policies that make it more difficult for the group in question to complete work requirements. For the elderly and those with disabilities, I expect organizations representing these constituencies to be in favor of more allowable work activities, more work exemptions, and longer time limits with exemptions or extensions. Survey data from 2005 and 2006 shows that TANF recipients are far more likely than the average US adult to have activity limitations; more than a quarter indicate they are limited in the type of work they can complete.[151] A greater range of allowable work activities could include counseling or life skills training, which may be more easily completed than paid employment or other labor force–related activities. Exemptions from work activities allow the recipient to continue receiving benefits even when they do not meet work requirements, and exemptions or extensions to time limits allow recipients to continue receiving benefits past the normal time limit.

Disability rights activists may also abandon advocacy around TANF in favor of other social safety net programs. In the aftermath of PRWORA's passage, some researchers speculated that the work requirements and time limits would move individuals from TANF to Supplemental Security Income (SSI).[152] This transfer could be beneficial to both recipients and states: SSI does not have time limits, recipients receive larger monthly payments, and it is fully federally funded.[153] Some states require TANF recipients with disabilities to apply for SSI or SSDI.

One of the most powerful interest groups in the country, the AARP, is a strong supporter of Medicare and Social Security and its policy preferences often align with the interests of low-income Americans.[154] These programs are specifically targeted at their constituents, so it is not clear how their presence would influence state TANF programs. Moreover, Gilens argues that the unique characteristics of the AARP—its large membership and extensive financial resources—do not present an ideal model of an interest group advocating for the interests of the poor.[155]

Women's Groups

In my analysis I include both organizations that are explicitly feminist in their ideology and other organizations that represent women more broadly. In her analysis of women's organizations' participation in rulemaking, English finds that organizations were least likely to mention socioeconomic status, but more likely to discuss gender identity and sexual orientation.[156] I expect feminist organizations to show their strongest opposition to policies that attempt to regulate a woman's sexuality, such as the family cap, and dictate how she should parent through behavioral requirements, such as mandatory parenting classes and required immunizations for children. Other women's organizations may choose to be less involved in the rules that appear to regulate the sexuality of welfare recipients.

Women's organizations more generally may be interested in the types of activities available to welfare recipients. As Hays points out, "the need of millions of women for welfare may be seen as product of the more limited opportunities and earning power of women in general."[157] In an effort to get welfare recipients out of low-paying, unstable jobs, organizations may advocate for more education and training activities to count in meeting the activity requirements. Under AFDC, for instance, the Institute for Women's Policy Research framed welfare benefits as an important form of income when the job market is unreliable.[158] Women with more training and education will qualify for higher-paying positions, which in turn may help them become self-sufficient. Moreover, "care feminism" emphasizes the value of care work, and organizations aligning with this strand of thought may support counting activities such as caring for the ill or young children as meeting work requirements.[159]

Latino, Immigration Rights, and Other Minority Groups

Historically, Latino organizations have taken the form of community service organizations rather than advocacy organizations.[160] These groups may not be interested in influencing state welfare rules, though they may be able to represent a population who is eligible for welfare. Among groups that are more expressly political, groups representing Latinos and other ethnic or racial minorities may also be in favor of more allowable activities, especially as they concern English as a Second Language classes or other forms of education and training. In a survey of poor immigrant women living in Santa Clara County, California, a majority of respondents reported limited English proficiency as a barrier to getting a job and accessing services. Most of the respondents had never received job training and felt they lacked the skills necessary to achieve self-sufficiency.[161]

They may also advocate on behalf of noncitizen eligibility. In the mid-1990s the Hispanic Association of New Jersey, which represented twenty-six member agencies, voiced its opposition to any provisions that would limit access to Work First New Jersey to citizens.[162] On the national level, the NAACP has worked with Latino organizations such as the League of United Latin American Citizens and National Council of La Raza (now UnidosUS) to fight strict immigration policies in states such as Arizona.[163] This group representation is important for noncitizen immigrants because they cannot use the right to vote as a way of expressing their policy preferences.

Social Welfare Groups

Social welfare groups encompass a wide variety of groups, including those that advocate on behalf of issues related to child welfare, poverty, homelessness, and food scarcity. Some of these groups provide services, while others do not. Among those that provide services, I anticipate they will support an expanded welfare policy because it reduces the burden placed on them. Describing the lobbying activity of Catholic groups, Cammisa and Manuel write, "many of the policies for which these groups lobby involve services that they provide."[164] In the Multi-City Survey of Social Service Providers, 75 percent of faith-based organizations stated that they served welfare recipients, with services ranging from cash and food assistance to treatment for mental health and substance abuse.[165]

I anticipate social service providers will support a variety of welfare rules. For example, I expect these groups will support state assistance to noncitizens. During the debate over welfare reform in Maryland, religious organizations including Catholic Charities came out in support of providing assistance for immigrants.[166] I also anticipate that social welfare groups will advocate against the family cap. At the national level, Catholic groups allied with feminist organizations to oppose family caps. Catholic groups expressed concern that the rule punished children for the behavior of their parents and may increase abortions.[167] Finally, I anticipate that social service organizations will be in favor of policies that allow states to tailor programs according to the needs of the recipient. Catholic groups have opposed time limits, for instance, because such restrictions do not address the reality that some recipients (such as drug and alcohol abusers) will not be ready to join the workforce in just a few years.[168]

Health Providers and Associations

While TANF does not provide direct medical assistance to low-income families, organizations focused on health issues may take an interest in certain welfare rules. For example, these organizations may be in favor of time limit and activity requirement exemptions for recipients who are ill or disabled; they may also support providing exemptions to their caretakers. In other cases, debates within the health industry spill over into welfare policy. The immunization requirements adopted by some states are part of the debate surrounding childhood vaccinations. An estimated 322 million illnesses will be prevented because of the routine childhood vaccinations among children born from 1994 to 2013, and immunizations will also provide a net savings of $296 billion in direct health costs.[169] Given this large public health impact, I anticipate that health-related organizations, from associations representing health professionals to health advocacy groups, will support required immunizations.

Economically Conservative Groups

I expect that conservative groups (e.g., Tea Party groups or other organizations in favor of small government) will favor more stringent policies that limit eligibility and make it more difficult for recipients to continue receiving assistance. With regard to limiting eligibility, I expect these groups to be against extending eligibility to noncitizens. In relation to making it more difficult for recipients to stay on the rolls, I expect these organizations to favor shorter time limits, with fewer exemptions and extensions, as well as fewer activity requirement exemptions. I also expect a small portion of conservative groups—mainly nativist groups seeking to limit immigration, hate groups opposed to multiculturalism, and white supremacy groups—will be against extending TANF benefits to noncitizens.

Pro-Life and Socially Conservative Groups

As proof that politics does make strange bedfellows, some religious groups and pro-life organizations aligned with feminist organizations to advocate against a family cap. At the federal level, for example, the National Right to Life Committee broke away from other conservative organizations with its stance against the family cap.[170] For socially conservative groups, however, their opposition to the family cap was rooted in a fear that the policy would lead to an increase in abortions. I expect similar coalitions at the state level.

On the whole, I expect conservative family organizations that promote traditional family values to favor more stringent policies in many of the areas in which feminist organizations favor more lenient policies. I expect these organizations to be in support of family cap policies and parenting class requirements because both policies can be seen as ways of promoting family formation, which conservative groups have argued is needed to fight childhood poverty.[171] Conservative family organizations that believe poverty is the result of an individual's moral failings may also be supportive of drug testing/screening of TANF applicants because drug users have proven themselves to be "undeserving" of such aid.

Labor Unions

Labor unions have several potential interests in TANF policy. Some labor unions may represent workers who could potentially be displaced by TANF recipients, which may lead them to oppose subsidized employment or community work experience. Public sector labor unions may represent the street-level bureaucrats who interact with TANF recipients. Under these circumstances, labor unions may oppose policies that increase the workload for employees, such as stricter eligibility requirements, or take jobs away from union members, such as through privatizing job training programs.[172]

Chambers of Commerce and Industry Groups

Gilens found no evidence that the preferences of business organizations were positively correlated with the interests of low-income Americans.[173] This does not mean, however, that business is uninterested in welfare policy; in fact, I anticipate that business organizations will be in favor of more stringent policies. I predict their interest in welfare rules to be directly tied to the possibility of employing welfare recipients in low-wage jobs. Therefore, I expect that business interests will be in favor of policies that focus on turning welfare recipients into workers. These include limits on the types of work exemptions and the activities allowed to count toward work requirements, as well as more stringent time limits. Fewer exemptions and allowable activities will force more welfare recipients into labor market activities (as opposed to education or training activities). A shorter time limit forces welfare recipients back into the job market more quickly and may make them more inclined to take low-paying jobs that they would otherwise not accept.

Low-wage industries in particular may have an interest in welfare policy because they are most likely to employ welfare workers. A Center on Budget and Policy Priorities (CBPP) review of studies examining the employment and earnings of current and former welfare recipients found that workers typically made less than eight dollars an hour, and a significant portion made less than six dollars an hour, putting their earnings well below the poverty line.[174] In one study of former welfare recipients in Maryland, more than a third worked in the wholesale and retail trade industry, including food service, department stores, and grocery stores.[175] In South Carolina, nearly half of the former welfare recipients surveyed worked in service industries.[176] In addition to the retail and food and beverage industries having an interest in welfare policy, agriculture and construction industries may have an interest in welfare policies as well. I expect that these industries will also be interested in noncitizen eligibility policies, given the prevalence of immigrant workers in these areas.

Conclusion

Political representation comes through many avenues. An individual may find herself represented by an elected official who shares similar characteristics or life experiences. In sharing these similarities, the voter hopes that the elected official will also share similar values and opinions on policy matters. More broadly, a political party may represent the interests of a group. Due to the two-party nature of the US political system, however, marginalized groups may find themselves choosing between the lesser of two evils. Citizens can also join organized groups that will advocate on their behalf. The effects of interest groups may also be wrapped up in these other methods of representation. Fording finds that Republican control of the executive increases the probability of a state adopting welfare waivers, but this is significant only in states where the Christian Right has a strong presence.[177] Women's interest groups may be more effective in their lobbying as the percentage of women in the legislature increases, as research has shown that female legislators are more responsive to women's organizations than their male colleagues.[178] Thus, the effect of interest groups may be channeled through both individual legislators and political parties.

Often there are financial or time barriers that prevent the most disadvantaged from active participation in interest groups, and so they may not have their interests fully represented. Instead, their interests may be represented by those who stand to benefit from a policy change, but not necessarily from the improved well-being of the group. Welfare recipients are maligned as promiscuous women and negligent mothers, reluctant workers, state dependents, and greedy noncitizens. Each framing of welfare recipients provides interest groups with the opportunity to pursue their own interests through welfare rules. Take the stereotypical assumption about welfare recipients' sexuality and parenting. Within this frame, feminist organizations may choose to advocate against policies placing restrictions on women's freedom, while groups from the Christian Right and those advocating traditional family values will be in support of more stringent policies. If a welfare recipient is seen as lazy and dependent on the state, business interests that may benefit from low-skilled labor may take an interest in policies that get recipients back to work. Finally, the same actors involved in immigration debates will be interested in the eligibility of noncitizen welfare recipients. Notably missing from this puzzle, however, are organizations that represent the target population of a state's TANF rules—the welfare recipients.

Regardless of interest group influence, racial stereotypes are a driving force in welfare policymaking. Gilens's work provides strong evidence that the American public strongly associates welfare with African Americans.[179] At the elite level, Neubeck and Cazenave note that when President Clinton signed PRWORA in 1996, African American women were at his side—a clear message that his promise to "end welfare as we know it" was directed at a particular subgroup of low-income women.[180] A lack of interest group influence may suggest that the public identity of the welfare queen—the poor, single African American woman whose poverty was caused by her own laziness and promiscuity—is still the driving force in creating welfare policy.[181] The history of welfare in the United States may be so deeply intertwined with racial stereotypes that even powerful interest groups do not have a significant impact on state welfare rules.

3

Morality and Motherhood

The Politics of Behavioral Requirements

Senator Marco Rubio, speaking in 2014 on the fiftieth anniversary of Lyndon Johnson's address to a joint session of Congress declaring a "War on Poverty," said, "The truth is, the greatest tool to lift children and families from poverty is one that decreases the probability of child poverty by 82%. But it isn't a government spending program. It's called marriage."[1] Two decades earlier, Jeb Bush, then a Republican gubernatorial candidate in Florida, conveyed a similar sentiment when he said that "if people are honest about the welfare system we have today, how you get on welfare is not having a husband in the house."[2] Implied in both of these statements is that unmarried mothers are to blame for their poverty.

In accordance with the fourth purpose of PRWORA, states may spend part of their TANF block grant on marriage promotion programs. For years, Oklahoma has dedicated millions of dollars of its TANF budget to promoting marriage and preventing out-of-wedlock births.[3] Ohio allocated $200,000 for couples group counseling in 2021, even as low-income families struggled amid the pandemic.[4] The promotion of the two-parent family ideal is seen within TANF rules as well, as states are given the option to mandate certain aspects of parenting, require cooperation with child support enforcement, and punish women when they give birth while receiving assistance through the family cap. In both rhetoric and policy, the traditional nuclear family is cast as a panacea for societal ills.

The cash assistance first provided in state's mothers' pensions were intended to enforce traditional family structures by providing financial assistance to keep women at home when they otherwise would have needed to find paid work. The passage of the Social Security Act in 1935, which created Aid to Dependent Children (later renamed Aid to Families with Dependent Children), was intended to provide aid to the less than approximately 1.5 million families headed by women who found themselves with children but without a male breadwinner.[5] The population of women-headed households increased throughout the twentieth century. In 1950, 7.3 percent of households with children under eighteen were headed by a single parent (and approximately 85 percent of those households were headed by women). By 2022, the share of single-parent households had increased to 31 percent.[6] As the prevalence of single-parent households has increased, Americans' opinions about single-parent households have shifted as well. A survey in 1994 showed that approximately half of respondents either disagreed or strongly disagreed with the idea that a single parent could raise children as well as two parents. By 2012, that had decreased to 42 percent.[7] Public opinion on parenting may be changing, but TANF rules remain remarkably consistent.

Mothering and Race

Cash assistance in the United States is as strongly driven by a desire to keep women in their traditional roles as wives and mothers as it is to provide relief to the poor. Under Aid to Families with Dependent Children (AFDC), widowed and abandoned mothers received enough aid to care for their children without having to search for work outside the home. Even prior to federal aid, local women's organizations advocated for mothers' pensions to promote the same cause.

The generosity under states' mothers' pensions extended only to white women, however; Black mothers have always been expected to work, from slaves required to work in the field immediately before and after giving birth, to Black women serving as domestic help for white families. State discretion allowed Southern states to exclude agricultural workers and domestic servants from receiving AFDC—not surprisingly, the majority of the people affected by these rules were Black.[8] In the 1950s the rules were revised, and in combination with the mass migration of Blacks from the South to the North, the AFDC caseload steadily became less white. Although African Americans have never constituted the majority of the welfare caseload, they are overrepresented in proportion to their population. Moreover, while the original recipients of AFDC were widows and their children, the number of unmarried women increased over time and the welfare caseload increasingly comprised divorced and never married mothers.[9]

The changing demographics of welfare recipients combined with a long racial history to perpetuate the stereotype of a promiscuous Black woman receiving welfare. Welfare recipients are viewed as morally deficient in all aspects of their lives; Hancock argues that this deficiency can be simplified into two dimensions: hyperfertility and laziness.[10] The hyperfertility associated with welfare recipients has a long, racialized history dating back to slavery. Stereotypes of promiscuous Black women were used to justify white slave owners' sexual abuse of their female slaves for their own pleasure and to maintain the slave population.[11] Collins describes the controlling image of the welfare mother as the "updated version of the breeder woman image."[12] Through the twentieth century, Black women have been forcibly sterilized and made to accept the birth control implant Norplant in order to receive aid.[13]

In her critique of welfare reform, Gwendolyn Mink argues that many policies are rooted in the stereotype of "reckless breeders who bear children to avoid work."[14] During ADC, these policies took the form of "substitute father" and "suitable homes" rules; by 1941, more than half of states had instituted some version of the rules into their ADC program.[15] Substitute father rules stated that any able-bodied man living in the same house as a welfare recipient could be considered financially responsible for the child.[16] As a consequence, a woman living with a man frequently became ineligible for welfare benefits. Welfare officials would conduct midnight raids of recipients' homes to search for evidence of a man living in the house.[17] Suitable home policies were arbitrary guidelines that required caseworkers to make decisions on the "deservingness" of a welfare recipient; the lack of clear guidelines led to increased discrimination against single African American women.[18]

Wrapped up in the stereotype of promiscuity is the belief that welfare recipients are "sly profit-maximizer[s]" who have more children for the sole purpose of increasing their welfare benefits.[19] Governor Jimmie Davis of Louisiana once referred to mothers on welfare as a "bunch of professional prostitutes."[20] As Daniel Patrick Moynihan described it, while someone in the middle class "would never dream of having another baby in order to get hold of an additional eight or twelve dollars a month," those living in poverty, "out of depravity, cu-pidity, ignorance, or whatever" would.[21] The idea that women had more children to receive more in cash assistance later gave rise to the family cap.

The welfare recipients spoken of by Governor Davis were not the good, deserving mothers who had fallen on hard times and needed gov-ernment aid to stay with their children; in the eyes of policymakers and the public, welfare recipients are assumed to be incompetent mothers. Transforming welfare recipients into better mothers was seen as one of the most effective ways to solve a variety of social ills. Policymak-ers argued that the disintegration of the Black family, which was largely blamed on Black mothers entering the labor force, led to increased riot-ing in urban areas and poor educational outcomes.[22]

The Moynihan Report

Daniel Patrick Moynihan's report, *The Negro Family: The Case for National Action*, confirmed preexisting stereotypes and influenced welfare policy for decades after its publication. Moynihan, the assis-tant secretary of labor under President Johnson and a domestic policy advisor to President Nixon, described the "deterioration of the Negro family" as the "fundamental source of the weakness of the Negro com-munity at the present time." He argued that Black families in America were "highly unstable" and "approaching complete breakdown" because of high divorce rates and even higher rates of out-of-wedlock births. To Moynihan, the connection between single parent households and wel-fare was clear; whereas initially following the creation of AFDC only a third of women were single parents because of desertion, that share had increased to two-thirds by the mid-1960s.[23]

What was behind the deterioration of the Black family? The Moyni-han report acknowledges the negative influence of slavery and racial discrimination. It also suggests, however, that Black women—or more specifically, the matriarchy—were to blame. Patricia Hill Collins de-scribes how the image of the Black matriarch was used to propel a nar-rative based in classed, gendered, and racial oppression.[24] Black women dominated family life in response to high unemployment among Black men.[25] According to Moynihan, this role reversal, where the woman was the main breadwinner, broke apart the traditional nuclear family. In turn, Black families turned to welfare and Black women were blamed for the pathology in which "the cycle of poverty and disadvantage will continue to repeat itself."[26]

Not only were dominant women destroying their families by daring to "reject the image of the submissive, hardworking servant," but they were also bad mothers.[27] While Moynihan did not explicitly blame Black women for having too many children, the report does remark that Black women "not only have more children, but have them earlier" and that "children are being born most rapidly" in "families with the least financial resources."[28] Moynihan also argued that Black children were at a disadvantage academically because they lacked father figures; young men were also less likely to be juvenile delinquents when they came from two-parent families.[29] In this way, growing economic disparity was blamed on Black women's personal choices.

The matriarch was also used to explain absent Black fathers. Naturally, men would feel emasculated if they were in a relationship with a woman who challenged gender roles. It should be no surprise that a man would refuse to marry such a woman. The need to correct for absent fathers led to a variety of government initiatives, backed by both Republicans and Democrats. The National Responsible Fatherhood Clearinghouse, which provides resources for all those "who are serving or interested in supporting strong fathers and families," was created following the passage of the 2005 TANF reauthorization.[30] While still a senator in 2008, Barack Obama declared on Father's Day that fathers were "missing from too many lives and too many homes" and had "abandoned their responsibilities, acting like boys instead of men."[31] As president, Obama established an initiative, My Brother's Keeper, to connect young Black men with mentors. On these occasions, and others, Obama has been criticized by academics and journalists for playing into racial stereotypes. Ta-Nehisi Coates wrote that Obama's tendency to lecture Black audiences about responsibility was troubling.[32] Frederick Harris expressed concern that much of My Brother's Keeper's "rhetoric about the lack of responsibility [. . .] reinforces existing stereotypes about black men, particularly as fathers."[33] Policies such as strict child support reporting requirements attempted to not only police women's sexuality but also hold so-called "deadbeat dads" responsible.

The image of an aggressive, domineering Black woman was used to explain the state of Black families in twentieth-century America. Their aggression emasculated men and pushed them to be absent fathers. Absent fathers, combined with a strong matriarch, led to poorly behaved children, and those children grew up to perpetuate a cycle of poverty and government dependence. Given all the blame placed on Black women, it is no wonder that welfare reform sought to regulate welfare recipients' morality.

Addressing Morality under PRWORA

During the 1970s and 1980s, the share of two-parent Black families decreased by more than 20 percentage points, and the share of children born out of wedlock increased from 35.1 to 62.6 percent.[34] The shift toward regulating personal responsibility began with the passage of the Family Support Act in 1988, which required single mothers to establish paternity and minor parents to complete their education and live in a supervised living situation if they were not married.[35] Public opinion also reflected a moralizing tone; the news media frequently covered welfare recipients as teen mothers with illegitimate children.[36] These were not the same women and children eligible for AFDC benefits fifty years earlier.

The Personal Responsibility and Work Opportunity Reconciliation Act completed the shift from an entitlement, in which someone who met the income requirements could receive aid without having to also meet behavior requirements, to a paternalist model in which welfare recipients must conform to society's values in order to receive aid.[37] PRWORA directly addressed the behavior and perceived immorality of welfare recipients in the stated purpose of TANF. In addition to providing assistance to low-income families, TANF is supposed to "prevent and reduce the incidence of out-of-wedlock pregnancies and establish numerical goals for preventing and reducing the incidence of these pregnancies" and "encourage the formation and maintenance of two-parent families." To encourage states to pursue these goals, the federal government provided monetary incentives to the states that decreased their out-of-wedlock pregnancies the most without increasing abortions.

With increased discretion over how to spend federal money under TANF, states have been experimenting with ways to promote marriage.

Arizona, for instance, allocated $1 million a year to marriage skills courses and designing a "healthy marriage" handbook. Michigan and Oklahoma have used funding to pay for marital counseling.[38] Nine states offer financial incentives for welfare recipients that marry; West Virginia provides a $100 monthly bonus to women who marry the father of their children. States dedicate funding to responsible fatherhood programs that provide employment services, parenting classes, legal assistance, and group and individual counseling to noncustodial fathers.[39]

The state's decision to promote two-parent families is driven as much by financial motives as it is by any moral imperative to help citizens establish healthy relationships. In 2021, only 6 percent of married couple families had incomes that fell below the poverty line, compared to 29 percent of single parent families.[40] Promoting marriage is an investment that aims to yield a long-term decrease in the number of families who meet the TANF income eligibility requirements. Even if a couple is not married, the state can force noncustodial parents (typically fathers) to pay child support, which is seen as a way of recovering the costs of government assistance.[41]

PRWORA also provided states with more discretion in determining the requirements for initial and continuing eligibility. While much of the attention on these requirements centers around the work requirements, the wide latitude given to states permitted them to institute behavioral requirements seemingly not related to obtaining or retaining employment. There are several common behavioral requirements imposed upon welfare recipients and two other common policies—child support reporting requirements and family caps—that center on a welfare recipient's sexuality and parenting.

The Rules

Behavioral Requirements

The behavioral requirements adopted by states are often included in a formal contract or behavioral agreement signed by the recipient when they begin receiving assistance. The details of these contracts range across the states; in some states, individuals meet with caseworkers to create an agreement specific to their situation, while in other states there are standard contracts signed by every recipient. To create a measure of state paternalism, I created an index comprising some of the most common behavioral requirements: drug screening/random testing, parenting classes, child immunizations, and school attendance. There has been a steady increase in the number of states adopting these behavioral requirements. In 1997, there were nineteen states that required none of the four behavioral requirements included in the index, and the average number of requirements per state was 1.5. By 2016, however, states had on average adopted 2.3 requirements and only seven states did not have any of the requirements. Figure 3.1 shows how many states had each requirement in place from 1997 to 2016.

During the welfare reform debate of the mid-1990s, welfare recipients were often linked to drug use. William Bennett, the first director of national drug control policy, told a House committee that "the day the welfare checks go out is a big day for drug buys."[42] Not only did this create the perception that taxpayer money was supporting drug habits, but politicians also connected drug use to poor parenting.[43] This national discourse around drug use and welfare prompted many states to require welfare recipients to undergo drug screening and random drug testing. This rule became the subject of increasing media coverage in the early 2010s. A LexisNexis search of "welfare" and "drug testing" produces over eighteen hundred newspaper stories between 1997 and 2018, with over two-thirds of those stories being published since 2010.

States may also require welfare recipients to attend parenting classes. Frequently these requirements stem from concerns about teen pregnancy and studies showing that minor parents are more likely to receive welfare and stay on welfare for longer periods of time than their peers who did not have children. Members of Congress frequently invoked the image of "children having children" and argued that not only were unmarried teenagers having unprotected sex, but that they were intentionally becoming pregnant.[44] Supporters of mandatory programs and training for unmarried teenage parents argue that participation in such programs increases dramatically when participation changes from voluntary to mandatory.[45] What these supporters do not recognize, however, is the class and race bias built into this participation requirement. An unmarried teenager who comes from a wealthy family may become pregnant, leave school, and face no penalty from the state. A wealthy minor parent can decide for herself if, and when, she wants to look for work. For poor minor parents, however, their dependence on cash assistance means that they have to comply with the behavioral requirements outlined by the state.

Behavioral requirements also focus on a parent's involvement in a child's schooling. By 1999, forty states had provisions requiring school attendance for dependent children in recipient households; in some states, such as Maryland and Delaware, social workers verify the attendance of school-age children by contacting the school.[46] States may also require parents to be involved in their child's education through activities such as parent-teacher conferences. The penalty for not meeting these requirements includes a reduction in benefit or case closure. Just as with work requirements for parents, school attendance policies for dependent children reinforce the importance of personal responsibility.[47] Women wealthy enough to not need government assistance do not have to comply with such requirements. These additional requirements on parents imply that welfare recipients are not good parents who would naturally be involved in their children's education.

Finally, there are the immunization requirements for dependent children. There has been little change in states' immunization requirements for TANF recipients over time; only Kentucky and Montana have changed their requirement since 1998. Immunization requirements reinforce the same paternalism as other behavioral requirements. Even though childhood vaccinations are commonly required for children to attend school or daycare, it is only low-income women who are financially penalized for not meeting this requirement. In many states, a family wealthy enough to not need cash assistance could avoid vaccination requirements by keeping their child out of public schools or daycare, or by claiming a religious or philosophical objection.

Child Support Reporting Requirements

One of the ways the state becomes involved with a TANF recipient's personal relationships and childrearing is through child support requirements. Even prior to welfare reform, women were often required by local welfare departments to sue their partners for nonsupport.[48] Child support enforcement policy changed significantly in 1975 when the Federal Office of Child Support Enforcement was created and

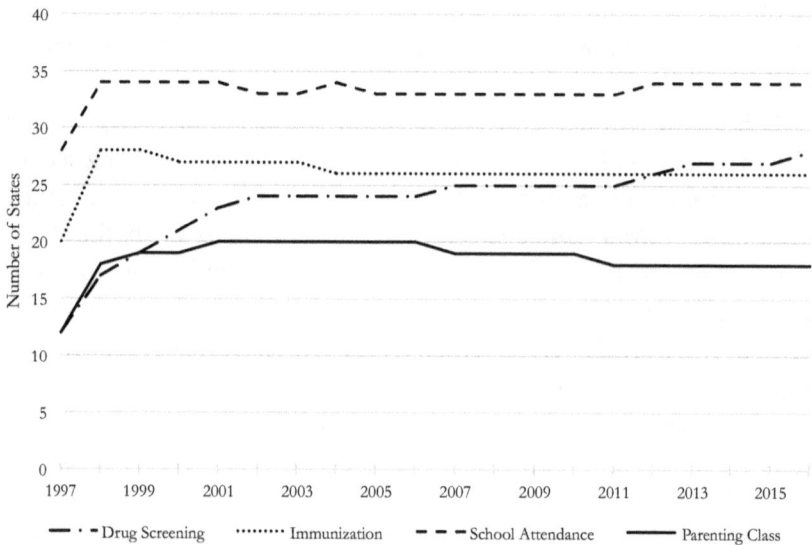

Figure 3.1. Number of States with Behavioral Requirements, 1997–2016.
Source: Urban Institute's Welfare Rules Database.

amendments to the Social Security Act mandated that states create their own enforcement agencies. Since then, to varying degrees of enforcement, states have required an unmarried mother to name the father of her children, whether that is her former husband or the biological father of the child.[49] In 1988, under the Family Support Act, states were required to establish paternity for 50 percent of child support cases receiving welfare; that requirement was increased to 90 percent under PRWORA.[50] Under TANF, child support requirements may include mandating the woman locate the absent parent and/or conduct a paternity test, among other conditions. The state expects women to be responsible for their relationships, while also implying that good mothers seek out child support. Pursuing child support is also beneficial to the state, because often any child support received is deducted from a recipient's total benefits. New Jersey Department of Human Services Commissioner William Waldman articulated the motivation behind child support enforcement during his testimony before the state senate's judiciary committee:

As welfare is now a block grant, every dollar collected for a family on welfare or for one who might otherwise need it is a dollar less of cap taxpayer funds that we'll need to spend on public assistance. Fundamentally supporting children should be a primary responsibility of parents. This legislation will make sure that the New Jersey parents fulfill this personal responsibility.[51]

There have been debates among feminists and welfare advocates as to whether recipients should be required to pursue child support. Those in favor of the requirement argue that child support is a guaranteed way to prevent an estranged spouse from becoming a "deadbeat dad." Those in opposition argue that communication between a woman and her ex should be a personal decision. Smith compares child support systems after a divorce and the policies for welfare recipients. "A divorced custodial mother," Smith writes, "is not pressed by the law to pursue her former spouse for child support."[52] She may fear retribution from the father, decide that she does not want him to be involved in the child's life, or not want to compromise a new relationship.[53] At no point in time is she required by the state to pursue child support—unless she is receiving public assistance. Smith writes that "the single mother who wants to live entirely apart from the biological father of her children must be wealthy enough to purchase governmental respect for her autonomy."[54]

To measure the stringency of a state's child support reporting requirement, I created an index of nine possible requirements: identify noncustodial parent, locate noncustodial parent, help determine paternity, appear at an agency, appear at and testify in court, obtain child support payments, obtain other support payments, sign over payments to the state, and other requirements. Not every recipient in a state may be subject to every requirement, but a higher number on the index indicates that the state has a stricter policy toward child support reporting. The average number of requirements by state is approximately six, and every state has at least two requirements.

Family Cap

States have tried to discourage women from having more children while receiving TANF benefits through family cap policies, which place an upper bound on a household's benefit level regardless of whether more children enter into the home. Much of the rhetoric around family caps emphasizes preventing out-of-wedlock pregnancies, even though caps affect both unmarried and married women.[55] Feminists, and feminist organizations, frequently take a strong position against these policies because of their infringement on women's sexual freedom.[56] The family cap also takes on a racialized tone with its underlying effort to stop "welfare queens" from having more children to increase their benefits and the overt concern about the number of "out-of-wedlock" births, which is largely viewed as a Black problem.[57] As a result, family caps are more frequently implemented in states with a higher proportion of Blacks and Hispanics in the population.[58]

In 1997, eighteen states had a family cap in place; by 2003 that number had increased to twenty-two states. Several studies have shown that family caps are unsuccessful at decreasing birth rates among welfare recipients.[59] As a result, states have reversed their policies; as of 2016, only sixteen states still apply family caps. Often when a state adopts a family cap policy it will allow for exemptions. The most frequent exemption to a family cap is in the case of rape or incest; in 1997, fifteen out of the eighteen states with a family cap allowed for this exemption. A few states allow for exemptions if the child or mother is disabled, or if the child is adopted into a family. In a departure from other literature that analyzes states' use of family caps, I use a measure of family cap stringency that takes into account the flexibility provided through these exemptions.[60] States without family cap policies are coded "0." States with family caps and one or more exemptions are coded "1" and states with family cap policies but no exemptions are coded "2."

Explaining Adoption of Paternalist Policies

In the following sections I outline the possible forces influencing a state's decision to implement behavioral requirements, child support reporting requirements, and a family cap. I theorize that the main influence is that of interest groups, many of whom are interested in the ethical and moral questions surrounding these paternalist policies. I also discuss how a state's level of need, political environment, and the larger welfare context may influence the adoption of these policies.

Interest Groups

While the welfare rights movement was not as prominent as some of the other social movements of the 1960s and 1970s, it did create some organizations that advocated on behalf of welfare recipients. The most prominent was the National Welfare Rights Organization, which actively pushed against the stereotype of a welfare recipient interested primarily in monetary gain and indifferent toward her children.[61] The organization was most vocal against this stereotype when it was run by the poor, Black women it was representing. Given the history of welfare advocacy, I anticipate that states with a greater diversity of interest groups representing welfare recipients will be less likely to adopt behavioral requirements and the family cap, and will require fewer child support reporting requirements.

I primarily anticipate that feminist organizations, African American organizations, and social welfare organizations will be the ones advocating in favor of more lenient behavioral policies because each type of group represents a component of the stereotypical welfare recipient's identity. The National Organization for Women (NOW) worked with child welfare advocacy groups such as the Children's Defense Fund and the Center for Law and Social Policy (CLASP) on issues like the family cap at the national level. Weaver writes that children's advocacy groups were unsuccessful in fighting PRWORA because of their "limited ability to mobilize grassroots support to force legislators or the president to be responsive to their views."[62] At the state level, though, child welfare advocates may have greater grassroots support and exert more influence over lawmakers.

In contrast, I anticipate that states with a greater diversity of conservative interest groups will be more likely to adopt behavioral requirements, strict child support reporting requirements, and the family cap. In the analysis I distinguish between three types of conservative organizations: socially conservative, pro-life, and fiscally conservative. The socially conservative organizations, such as the Christian Coalition, include members of the religious Right and those that advocate for traditional family values. They may oppose abortion, but they differ from pro-life organizations in that abortion is not their primary issue. The missions of these organizations align with the third and fourth purposes of TANF, decreasing out-of-wedlock pregnancies and supporting stable, two-parent families; therefore, I expect these groups to support behavioral requirements. During the national debate around welfare reform, however, pro-life organizations aligned with more liberal organizations in opposition to the family cap for fear that family caps would increase abortion rates.[63] Economically conservative groups include those that want to rein in government spending on social programs and decrease taxes. I anticipate these groups to be strongly in favor of the family cap because it limits government spending; similarly, I expect them to favor stricter child support reporting requirements because greater child support payments decrease the financial burden on the government.

I also anticipate that civil rights organizations will take an interest in these policies. A civil rights organization such as the NAACP may see these requirements as unfairly targeting a racial or ethnic group. Moreover, civil rights organizations may perceive these behavioral requirements to be infringements on personal liberty. The ACLU, for instance, (unsuccessfully) challenged New Jersey's family cap policy in court.[64] Finally, I anticipate that health organizations will be in favor of immunization requirements. Childhood immunizations prevent the spread of disease and are far more cost-effective than treating preventable illnesses.

As shown in table 3.1, social welfare groups greatly outnumber the number of organizations representing other interests. Social welfare is broadly defined to include child welfare groups, as well as general poverty advocacy organizations. There are also a large number of health organizations; this category includes professional associations such as state chapters of the American Academy of Pediatrics as well as many community health clinics. In contrast, the number of socially conservative organizations is quite small in the sample (twenty-four groups). In some models, these groups are combined with pro-life organizations to represent a broader contingent of pro-family conservative organizations.

Just as gender and politics scholars have debated whether "women's interests" or "women's issues" include only feminist causes or all issues pertaining to women, I debated whether to create a category of "women's organizations" that included not only feminist organizations, but all organizations that described themselves as representing women.[65] I chose to limit the category to feminist organizations because I expect

Table 3.1. Descriptive Statistics on Interest Groups

	Total in Dataset	Minimum in State	Maximum in State
Feminist	220	1	34
African American	477	0	45
Social Welfare	1536	7	157
Civil Rights	460	1	51
Economic Conservative	99	0	7
Social Conservative	24	0	3
Pro-Life	143	0	15
Health	2025	8	158

feminist organizations to oppose the paternalist policies under TANF; I cannot make the same assumption for all organizations that represent women. In subsequent chapters, I combine these "feminist" organizations with other groups representing women to capture a broader range of advocacy organizations.

State Need

I anticipate that a state's welfare policy will respond to the level of need within the state. To capture this level of need I include a number of variables measuring the demographic and economic characteristics of the state. Demographically, I include the percentage of the population that is Black and the percentage of the population that is Hispanic. Even though the majority of welfare recipients are white, racial stereotypes are still a strong driver in creating policy and shaping public opinion, and previous research has shown that states with greater minority populations have more stringent policies.[66] I also include the percentage of births to unmarried mothers; states with a higher percentage of births to unmarried mothers are likely to have greater need for TANF. Finally, I include the percentage of the population living below the poverty line and the percentage of the population currently on the TANF rolls.

The Political Environment

The political environment of a state may also be expected to influence a state's adoption of paternal policies, as Democrats are traditionally associated with more liberal social policies and Republicans have supported paternal policies. During the national debate over welfare reform, both Democrats and Republicans called for the federal government to become more involved in welfare recipients' personal lives. At the state level, I anticipate that states controlled by Democratic legislatures and Democratic governors will be less likely to adopt these policies, while Republican-controlled state governments will be more likely to adopt paternal policies. I include a dichotomous variable to capture whether the governor is a Democrat, and a dichotomous variable to measure control of the legislature (1 = Democratic-controlled legislature; 0 = not Democratic-controlled).[67]

Party control is not the only consideration, however. Given that the vast majority of welfare recipients are women, I anticipate that descriptive representation will be influential in creating welfare policy. As a measure of descriptive representation, I include the percentage of the legislature that is female. Finally, I include a measure of citizen ideology, with the expectation that states with more liberal populations will be less likely to adopt paternal policies.

Welfare Context

States often adopt policies after their neighbors do so, and with welfare policy in particular, research shows that some rules spread through policy diffusion. One theory is that welfare policy is governed by a "race to the bottom" in which states adopt increasingly more stringent policies to avoid becoming the "welfare magnet" for poor people in the region. Even without the "race to the bottom" theory, legislators and other state policymakers do meet with their counterparts across the country and share best practices and often are lobbied by the same organizations. We might expect then that a state will react to the welfare policy of its neighbors. This variable is captured by taking the mean of the neighboring states' policies.[68]

Finally, I include a set of variables designed to take into account the overall generosity of a state's welfare program. The first variable is the maximum monthly benefit value for a family of three, adjusted for the state cost of living. The AFDC or TANF monthly benefit has been widely used as a measure of generosity; previous research has shown the measure to be related to party competition, policy diffusion, descriptive representation, and the use of welfare boards.[69] In each model I also include a measure of the other morality policies; for example, in the child support model, I control for the presence of a family cap and the total number of behavioral requirements. Controlling for these other policies with similar objectives allows me to discern whether the state adopts conservative paternalist rules or if the state is likely to adopt strict policies across the board.

Results

I ran partial models that included all of the interest groups as independent variables, but did not include any of the control variables outlined above. For all of these models, and the full models discussed below, the data runs from 1997 to 2016. Each model includes year indicator variables and standard errors clustered on states. I chose to analyze the contemporaneous effects of interest group activity rather than lagging the effects. Previous research has shown that lagging interest group variables does not have a significant effect in predicting legislative activity.[70] Moreover, while some interest groups may spur political activity (thus necessitating a lag of the interest group variable), other organizations may form as a response to political activity (suggesting a lag of the policy variable). In a dataset with so many organizations, it is impossible to parse out this temporal relationship.

There are five models for the behavioral requirements: one for each individual requirement, and one for the index of requirements. The individual requirement models are modeled with logistic regressions, and the index model uses OLS regression (table B.1). The results of the partial models show little support for a relationship between interest group advocacy and state welfare policy. The percentage of feminist interest groups in a state, for example, is negatively associated with adopting a parenting class requirement, but the relationship is not statistically significant. States with a higher percentage of civil rights organizations are less likely to have any of the four behavioral requirements, but again the relationship is not statistically significant. In contrast, the percentage of African American organizations is positively associated with adopting behavioral requirements, though again the relationship is not statistically significant. I anticipated that such groups would advocate against these policies; the positive relationship here may be reflecting the relationship between a state's African American population and its policies, however, given the high correlation between the percentage of African American interest groups and percentage of the population that is African American (the correlation is 0.66). Drug screening and immunization requirements appear to be less likely in states with a greater percentage of social welfare groups and socially conservative groups. Moreover, in states with a greater percentage of social welfare organizations there are fewer total behavioral requirements. This aligns with my expectations that these groups want to increase access to benefits.

The partial model for the family cap is an ordered logit (table B.2). The results do not show any significant relationship between a state's interest group density or diversity and its decision to adopt a family cap. The child support reporting requirement model is an OLS regression. In support of my expectations, the number of reporting requirements decreases as the percentage of social welfare organizations increases in a state. Contrary to expectations, however, an increased percentage of feminist groups, African American groups, and civil rights groups are not significantly related to fewer child support reporting requirements adopted by a state.

Behavioral Requirements

Based on the logistic regressions that control for a state's level of need, political environment, and broader welfare context, there is limited support for my theory of interest group involvement in welfare rule creation as it pertains to behavioral requirements. There is no statistically significant relationship between a state's interest group community and immunization requirements for TANF recipients. Among the case study states, legislative debates around immunizations did not focus on welfare recipients, but reflected the larger anti-vax movement. Overall, the composition of a state's interest group community also appears to have no significant relationship to parenting class requirements. There is also no statistically significant relationship between the density and diversity of interest groups within a state and the adoption of drug screening requirements. There was frequent debate over drug screening requirements, however, with representation from a variety of interest groups. Among the states studied in detail here, Alaska, Nebraska, Texas, South Dakota, and Wisconsin all considered legislation related to drug testing or screening for welfare recipients.

Contrary to my expectations, states with a greater percentage of feminist organizations and social welfare organizations are significantly more likely to have school attendance requirements. This positive relationship shows the difficulty in separating cause and effect in the relationship between interest groups and public policy. States that require school attendance in behavioral contracts may be more likely to have feminist or social welfare organizations *because* of this paternalist policy; the interest groups could be responding to policy rather than advocating for its implementation. The percentage of civil rights organizations in a state, however, is negatively associated with school attendance requirements, which supports my hypothesis.

With regard to the other sets of variables, there is no overwhelming evidence of state need predicting a state's adoption of behavioral requirements. The Black population is not significantly related to any of the requirements; the lack of a relationship calls into question the belief that policymakers are heavily influenced by racial stereotypes in crafting policy. There is a positive relationship between a state's Hispanic population and the likelihood of requiring school attendance and childhood immunizations. To extend the stereotype of the Black welfare queen to include all women of color, this relationship makes sense—a greater Hispanic population may spur policymakers to adopt stricter policies. In contrast, however, there is a negative relationship between a state's Hispanic population and the likelihood that it will adopt parenting class requirements. The relationship between behavioral requirements and Hispanic population does not provide a consistent narrative.

The political environment in a state also appears to have little influence on behavioral requirements. Party control of the legislature is not significant in any of the models, and citizen ideology is significant only in the school attendance model. States with Democratic governors are less likely to have immunization requirements or parenting class requirements for TANF recipients; both results confirm my expectation that more liberal governments will support fewer paternalist policies. The percentage of women in the legislature is positively related to the likelihood of a state requiring parenting classes, which goes against descriptive representation arguments. States with a greater percentage of women in the legislature are less likely to adopt school attendance requirements for welfare recipients, however; this confirms expectations that women will advocate against policies that police motherhood.

The wider welfare context appears to be the most consistent predictor of whether a state will adopt behavioral requirements. In all four models, a state is more likely to adopt a given behavioral requirement if it has other behavioral requirements in place. States also appear to distinguish themselves from their neighbors, at least as it pertains to immunization and school involvement policies. A state whose neighbors have adopted these requirements is less likely to do so itself.

Stigma and Stereotyping

Representative Wes Keller (R) introduced HB 16 to the Alaska House in 2013, which would have required public assistance applicants to sign a statement that they were not abusing drugs or alcohol. Keller justified the bill by pointing out the mission of TANF to "promote self-sufficiency" and noted that addiction and self-sufficiency were "at least in tension."[71] When Representative Geran Tarr (D) questioned whether drug testing would be a good use of public resources and cited a study finding that only 2.6 percent of Florida public assistance recipients tested positive for drug and alcohol use, she was met with disbelief. Rep. Keller said he was "stunned" by the statistic and questioned its legitimacy; such skepticism is emblematic of the stereotyping of welfare recipients.[72]

Opponents to drug testing or screening requirements included civil rights organizations, religious groups, and service providers. Not surprisingly, religious leaders often presented their opposition to drug testing welfare recipients as a matter of faith and principle. A coalition of religious leaders submitted testimony to the Wisconsin State Assembly in 2015 to express their opposition to drug testing:

> In our respective religious traditions poverty and joblessness are not indicators of bad character. Thus, we do not believe it is just to craft policies that punish those who face these trials while also suffering from the illness of addiction. [...] Subjecting applicants for federal assistance to drug

screening and testing only because they are dealing with poverty or loss of income is degrading and humiliating. It adds to the stigma of applying for public assistance. Moreover, it may discourage some from seeking the very help they and their families need.[73]

While some conservative organizations and legislators questioned the deservingness of welfare recipients, religious leaders spoke about the inherent deservingness of every human being. Social welfare groups often expressed concern that such requirements would be ineffective at preventing drug use and would hurt the children in these families. Instead, advocates promoted policies that would increase access to treatment, reflecting a societal shift toward understanding addiction as a disease rather than a moral failing.

Playing into another stereotype, in 2005 the Wisconsin General Assembly considered a bill that would have required a Wisconsin Works recipient with an infant to attend parenting skills training and meet with a financial and employment planner. The sponsor of the bill, Representative Debbi Towns, argued that the measure was necessary because:

[c]ounties are seeing many young women apply for [W-2] eligibility immediately prior to delivery, collect the three monthly payments, and then never show up to participate in the valuable part of the W-2 program—the work component. Furthermore, if they become pregnant again, they can re-apply for eligibility and collect the monthly grant a second time—or even a third time—and never participate in any W-2 employment planning, training or work experience.[74]

Representative Towns believes that young women are abusing the state's welfare system; she suggests that women may become pregnant multiple times just to receive state benefits. This is eerily reminiscent of earlier arguments around the "welfare queen." Testifying against the bill, Christopher Ahmuty from the ACLU of Wisconsin said:

We agree that W-2 agencies should be required to offer parenting classes to, and discuss supportive services with, parents of newborn infants. AB 754, however, goes too far. By forcing all parents to attend such classes, the proposed statute presupposes a lack of competency of new mothers simply by virtue of their being poor enough to require W-2. [. . . T]he proposed legislation disregards the actual needs and circumstances of parents of newborns.[75]

Civil servants also testified against the parenting skills bill. JoAnna Richard from the Department of Workforce Development told legislators that the bill "assumes that because these parents are poor they are poor parents" and the department disagreed with such an assumption.[76] The differing views presented by bureaucrats and legislators demonstrate that stereotypes may be driving policymaking, even when those who work with welfare recipients know these stereotypes do not reflect reality.

Replicating the Working World

Debates around behavioral requirements often focused on the extent to which the experience of welfare recipients mirrored the experience of hardworking, employed taxpayers. Implicit in this comparison is that welfare recipients are not hardworking, are living off the generosity of the state, and do not understand the "real world." When Senator Charlie Janssen introduced LB 221 to the Nebraska state legislature in March 2011, for example, he framed the bill as a response to constituent concerns:

> I introduced LB221 after hearing from numerous Nebraskans, both in Dodge County and across the state, who asked me why they have to undergo drug testing in order to qualify for many jobs in our state but recipients of our state's cash assistance program did not have to be drug free in order to receive cash assistance.[77]

During that same hearing, Nebraska resident Daniel Maas expressed his frustration that he, as a private employer, could randomly drug test his staff and fire them at will if they tested positive, but the state did not have a similar policy for welfare recipients. Maas was not alone in his frustration. In a letter to one of his legislators in 2013, an Alaska resident wrote that both he and his wife "had to pass alcohol and drug tests" to obtain employment and were subject to random drug tests. Since taxes are taken out of their paychecks to pay for government assistance, he reasoned, "we think it only logical that individuals who receive assistance from hard working taxpayers should be subject to the same rules and requirements." Moreover, he "would hate to think that [his] hard earned tax dollars are enabling individuals' drug and alcohol addictions."[78] This sentiment reappeared when Wisconsin debated a drug testing bill in 2015.

In 2013, the Texas Senate considered a bill (SB 11) that would have required any TANF applicant suspected of using a controlled substance to submit to a drug test; applicants who tested positive would have been disqualified from receiving assistance. The executive director of the Texas Conservative Coalition testified in favor of the bill, stating:

> Fundamentally it is a violation of the welfare system for recipients of taxpayer-funded cash assistance benefits to be purchasing and using controlled substances while they are relying on the financial support of their fellow Texans. [. . .] This would encourage not only self-sufficiency, but improvements in family life and community life.[79]

SB 11 passed the Senate but was never voted on by the House. Two years later, Texas's House Human Services Committee considered a similar bill, though it would have also required the Health and Human Services Commission to provide a list of treatment providers to any applicant denied TANF benefits. Notably, Texas has required some form of drug screening for TANF recipients since welfare reform began; bills introduced in the mid-2010s were designed to tweak existing policy.

In several states considering drug screening or testing bills, the state branch of the ACLU testified against the bill. Nationally, the ACLU takes a clear stance on the issue: "Drug testing welfare recipients as a condition of eligibility is a policy that is scientifically, fiscally, and constitutionally unsound."[80] Amy Miller, representing ACLU Nebraska in 2011, explained to legislators what differentiates welfare recipients from private employees:

> We've heard several testifiers ask the question: Why does my employer test me but state recipients of public assistance do not get drug tested? And the answer is simple. It's the Bill of Rights. The Fourth Amendment

protects us from unreasonable searches and seizures or intrusion into our privacy. The Fourth Amendment only protects us from the government.[81]

Jeffrey Mittman, executive director of the ACLU of Alaska, also framed his argument against drug screening as a legal issue, asserting that the "state's need to prevent drug use among cash assistance recipients would not be more compelling than its interest in preventing drug use among the general population."[82] Neither state—Alaska nor Nebraska— required drug screening among TANF recipients when these bills were being considered in the state legislature. In the legal debate over drug screening and testing, ACLU representatives cited failed measures in other states, with Florida being the most common example.

The comparison between receiving government assistance and working also came up in debates around the 2005 Wisconsin bill that would have required Wisconsin Works recipients with an infant to attend parenting skills training. In this case, however, those who were opposed to behavioral requirements reminded legislators that their program had been designed to mirror the experience of those in the working world. Bob Andersen from the Wisconsin Council on Children and Families explained the rationale behind exempting new parents from any work-related requirements (including parenting classes): "It is widely acknowledged that the philosophy behind current law is, and always has been since the inception of W-2, that the legislature desires to have the CNI program mirror the current practice and experience that thousands of families have in the private workplace." Others testifying before the legislature noted that the parenting class requirement was "not in keeping with the norm in terms of welfare policy or the real world of work" and that "it is illogical to establish conditions for parents that are contrary to the precedent and customary practices of the work world regarding maternity leave."[83]

Mandating that welfare recipients both submit to drug tests because that is "normal" for workers and go back to work immediately after birth presents a contradiction. These policies suggest that welfare recipients should be subject to all the punitive policies of the working world but enjoy none of the benefits or protections. Social welfare and civil rights organizations in multiple states have fought against punitive provisions that further stigmatize TANF recipients by treating them differently from other citizens.

Family Cap

I predict the severity of a state's family cap policy using an ordered logistic regression; the results show that a state's family cap policy becomes less strict as the percentage of pro-life organizations within the state's interest group community increases (see table B.4). This aligns with my expectations, as abortion opponents have spoken out about the potential for a family cap to increase abortion for decades. When Nebraska debated removing its family cap in 2006, for instance, Jim Cunningham from the Nebraska Catholic Bishops Conference testified before legislators:

> We also are concerned that the punitive nature of the child exclusion policy can pressure a poor woman's decision to turn to abortion rather than to carry her child to term. The welfare-eligible woman in this situation faces the financial penalty of giving birth to her child, and it is well established over the years that abortions often are attributed to socioeconomic considerations.[84]

Advocates in Nebraska did not frame their opposition to the family cap solely as a pro-life argument. Like arguments against other punitive behavioral policies, Becky Gould from Nebraska Appleseed pointed out the contradiction in implementing a family cap because it mirrors the experience of working families:

> It is sometimes argued that the family cap maintains reality for families on welfare because working families do not receive a raise when they decide to have additional children. Putting the differences between ADC families and working families aside, working families do receive a benefit when they have an additional child in the form of tax relief, such as income tax exemptions, child tax credits, and childcare tax credits.[85]

Nebraska repealed its family cap policy, effective October 2007. There is no way of knowing whether this testimony was the deciding factor in the legislators' decision to repeal the family cap, but it is clear that there was vocal opposition to the policy.

Another state that reconsidered its family cap policy was Connecticut, as part of a broader reform of its TANF program in 2015. Carolyn

Treiss from the Permanent Commission on the Status of Women told lawmakers that "family caps make several inaccurate assumptions about women living in poverty and their decision making with regard to child bearing." When she was asked by a representative to explain those assumptions, she answered:

> Well, you know one of the assumptions it makes is that women have ready access that all women and women in poverty have, you know, ready access to effective contraception so that they can make childbearing choices the way middleclass women can. [. . .] I think you also have to think about this economically. [. . . I]f I already have children I have to think about what my life is going to look like with more children and I'm going to get about fifty bucks more. So, is that whole experience of getting pregnant, of going through pregnancy, having a child, is that really worth the $50.00?[86]

Other advocates in favor of repealing Connecticut's family cap also mentioned that the policy was rooted in stereotypes. Jean Mills Aranha from Connecticut Legal Services explained to legislators that family cap provisions were an attempt to combat Ronald Reagan's image of the welfare queen—a woman "collecting huge amounts of money by having lots of children." She pointed out that the increase in benefit levels was "not even enough to cover the cost of diapers, formula, and clothing for a new child."[87] Both advocates used their allotted time to dispel the myth that welfare recipients have more children with the explicit purpose of collecting more benefits. They also expressed concern that women receiving government assistance did not have sufficient access to contraception. Aranha pointed out to legislators that, even with access to contraception, "it's not a hundred percent, you know, effective in all situations. People are in abusive situations where they're not allowed to pursue contraception."[88] Some states with family caps makes exemptions for exactly these types of situations; Connecticut allows for exemptions in the case of rape or incest, but not for these other circumstances.

Aside from the influence of pro-life interest groups, the model shows that a state is more likely to adopt a family cap as the percentage of its population that is Black increases. This confirms previous research and suggests that racialized stereotypes may be driving family cap policies. A state's unmarried birth rate is not significantly related to the state's family cap policy; given that family caps are established largely as a way to discourage unmarried women from giving birth, this result is especially surprising. Neighboring state policy does appear to matter, though—a state is significantly less likely to adopt a more stringent family cap policy as the family cap policy of its neighbors becomes more stringent. This runs against expectations that states adopt strict policies to avoid becoming "welfare magnets."

The lack of significant results may be caused by the fact that many states started adopting family caps before welfare reform passed in 1996. New Jersey was the first state to create a family cap in 1992; several other states, including Arkansas, Georgia, Maryland, Massachusetts, and Wisconsin, followed in the next four years.[89] In a few of these states, the exemptions have changed—Georgia began allowing exemptions in the case of rape or incest in 2000, for example—but a state that already had a family cap pre-TANF may be less likely to change its policy on account of interest group lobbying.

Moreover, states have found other ways to discourage reproduction without enforcing an explicit family cap. Richard Armstrong, director of the Idaho Department of Health and Welfare, spoke before state legislators about some common welfare myths. Armstrong disabused legislators of the notion that families received more assistance as the family size grew:

> That's not true in Idaho, and I don't think that's true anywhere else in the country because of reform. Actually, you could be the octomom and you're only going to get $309 a month. [. . .] It used to be, prior to [']96, there was an elevated level of cash assistance, but that's not happening anymore. Furthermore, we subtract from that allowance anything—any money that the individual is earning, so you really end up with very, very few people that are receiving any kind of cash assistance. I think, as we looked at it recently, there are 204 family households in the state of Idaho—in the whole state of Idaho—that are receiving any kind of cash assistance but it does not escalate with the number of children.

Armstrong is factually incorrect (many states do increase TANF benefits as the size of the household increases), but Idaho does maintain a flat benefit level regardless of the family size. Wisconsin has a similar policy for those participating in the W-2T and community service jobs programs. Other states have such a negligible increase in benefits (benefits increase twenty-four dollars a month for each additional person in Mississippi, for instance) that it effectively acts as a cap.[90]

Child Support Reporting Requirements

The child support reporting requirements model is an OLS regression. The results indicate that states with a greater percentage of socially conservative groups adopt more reporting requirements for parents (see table B.4). Socially conservative groups such as the Christian Coalition and chapters of the American Family Association may welcome policies punishing unmarried women. Some opponents to child support enforcement policies argue that "the notion of supporting the potential of the parents to work together [. . .] reeks of conservative marriage promotion efforts."[91]

Child support reporting requirements are not significantly related to a state's political environment, though the number of requirements increases as the unmarried birth rate in a state increases. In addition to concerns about noncustodial parents' bearing responsibility for their children, legislators are also concerned about the economic effects of unpaid child support. Nebraska senator Jeremy Nordquist (D) explained the state's interest in ensuring child support enforcement:

> This means that when more custodial parents receive child support, they will be less likely to have incomes low enough to qualify for public assistance. Or if the families are receiving public assistance, the state will be reimbursed. It's estimated that if all custodial families had child support orders and those orders were fully enforced, cash assistance, or welfare, costs for those families would drop by 26 percent; food stamp costs would be reduced by 19 percent; and Medicaid costs to the state would be 5 percent lower.[92]

The results show no relationships between the percentage of feminist organizations in a state and their child support reporting requirements, however. Looking at committee testimony provides insight into why this might be the case. During a New Jersey Senate Judiciary Committee hearing on child support enforcement, Bear Atwood—a representative from the New Jersey chapter of NOW—expressed her concerns about the child support enforcement system. She begins her testimony with what could be an argument against strict child support reporting requirements:

> What we would ask if that in making decisions about consolidation that the Legislature really step back and think about the women who are collecting child support. [. . .] It is women who have to take a day off from work to go to court, to go to hearings, and unfortunately, in New Jersey, a large number of those women still work at jobs where they are paid by the hour, and they lose a day's pay every time they have to go to court.[93]

In this quotation, Atwood refers to the general burden placed on women navigating the child support enforcement system. This argument could easily be applied to welfare recipients. Given a welfare recipient's work requirements, she may not be able to take off work to testify in court or travel around the state to collect child support. As she continues her testimony, however, it becomes clear that Atwood does not see herself as representing welfare recipients:

> The other concern that I have, and I really think this is a serious concern for the women who will be struggling with this, is the consolidation in the executive branch. Last spring, I guess, when this first legislation first started to be talked about and there was some newspaper articles, we got a flood of calls from women who said, "You mean now we are going to have to go down to welfare to collect our child support?" That's a real issue for women in New Jersey. There is truly a stigma to being on welfare. The thought of being seen coming out of that building is serious for a lot of women.[94]

Atwood's testimony provides a perfect example of why feminist organizations such as NOW may not have strong influence on welfare policy. NOW is certainly concerned about child support and the burden its collection places on women—including on low-income women who work hourly jobs. She makes clear, though, that the women she represents are not on welfare, and they do not want to be associated with the stigma of welfare. Later she expresses concerns that a disproportionate amount of resources will be spent collecting child support for those on welfare. While 90 percent of adult welfare recipients are women, the stigma attached to receiving cash assistance prevents them from being represented by major feminist organizations.

Conclusion

The stereotype of the welfare recipient as a promiscuous woman intent on abusing the welfare system has been perpetuated for decades. In response to that narrative, policymakers have adopted welfare rules that seek to regulate recipients' personal moral decisions, ranging from whether they should have another child to how involved they should become in their child's education. Based on the stereotype of the "welfare queen" as a poor woman of color, I expected that advocacy organizations representing women and African Americans, as well as those providing social services, would have an influence on a state's decision to adopt some of these requirements. During the national debate over welfare reform before the passage of PRWORA, these interest groups were some of the most vocal in opposition to the reforms.

The results largely suggest, however, that the diversity of interest groups in a state have no consistent relationship to a state's behavioral requirements, child support reporting requirements, or family cap. The higher the percentage of pro-life groups in the state the lower the state's likelihood of having a family cap policy, which aligns with concerns that a family cap may push a woman to choose abortion. An increase in the percentage of socially conservative groups in a state is associated with a greater number of child support requirements; this result is expected as social conservatives promote traditional family values and child support enforcement is viewed as promoting a two-parent family (even if it is through child support cooperation rather than marriage).

It is possible that interest groups have little influence when it comes to a state's welfare rules as a whole, or just as they pertain to morality and personal decision-making. The lack of significant results may also be a result of the lack of variation over time; few states changed their behavioral requirements, reporting requirements, or family cap policy during the period analyzed. Analyzing interest group influence in a more dynamic policy setting may produce more significant results. Finally, morality may be so deeply ingrained in state culture that not even the strongest advocates could change the expectations policymakers set for welfare recipients or overcome the stereotype that has been portrayed for so long.

4

Working for the Man

Inside Welfare-to-Work Policies

In a guest column published in the *Idaho Falls Post Register* over Labor Day weekend in 2015, state senator Brent Hill reflected on Americans' changing view of work. "Somewhere along the line we have been fed the idea that a life full of free time, leisure, and relaxation is the most satisfying," he wrote. "The truth, however, is that our greatest achievement of self-worth, of accomplishment and satisfaction, comes not from the work we avoid, but the work we achieve." From Senator Hill's perspective, individuals' inability to appreciate work was inextricably tied with a government welfare system that "rewards idleness and creates dependency."[1]

Senator Hill is certainly not the first politician to express such sentiments. The importance of work in establishing independence has a long tradition in America. The Puritan ethos equated work with not only economic independence but also control over one's spiritual destiny. Benjamin Franklin in *Poor Richard's Almanack* frequently referenced a strong work ethic with lines like "sloth makes all things difficult, but industry all easy" and "laziness travels so slowly that poverty soon overtakes him."[2] Centuries later, feminist activists argued that working outside the home was liberatory, even though plenty of poor and working-class women knew from experience that work did not necessarily lead to liberation.[3] This relationship was codified in the second goal of PRWORA: "end the dependence of needy parents on government benefits by promoting job preparation, work, and marriage."[4]

Implied in PRWORA's second goal for TANF is that welfare recipients are lazy, unwilling to work, or lack the intrinsic motivation to find employment. These stereotypes are also translated into welfare rules. Because the welfare recipient stereotype depicts someone who would rather collect public assistance than be self-sufficient, public policies are designed to discourage this behavior and provide an incentive to work.

Some states will choose to adopt strict requirements in order to "punish" a recipient and keep them under tight control. In other cases, the state may create more generous policies to meet its lower standards for the target population.[5]

Working Women and Welfare Queens

Under Aid to Dependent Children (ADC), many welfare recipients were not required to work; for white women especially, the expectation early on was that women received aid specifically so they would not have to find employment outside of the house. When the program was created, the norm was a family with a sole (male) breadwinner; the mother stayed out of the workforce to care for the children and the home. Over the years, however, the percentage of women working outside the home increased, and both the public and policymakers became more accepting of women's participation in the labor force.[6] By 1960 over 30 percent of married women were working or looking for work; among nonmarried women with children that figure was 56 percent.[7] Critics of the welfare system questioned why welfare recipients were not required to work when so many middle-class women were joining the workforce to supplement their family's income.

Furthermore, many Black women had been forced to work since the inception of ADC. Southern states, which often had a higher percentage of Black ADC recipients, often denied assistance to "employable mothers."[8] These women were often asked to perform seasonal farm work or domestic labor. Piven and Cloward describe the policies of Southern states as an example of how "relief policies can be used to support a caste labor system, one in which the subjugation of particular ethnic or racial groups (in this case, blacks) serves to lower the price of labor generally."[9] States not only denied assistance to those deemed "employable," they also kept monthly benefits so low that it would be impossible for a family to support itself on government assistance alone.[10]

Becoming Undeserving

Even though many welfare recipients were working, and many who were unemployed were interested in working, the perception of welfare recipients gradually shifted from one of deserving mothers who needed assistance to raise their children to women who refused to get a job. Closely related to the stereotype of welfare recipients having more children to stay on welfare, welfare mothers (and particularly Black mothers) have been blamed for failing to pass on a strong work ethic to their children, thus creating a culture of dependency.[11] Stereotypes of the "welfare queen" depicted a woman living a life of luxury on welfare benefits—someone "shirking her duty to carry her part of the load as an American citizen."[12] In an in-depth interview conducted by Seccombe and her colleagues, one welfare recipient described people's misconceptions about her life: "They say you lazy and you don't want to work. You want people to take care of you. You want to sit home and watch stories all day, which I don't."[13]

While a welfare recipient may be quick to dismiss the assumption that she is lazy, welfare recipients are not immune to the stereotypes held by the general public. One young mother interviewed by Seccombe described some welfare recipients as "[l]azy. Don't want to do nothing. [. . .] A lot of women are abusing the system."[14] That welfare recipient's testimony aligns with public opinion of welfare recipients during the 1990s. When asked whether they thought welfare recipients were genuinely in need or were taking advantage of the system, two-thirds of respondents in a 1994 poll said that welfare recipients were taking advantage of the system.[15] Similarly, a majority of survey respondents believed that welfare recipients could manage without welfare; it was their impression that able-bodied welfare recipients preferred to sit home rather than work.[16] In this environment Congress passed PRWORA and the states started crafting their individual TANF programs.

Racialized Perceptions of Dependency

The perception of welfare recipients as lazy and dependent has, like many aspects of welfare policy, strong racial undertones. Piven and Cloward wrote that Southern opposition to AFDC-UP (AFDC for unemployed parents) was "expressed by a county welfare director in Alabama who opposed the program on the ground that 'Negroes just do not want to work.'"[17] When the Work Incentive Program (WIN) was instituted in 1967, AFDC recipients were required to participate in low-wage jobs that traditionally employed poor Black women.[18] In her book on the welfare rights movement, Mary Triece notes that "poor black women, viewed as a ready pool of domestic workers and field hands, were labeled lazy if they received public assistance."[19]

Respondents in the 1990 and 1994 General Social Survey were asked if Blacks tend to be lazy or hardworking—40 percent placed Blacks on the "lazy" side of a seven-point scale, while only 20 percent of respondents thought they were hardworking.[20] Scholars have hypothesized that the media's portrayal of poverty has played at least some role in the creation, and permanence, of these stereotypes. In an analysis of 412 newspaper articles mentioning poverty and welfare in 1999, Bullock and colleagues found that only two articles identified individuals as white. In contrast, there were 32 articles identifying individuals as Hispanic, and 29 articles identifying individuals as African American.[21] In the articles about African Americans, 13 stories focused on chronic poverty, single motherhood, or welfare fraud; only 6 articles were categorized as success stories.

Defending mandatory work programs, Lawrence Mead argued that welfare recipients who were working did so under the table so they could keep their benefits, or received financial assistance from their friends and family. Policymakers argued that there was no incentive for women to get off welfare—they were better off if they stayed on the rolls than if they tried to find employment. The solution to the welfare queen appeared to be work requirements; as Mead described it, "work programs have the power to tame dependency."[22]

The Importance of Work under TANF

One of the most significant differences between TANF and AFDC is the work requirement placed on TANF recipients. The introduction of work mandates into welfare did not begin with TANF, however. As mentioned previously, states began requiring work activities from some recipients as early as the 1940s. Beginning in 1967 with the Work Incentive Program, the federal government began providing services and financial benefits to recipients who volunteered to participate in work training activities.[23] In 1988, under the Family Support Act, recipients with children over three years of age were required to participate in work training programs.[24]

There are two levels to the work requirements adopted under TANF. First, because TANF is no longer an entitlement but is distributed as a block grant, the federal government holds states to a work participation rate. The work participation rate is the percentage of able-bodied adult recipients who are meeting their work activity requirements. Failure to meet this target can result in loss of federal funds. In 1997, 25 percent of a state's TANF caseload was expected to participate in work activities at least twenty hours per week; by 2002, 50 percent of the caseload was to be engaged in work activities for thirty hours per week.[25] Under federal guidelines, states are allowed to exclude up to 20 percent of their caseload from the work participation rate; the state can decide which recipients they choose to exempt from these requirements. Common exemptions include those for the elderly, the ill or incapacitated, and parents caring for young children.[26]

To meet the work participation rate, states enforce work requirements on individuals. Federal guidelines dictate that recipients with children six years of age or older work thirty hours per week to remain eligible, though states may require recipients to work more hours. In the section below, I outline more of the rules that apply to individuals receiving welfare. Specifically, I focus on the activities they must complete to meet their work requirements and the exemptions provided to these requirements.

Work-Related Welfare Rules

Previous literature on TANF's work requirements has combined all rules regarding work requirements into one index of work flexibility; one commonly used index comes from Fellowes and Rowe, and it has been reproduced or adapted in several other studies.[27] The Fellowes and Rowe index consists of twelve rules capturing flexibility on work activity exemptions, the types of activities allowed, the number of hours required, and the sanctions for noncompliance.[28] Fellowes and Rowe do not provide a comprehensive list of exemptions or work activities, however, which may underestimate the flexibility of some states while overestimating the flexibility of others. With regard to allowable activities, Fellowes and Rowe include only variables capturing whether "education and training activities" and "postsecondary education" are allowable activities. As I will discuss in further detail below, this narrow definition of work excludes care work traditionally performed by women.

Allowable Work Activities

The slogan "welfare to work" is something of a misnomer for the types of activities that welfare recipients are actually participating in to receive their benefits. When TANF was first created in 1996, there were twelve activities that could count toward a recipient's work requirement. Following the passage of the Deficit Reduction Act, these activities were further broken down into two subcategories: core activities and non-core activities (see table 4.1 for classification of activities). Core activities can count toward the first twenty hours per week for a recipient and include unsubsidized employment, subsidized private- or public-sector employment, work experience, on-the-job training, job search and job readiness assistance, community service programs, vocational education training, and providing childcare to another welfare recipient. Non-core activities can count toward meeting the activity requirement only after the first twenty hours. Non-core activities include education or job skills training directly related to employment and satisfactory attendance at a secondary school or GED program. These activities can be broadly categorized as educational activities or labor market-oriented activities.

Education Activities

There are four education activities that a state may choose to count toward the work requirement: basic education, high school education, English as a Second Language classes, and postsecondary education. Generally speaking, more education leads to increased earning potential. The same is true for welfare recipients: research has shown that recipients who receive two- or four-year degrees have higher wages and work more consistently than those with less education.[29] At the same time, TANF recipients are not given free rein to complete their activity requirements via education. In most states there is a one- or two-year time limit on how long postsecondary education can count as a work activity. Basic education and English as a Second Language classes, for example, may be available only if they directly relate to employment.[30] Completing the requirements for a high school degree may be available only to minor parents.

South Carolina is the only state to not count education activities toward work requirements for the majority of recipient types from 1997 to 2016. In South Carolina, however, TANF-eligible adults who are most likely to benefit from educational activities are moved to a separate, state-funded program called CARES (Challenging Adults Through Rehabilitation, Education, and Services).[31] This state-funded program allows the state to serve adults who may not be able to meet federal work requirements without bringing down the state's overall work participation rate. In contrast, nine states allowed all four educational activities to count toward the work requirement for all eight recipient types (see appendix table B.5 for details about the "types" of welfare recipients). Over the twenty years analyzed in this study, the average number of educational activities allowed was 3.3.

Labor Market Activities

Welfare recipients were increasingly encouraged to participate in the labor market as norms around women in the workplace changed in the latter part of the twentieth century. Policymakers pushed women to become self-sufficient rather than view public assistance as a replacement for a male head of household's wages. Plenty of welfare recipients lacked the skills to enter the labor force, however, and so states created job training and placement programs to move recipients "from welfare to work."

Almost universally under TANF, recipients are required to engage in job search; in an increasing number of states applicants must apply for jobs before they can even receive benefits. States also provide job skills training, which often teaches recipients how to "create resumes, write work histories, and [. . .] how to conduct oneself during an interview."[32] States also created work opportunities for TANF recipients through both subsidized job programs and community work experiences. Subsidized job programs provide financial incentives for private employers to hire TANF recipients, typically for a set time period. In 2012, Nebraska state senator Heath Mello explained how a subsidized job program would benefit both welfare recipients and employers:

> Under LB1136, employers would partner with nonprofit employment agencies and apply for wage subsidies to help bring on new employees who are currently participants in the ADC program. Over a six-month period, the employer would gradually take on more responsibility for paying wages until the employee is receiving 100 percent of their wages directly from the employer rather than from the subsidies. ADC recipients who participate in the program would gain job skills and obtain access to meaningful employment, while employers would benefit from the offset costs to train new employees.[33]

Community work experience is designed to give welfare recipients an opportunity to develop marketable skills, but unlike subsidized jobs, the position does not pay.[34] Although community work experience programs may lead to higher employment rates among those with significant barriers to work, the experience may not be enough to increase the future earnings of participants, unless it is combined with other training and job search activities.[35] If policymakers are focused on moving welfare recipients off the rolls and toward self-sufficiency, they may choose to limit the types of labor market activities available to recipients to those that are directly related to employment in the private sector.

Self-Improvement Activities

In addition to these twelve federally recognized activities mentioned above, some states allow recipients to participate in other activities. The time put into those activities helps the individual meet his or her requirement, but it does not help the state meet the requirement set by the federal government. These activities include counseling, self-employment, and life skills training. Discussing the larger purpose behind TANF work requirements, Zatz classifies these activities as "self-improvement" activities. While the recipient may not be earning money in these activities, they receive benefits such as "structure and discipline, opportunities for accomplishment, or immersion in social relationships."[36] Finally, a state may allow "other" activities, including rehabilitation services, to count toward the work requirements. The most consistent pattern among states that allow for this activity is the case-by-case basis on which these decisions are made. When a state allows an "other" activity to count toward the work requirement, it acknowledges the differences in women's backgrounds and their needs. Allowing a recipient to work with her caseworker to determine what she needs to do in order to become self-sufficient places trust in the woman and stands in sharp contrast to many of the paternalist overtones in TANF.

Generally speaking, states increased the total number of allowable activities over time. Not all activities are available to all recipients, however. Many states have a separate set of activities available to recipients who have received a high school degree versus those who have not. Those without a high school degree may be allowed to count more education activities toward the work requirement than those with a degree. Some states also delineate based on the age of the recipient's youngest child; still others apply different rules for recipients who are minors. To capture this variation, a state's measure of flexibility in any activity is defined as the number of recipient "types" that may count the activity as work (see appendix table B.5). A state in which 50 percent of recipient types can count basic education, for instance, is thus considered more flexible than a state in which only 25 percent of recipient types can count the activity toward the work requirement. Table 4.1 shows how many states allowed *at least* 50 percent of recipient types to count a given activity in 1997 and 2016.

As shown in table 4.1, only one activity was allowed in fewer states in 2016 than in 1997 (job development programs); all other activities were either adopted by more states or stayed the same. The average number of allowable activities increased from 10.4 in 1997 to 13.4 in 2016, with some of the greatest increases occurring among activities not federally recognized. The number of states allowing recipients to count counseling as an allowable activity more than tripled between 1997 and 2016, and four times as many states allowed recipients to count self-employment toward the work requirement in 2016 than in 1997. Given that these activities do not increase the state's work participation rate, why would a state allow these activities to count? In some states the hours requirement is higher than the federal requirement; whereas the

Table 4.1. Allowable Activities

Work Activity	Core, Non-core, or Not Federally Recognized?	States Allowing Activity, 1997	States Allowing Activity, 2016
Education			
Basic or remedial education	Not federally recognized	46	49
English as a second language	Non-core	44	46
High school education	Non-core	45	49
Postsecondary education	Non-core	37	46
Labor Market			
Community work experience	Core	43	47
Job development program	Not federally recognized	44	39
Job readiness assistance	Core	49	50
Job search	Core	50	50
Job skills training	Non-core	49	51
Nonsubsidized employment	Core	39	49
On-the-job training	Core	47	48
Self-employment	Not federally recognized	10	40
Subsidized employment	Core	40	47
Self-Improvement			
Community service	Core	19	43
Counseling	Not federally recognized	11	37
Life skills training	Not federally recognized	17	29
Providing child care for others	Core	13	28

Note: "Allowing Activity" means a majority of recipient types (as defined in appendix table B.5) may count the activity toward the work requirement.

federal requirement is that a recipient with a child under the age of six must complete twenty hours of "work" each week, a state may increase that to thirty hours. In these cases, the recipient could use activities not federally recognized to complete the rest of their hours.

Activity Requirement Exemptions

To receive an activity exemption, a recipient typically must show just cause—I argue that the source of this just cause is at times external to the recipient and at other times originates with the recipient. Table 4.2 lists the ten most common activity exemptions and the number of

Table 4.2. Activity Exemptions

Type of Exemption	Number of States with Exemption in 1997	Number of States with Exemption in 2016
Caring for ill/disabled family member	37	41
Caring for young child	47	42
Domestic violence survivor	8	23
No child care available	28	19
Other exemptions	33	29
Recipient elderly	34	27
Recipient ill/disabled	39	30
Recipient is a minor attending school	46	45
Recipient pregnant	27	14
Working unsubsidized job	21	9

states allowing each exemption in 1997 and 2016. The average number of exemptions allowed by a state did not change much over the twenty-year time period: in 1997, states allowed an average of 5.4 exemptions; by 2016, that average had decreased to 4.6. Every state provides at least one exemption (Montana and Utah provide only one) and some states provide up to nine (Nevada and New Mexico).

The first category of exemptions is granted to recipients who are performing care work; it is a responsibility to someone else that is taking them away from the labor force. These exemptions include those provided to caretakers for young children and caretakers for ill or disabled family members. The state may also exempt recipients when childcare is not available—in that case, staying home with a child becomes a reasonable excuse for not having a job. The assumption behind this exemption is that if childcare is available, a welfare recipient should be working. In a 1997 Associated Press poll, over half of respondents agree that a single mother should be exempt from work requirements if she has a child less than a year old.[37] In some sense, a state that allows recipients to assume caretaking responsibilities in exchange for activity requirements equates caretaking with work. It may not be an even exchange (the recipient may be limited in how long she can use a caretaking exemption), but it is a recognition that caretaking is work.

If the first category of exemptions includes circumstances in which the recipient is taking care of other people, the second category can be thought of as involving situations in which the recipient needs an exemption from activity requirements to care for herself. Recipients may be exempt from work requirements when they are sick or disabled, for example, or if they are considered elderly. There is strong public support for some of these exemptions. In a 1993 *U.S. News & World Report* poll, only 37 percent of respondents supported work requirements for a parent with a significant physical or mental disability.[38] Survivors of domestic violence may also receive exemptions from activity requirements, either because they face a danger in returning to work or because they are in need of counseling or other support services. In these cases, the recipient may be viewed as deserving of the exemption—due to limitations beyond their control, they cannot be expected to meet work requirements.

Straddling the line between caring for others and self-care is the activity exemption for pregnant women. Typically, activity exemptions are allowed to pregnant women when they are late in their pregnancy and work becomes more difficult, or if the woman's doctor recommends that she stop working. A pregnant woman's activity exemption may be seen as protecting her unborn child—it is in the best interests of the fetus that she not be required to work. An activity exemption may also be vital to the health of the mother. Alternatively, the argument could be made that women on welfare who choose to become pregnant should not be "rewarded" for such behavior by receiving activity exemptions.

Finally, states can provide activity exemptions based on other just causes. Some states, for instance, may permit an activity exemption to a recipient receiving mental health or substance abuse treatment. Other states exempt recipients from activity requirements if they do not have the transportation necessary to participate in activities, or if their immigration status prevents them from obtaining work. Finally, some states exempt recipients from certain requirements if they are meeting other commitments. For example, in some states a recipient with an unsubsidized job will be exempt from meeting activity requirements. A recipient could have an unsubsidized job where they work for twenty-five hours per week; under the federal guidelines they would not be considered as meeting the activity requirements. The state may determine, though, that having a twenty-five-hour paid position is worth more to the recipient in the long run than thirty hours of job search training or community service. Dependent children may also be exempt from meeting activity requirements if they are attending school. A state may exempt eighteen-year-old high school seniors from meeting the same activity requirements as their parents, for example, if they are in school. If the child were to drop out of school, however, they would be required to participate in work requirements in order to receive benefits. Frequently these exemptions are determined on a case-by-case basis.

In many cases, states provide fewer exemptions in 2016 than they did in 1997 (see appendix figures B.1 and B.2 for trends in activity exemptions over time). The only exemptions to grow more popular over time are those provided to recipients caring for an ill or disabled family member and exemptions for survivors of domestic violence. As states are confronted with the realities of the federal work participation rate, it may become more difficult to make their targets while allowing for a variety of activity exemptions.

Explaining the Adoption of Work Policies

Every state must adopt some combination of allowable activities and activity exemptions in order to meet the federal work participation rate. In the following sections, I explain how a variety of factors may influence a state's decision in these areas. I begin by reviewing the potential influence of a state's interest group community. Then I consider the state's demographics, politics, and the greater welfare context.

Interest Groups

Interest groups have several reasons to take an interest in work-related TANF policies. Some groups may be interested in defending the dignity of welfare recipients, whether that means advocating for an expansive list of allowable activities or providing work exemptions for the most marginalized recipients. Organizations may also be interested in work-related policies because of their effect on the labor force. Still others may be interested in the effect these policies have on government spending.

Organizations representing women and African Americans may be interested in TANF policy because of the gendered and racialized stereotypes assigned to welfare recipients. Welfare rights activists during the 1960s and 1970s fought against the conception of paid labor as the only valuable form of work. Many grassroots organizations, for example, included "Mother" in their names to emphasize the importance of child rearing. Welfare recipients "stood up to declare the importance of their work as mothers" and viewed welfare as a method of compensation.[39] As a relic of the welfare rights movement, states with a high percentage of social welfare groups are expected to adopt more expansive definitions of work and to grant exemptions to recipients performing care work.

The influence of feminist organizations on work-related welfare policies, however, is unclear. Many feminists did not object to work requirements because of their own desire to join the workforce, participate in a white man's world, and make "work outside the home a defining element of women's full and equal citizenship."[40] More recently, however, mainstream feminist organizations such as the National Organization for Women have placed an increased importance on valuing care work. In August 2015, for example, NOW issued an action alert to its members, urging them to call their members of Congress in support of the Social Security Caregiver Credit Act.[41] While this act did not specifically apply to TANF recipients, it did acknowledge that devaluing care work increases women's financial vulnerability.

The stereotypical TANF recipient may be viewed as lazy and unwilling to work, but there are some situations in which a recipient may be seen as having a legitimate reason to not meet work requirements. Domestic violence organizations, for instance, have argued that work exemptions are necessary for women who have experienced abuse because forcing women to go back into the workforce opens the possibility for their abuser to stalk or harass them at work.[42] They may also be in favor of counting counseling as an allowable activity. Other organizations representing the elderly and the disabled may also advocate for their constituents to be exempt from work requirements. In states where these organizations make up a greater percentage of the interest group population, I anticipate there will be more work exemptions.

While there is a moral element to encouraging welfare recipients to find work—those who rely on government assistance are often portrayed as taking money from hardworking taxpayers—there is also a vested business interest in work-related requirements. Some states provide tax incentives for companies that hire welfare recipients.[43] Other states profit from the welfare system; IBM, for example, earns more than $1 billion annually through contracts with state and local welfare agencies.[44]

Business's main interest in welfare policy, though, rests in the potential for low-wage labor. While collecting testimony in Illinois in 1966, a member of the US Commission on Civil Rights asked, "So you think, then, the ability of the farmers in this area to get labor for as little as 50 cents is by reason of the relationship between public aid, the recipient, and the necessity of taking that work?" The AFDC recipient replied, "That's right."[45] Similarly, in California much of the backlash against AFDC came from the Farm Bureau.[46] Under TANF, corporations like Burger King and CVS Pharmacy employ thousands of people participating in welfare-to-work programs.[47] I use the percentage of organizations in a state that are Chambers of Commerce as a rough measure of general business interest. I also create a measure of industry influence by adding the groups representing four low-wage industries: agriculture, construction, food and beverage, and retail. In states with a higher proportion of business organizations, I anticipate greater flexibility in work activities related to paid employment such as job search and subsidized employment and fewer activity exemptions that will remove recipients from the labor force.

Labor unions, depending on which workers they represent, have a variety of reasons to be interested in TANF work requirements. Some labor unions represent the public employees that provide social services—TANF caseworkers or those leading job skills training may be public employees. Other labor unions may represent workers who could potentially be displaced by welfare recipients completing community work experience or a subsidized job program. I anticipate that labor unions will be opposed to counting these activities as "work." There is also some evidence that the increased presence of labor unions reduces economic inequality, as labor unions fight for the interests of the working class.[48] Therefore, labor unions may advocate for policies that provide TANF recipients with the same rights as other low-income workers.

State Need

I include a number of variables to measure state need for welfare and the types of activities in which recipients may participate to meet their work requirements. The percentage of the population that is African American is included, as well as the percentage of the population that is Hispanic.

The unemployment rate is included to capture the population that is out of work. The primary goal of TANF is to help recipients achieve financial self-sufficiency through employment. When the unemployment rate is low, jobs may be easy to come by; during this time, a state may take a harsher stance on types of activities that may count toward the work requirement. When the unemployment rate is high, however, policymakers may adjust state programs accordingly. They may choose to provide more work exemptions or allow recipients to choose from a wider range of activities to complete their work requirements, knowing that paid employment is harder to obtain. I also include the percentage of the adult population with a high school degree as a control. I expect that states may change the work activities available to recipients depending on the education of the population. In a state with a highly educated population, it may not be necessary for welfare recipients to complete basic education classes. In a state with a lower percentage of high school graduates, however, there may be a greater emphasis on recipients' education before getting them into the workforce.

I also control for the percentage of the population that is receiving TANF. A state seeking to decrease its caseload may choose to allow fewer exemptions from the work requirements.

The Political Environment

I do not anticipate that partisan control will be strongly related to work policies. Both Democrats and Republicans favored work requirements under TANF. As Piven and Cloward write, "liberals and conservatives could readily agree that poor relief generated 'dependency,' and that funneling women into the labor force was the remedy."[49] The percentage of women in the legislature may have an effect on allowable activities and exemptions, however. Female legislators may feel a responsibility to represent the preferences of welfare recipients because a large majority of them are women. Given their common experiences, female legislators may show more empathy toward women with young children. I expect that states with a higher percentage of women in the legislature will be more likely to provide an activity exemption for pregnant recipients and recipients taking care of young children.

Finally, I include a measure of citizen ideology. If state policymakers are responsive to the preferences of their constituents, then I would expect states with more liberal populations to have more generous welfare policies, including a wider range of allowable activities and more exemptions to work requirements.

Welfare Context

The final group of control variables included in the models control for the greater welfare context. I include a measure of neighboring states' policies to account for policy diffusion and possible "race to the bottom" effects. Finally, the maximum monthly benefit for a family of three is included in the models as a rough measure of the generosity of a state's welfare policy.

How Do the Rules Interact?

Individual welfare rules are not made in a vacuum and it is possible that policymakers consider the entire scope of a state's welfare program before changing individual rules. Similarly, a state that allows recipients to count only a few activities toward their work requirements may offer many activity exemptions. A state may not offer counseling as an allowable activity, for instance, but it may allow recipients who are most likely to need counseling (those who have experienced domestic violence, those seeking mental health or substance abuse treatment, etc.) to be exempt from work requirements. Some states may be lenient in all their policies and have a generally more expansive welfare program. Other states may have more stringent policies across the board. Then, in the middle, there may be states that are strict in some respects but offer flexibility in other areas.

There are some allowable activities and exemptions that appear to mirror each other in that the end result is the same. For example, states can accommodate the individual needs of recipients either by exempting recipients on a case-by-case basis or by creating other activity requirements that address the recipient's needs. As shown in figure 4.1b, the number of states allowing other activities to count toward the work requirement has increased over time, while the number of states allowing for other exemptions has decreased. Similarly, over twenty states provided activity exemptions for recipients who had unsubsidized employment in 1997. Over time, the number of states permitting this exemption decreased, but more states began counting unsubsidized employment toward the work requirement (see figure 4.1c).

Another area of possible substitution concerns situations in which counseling may be prescribed for the recipient. In a number of states that do not provide activity exemptions for survivors of domestic violence, recipients may count counseling toward their activity requirement (seven states fell into this category in 1997; nineteen did in 2016). In an ideal situation for domestic violence advocates, states would expand activity requirements to include counseling and provide exemptions for survivors of domestic violence. If that option is not available, advocates may focus on getting one rule passed. As figure 4.1a shows, both the number of states counting counseling toward the work requirement and the number of states providing domestic violence exemptions has increased; this suggests a larger shift in states' priorities. Finally, a state can ensure that dependent children in school remain eligible for benefits either by exempting them from work activities, or the state can choose to count attending high school as meeting the work requirement. This may not be the case, however, given that so many states both count high school education as an allowable activity and exempt dependent children from work requirements (see figure 4.1d).

Figure 4.2 shows what substitution may look like on a larger scale by graphing the total number of activity exemptions allowed by a state (averaged over 1997 to 2016), as well as the total number of activities that may count toward the work requirement available to half of the state's recipient types.[50] The dashed horizontal line indicates the mean number of activity exemptions over all state-years (4.6), while the dashed vertical lines represents the mean number of activities available to recipients over all state-years (12.5). Thus, a state below the horizontal dashed line may be considered more stringent than the average state-year with regard to allowable activities; a state above the line may be considered more flexible than average. A state to the right of the vertical dashed line may be considered more flexible in terms of activity exemptions

(a) Domestic violence exemption & counseling activity

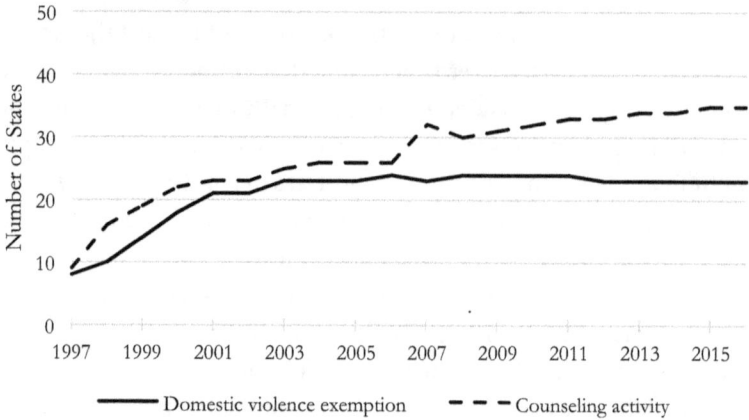

Number of States

1997   1999   2001   2003   2005   2007   2009   2011   2013   2015

——— Domestic violence exemption   – – – Counseling activity

(b) Other activity exemption & allowable activity

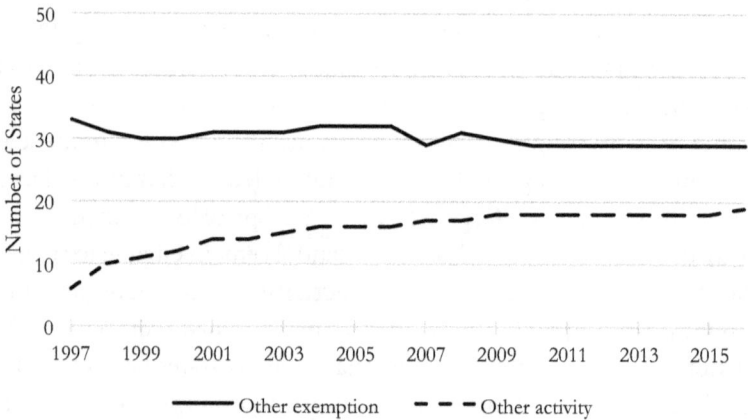

Number of States

1997   1999   2001   2003   2005   2007   2009   2011   2013   2015

——— Other exemption   – – – Other activity

(c) Unsubsidized job exemption & allowable activity

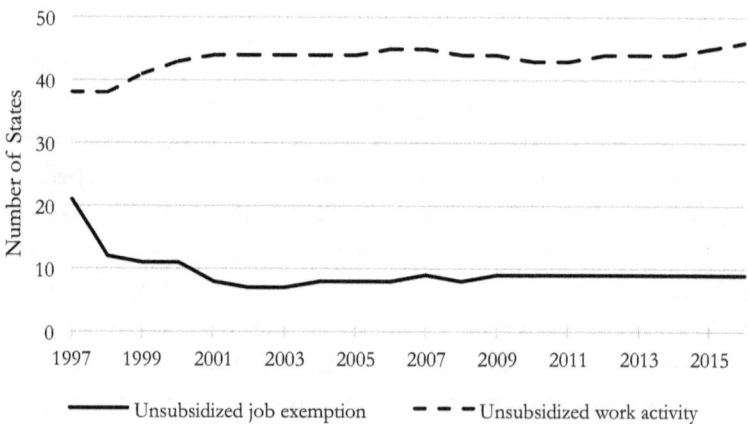

Number of States

1997   1999   2001   2003   2005   2007   2009   2011   2013   2015

——— Unsubsidized job exemption   – – – Unsubsidized work activity

(d) High school exemption & allowable activity

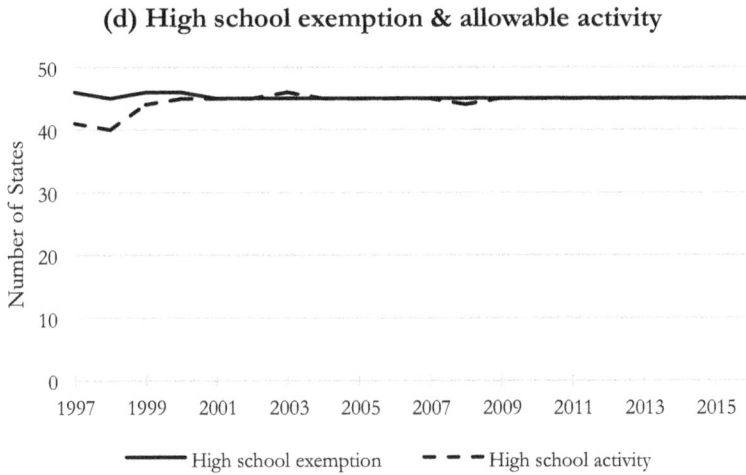

Figures 4.1a–d. Possible Areas of Exemption and Allowable Activity Substitutions.
Source: Urban Institute's Welfare Rules Database.

provided to recipients, while a state to the left is more stringent than the average state-year.

The states in the upper right quadrant are more flexible on both measures than the average state-year. It could be that these states are flexible just with respect to work-related policies, but have stringent time limits or behavioral requirements. This is the case with South Dakota, which in 1997 provided both more activity exemptions and more allowable activities than the average state-year, but also had a twenty-four-month lifetime time limit and several behavioral requirements for its recipients. In contrast, states in the lower left quadrant offer fewer exemptions and fewer allowable activities than the average state-year. Similar to South Dakota, Idaho had a twenty-four-month lifetime time limit in 1997, but the state provided far fewer reasons for activity exemptions and provided fewer work activity options. The vast differences in the two states' work-related policies suggest different policy priorities and perhaps agendas driven by different types of interests. While I analyze how channels of representation influence specific welfare rules, it is also important to keep in mind the big picture of the state's overall welfare program.

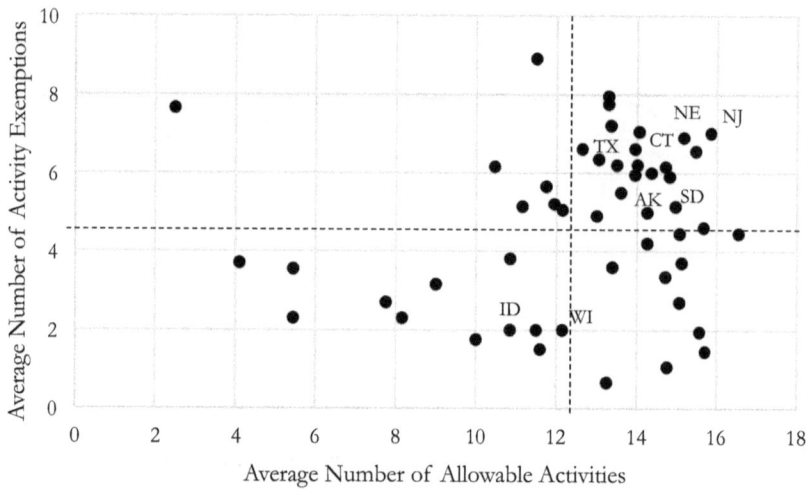

Figure 4.2. Number of Activity Exemptions and Allowable Activities.
Source: Urban Institute's Welfare Rules Database.

Results

To analyze the relationship between allowable activities, activity exemptions, and different channels of representation, I ran a series of logistic regressions, where the state-year serves as the unit of analysis (see tables B.6–8 and B.10–11) . Allowable activities are measured as binary variables, with 1 indicating at least four recipient types may count the activity toward their work requirement (see appendix table B.5 for description of recipient types). Activity exemptions are also measured as binary variables, with 1 indicating the state allows the exemption and 0 indicating the state does not allow the exemption.

Broadly speaking, I expect business and industry groups to be in favor of activities related to the labor force. I expect women's, civil rights, and social welfare organizations to be in favor of a broader definition of work, including education and self-improvement activities. If influence over policymakers is measured as the size of the interest group population given the state's interest group community, then states with more labor force–oriented allowable activities should have a greater proportion of business and industry groups. Conversely, states with more education and service or personal enrichment allowable activities should have a greater proportion of women's, civil rights, and social welfare groups.

Two major themes emerged from these results: the importance of care work and the widespread support for education. I first delve into how care work is incorporated into TANF rules and then discuss the support for education among various types of interest groups. I then review the extent to which TANF's activity requirements require "work" in the traditional sense.

The Importance of Care Work

There are both allowable activities and activity exemptions that recognize the importance of care work. In some cases, this care work is provided to others—this is the traditional care work that women provide to their families. I argue that another type of care work is also underlying some of the allowable activities and exemptions within TANF—that of self-care. First, I discuss the organized interests and environmental variables that increase the likelihood of a state supporting activities and exemptions focused on care of others. Then I discuss what factors in a state may contribute to activities and exemptions that support self-care.

Caring for Others

One of the principal fights of the welfare rights movement was over whether care work should count as work. Under TANF, there are few allowable activities that fall into this category; the one exception is providing childcare for others.[51] While few of the allowable activities under TANF focus on providing care, several of the activity exemptions do. Caretaker exemptions include those provided to recipients who are pregnant, without childcare, caring for ill or disabled family members, or caring for young children. On average, a state allowed for 2.3 caretaker exemptions between 1997 and 2016, a figure that remained relatively stable over time. I anticipated women's organizations would strongly support these exemptions for their recognition of the importance of care work. I also expected that disability rights groups and health organizations would be in favor of exemptions caring for ill or disabled. In contrast, I expected business and industry to be opposed to any activity exemption that takes potential workers out of the workforce. For example, caretakers of young children *can* work, provided that they have childcare. Therefore, I would expect that states with caretaker activity exemptions would have a smaller proportion of business and industry interest groups than states without these exemptions.

When analyzed together, only the proportion of labor groups is significantly related to the total number of caregiving exemptions allowed by the state (see table B.10). Contrary to expectations, the proportion of Chambers of Commerce is unrelated to the number of caretaking exemptions allowed by the state. There is not a significant relationship between the percentage of women's organizations in a state and any caretaker exemption. In most of the models (the exception being an exemption when no childcare is available), the relationship is negative but does not reach statistical significance. Similarly, the presence of more women in the legislature appears to have little relationship to caretaker exemptions.

PROVIDING CHILDCARE FOR OTHERS

I expected that an increase in the proportion of women's groups or African American groups in a state would increase the likelihood of a state allowing recipients to count providing childcare for others as work. This is not supported by the results of the logistic regression, however (see table B.7). Neither greater presence of women's organizations nor African American organizations are significantly related to allowing childcare to count toward the TANF work requirement.

States with a greater percentage of socially conservative organizations are more likely to count providing childcare as a work activity, however. These organizations may support women pursing childcare as an allowable activity because it fits in with the traditional role of the woman as caretaker. States with a larger Hispanic population are also more likely to expand the definition of work to include providing childcare for others. Walker and Schmit argue that center-based childcare may not meet the needs of Hispanic families.[52] Low-wage workers often work irregular hours and have inconsistent schedules, so a childcare center open during regular business hours may not provide adequate coverage. Allowing recipients to count providing childcare for others as work, however, could be a way for recipients to help those in their communities. On the other hand, this positive relationship between a state's Hispanic population and the option to provide childcare to others as "work" may be rooted in a belief that women of color should be taking care of other people's children.

While I do not find the expected relationship between interest groups and childcare as an allowable activity, the results do suggest that more liberal states are more likely to allow TANF recipients to count providing childcare as work. States with Democratic-controlled legislatures are significantly more likely to include providing childcare in the list of allowable activities, and states with a more liberal citizenry are also significantly more likely to count the activity as work. This confirms previous studies attesting to more generous welfare programs under liberal governments.

CARING FOR YOUNG CHILDREN/NO CHILDCARE AVAILABLE

States with more socially conservative organizations are more likely to provide exemptions for recipients without childcare (see table B.10). These socially conservative organizations include those that promote traditional family values, so it is unsurprising that they would be supportive of exemptions that would allow caretakers—primarily women—to stay at home fulfilling traditional gender roles.

Carol Kasabach, representing the Lutheran Office of Governmental Ministry in New Jersey, expressed concerns with the state's activity requirements for recipients with young children:

> Right now, the law says that anyone who has a child 12 weeks or over is required to take part in TANF—Temporary Assistance to Needy Families. I indicated how difficult it is to provide the infant care at that kind of ratio. There has to be an appropriate reimbursement rate or people will not be able to provide the childcare. [. . .] Another concern that some of us have is with sanctioning. If a mother is not comfortable with a particular childcare arrangement that seems to be available and says to her worker, "I am not comfortable with that," what if the worker says, "Well, I'm comfortable with it. That's available; you take it." We have to make absolutely sure that people are not being sanctioned indiscriminately.[53]

States with a greater proportion of interest groups representing industries that often employ TANF recipients are actually more likely to provide an exemption when a recipient has a young child. Businesses may be in favor of—or less opposed to—activity exemptions when they would not want to hire a recipient because of their circumstances. This issue came up in Wisconsin when addressing the requirement that recipients attend a parenting class while the child was still an infant. Anne DeLeo from the W-2 Monitoring Task Force told legislators in 2005 that "some employers are referring their pregnant employees to the W-2 program instead of offering them employer-paid maternity leave."[54]

As the state's Black population increases, a state is more likely to exempt recipients caring for young children. The state is no more likely, though, to provide an exemption for a recipient who does not have childcare. This may reflect a judgment of the target population—women who are caring for children may be seen as more sympathetic than those who have older children but cannot find childcare. It may be easier for policymakers to make the case that mothers should stay home with their newborns than to justify what may be perceived as laziness by mothers who are without childcare.

An alternate model specification also suggests this policy may be influenced by the state's interest group population (see table B.12). Looking only at the states that provide an exemption for recipients caring for young children, states with a greater proportion of African American organizations provide significantly longer exemptions. In a state where African American organizations make up 2 percent of the interest group community, the estimated length of the exemption is just over ten months. If the proportion of African American organizations in a state increases to 5 percent, the estimated length of the activity exemption is over fourteen months.

CARING FOR ILL/DISABLED FAMILY

The probability of a state providing an activity exemption for recipients caring for ill or disabled family members is significantly higher in 2013 through 2016 than in 1997. This may reflect a broader societal trend toward recognizing the labor involved in care work. There is no significant relationship, however, between a state's interest group community and providing an activity exemption for caring for family with an illness or disability (see table B.10). The presence of women's organizations or disability rights groups are not correlated with a greater likelihood that a state exempt this care work from the activity requirement. At the same time, larger proportions of business interests within a state are not significantly correlated with a lower probability that a state will exempt recipients performing this care work. Similarly, partisan control and citizen ideology is not significantly related to allowing this exemption. The only significant relationship found is that the probability of allowing the exemption increases as the percentage of the state's population receiving TANF increases. This suggests, at least, that states are not removing this exemption as a way to kick recipients off the rolls.

The lack of a relationship between a state's interest group community and work exemptions for those experiencing illness or disability, and/or their caretakers, may also reflect the strategic use of resources by advocacy organizations. Many organizations mobilized as states began proposing work requirements for Medicaid recipients. In Alaska, organizations as varied as the Alaska Primary Care Association (APCA), the Alaska State Hospital and Nursing Home Association (ASHNHA), and the American Diabetes Association submitted testimony against proposed work requirements.[55] Healthcare providers may be more likely to testify against Medicaid work requirements because denying applicants coverage will have negative financial consequences for them. When the Wisconsin legislature was reviewing a package of welfare reform measures, advocates from several disability rights organizations spoke out in opposition to BadgerCare (Wisconsin's name for Medicaid) work requirements.[56] Some of those speaking against the work requirements included caretakers, such as Courtney Waller, who described the challenges in retaining employment while caring for her daughter Theodora:

> In 2013 Theodora Elise came into the world with an ultra-rare disease, Timothy Syndrome. [. . .] I understand the challenges to the parents of children who are medically fragile in adequately being able to perform their jobs. Or unable to keep jobs due to the number of emergency or planned hours they must miss. If I am lucky enough to find employment that is very forgiving of the medical emergencies, appointments and surgeries Theodora has, I must find someone to care for her. When Theodora was first born, we quickly found that not a single day care in the

area would accept her. [. . .] It is imperative than any work requirements considered by the Assembly take into account families likes ours and the barriers to finding and retaining employment we face.[57]

For these caretakers, maintaining healthcare coverage may be a priority over receiving cash assistance. Given that the income thresholds and eligibility requirements are less strict for Medicaid than for TANF, advocating against Medicaid work requirements also appeals to a broader population. Finally, advocacy organizations may find it easier to make a case that people need or deserve access to medical care, especially when they have chronic conditions or disabilities. It is easier, therefore, to ask policymakers to make exemptions to work requirements to Medicaid than to exempt TANF recipients from work requirements.

RECIPIENT IS PREGNANT

The proportion of labor groups is significantly related to the likelihood that a state provides activity exemptions for pregnant recipients (see table B.10). Given that policymakers and advocates frequently compare welfare to the working world, labor groups may be in favor of providing caretaker exemptions when workers would normally be able to take off work. It is common for workers to take time off to care for sick family members, to care for young children, or to have maternity leave. Labor advocates may argue that this same opportunity should be extended to TANF recipients.

In contrast, there is a negative relationship between the proportion of African American organizations in a state and state exemptions for pregnant recipients. This negative relationship disappears in an alternative specification of the model that focuses solely on states that allow pregnancy exemptions (see table B.12). In that model, the percentage of African American groups in a state is not significantly related to when during her pregnancy a woman becomes eligible for an activity exemption. An increase in the percentage of economically conservative organizations is significantly related to a woman being allowed an exemption later in her pregnancy. This suggests that the negative relationship in the logistic regression may be driven by conservative states in the South that have a large proportion of African American organizations. For example, Louisiana has one of the largest proportions of African American groups in its interest group community—3.7 percent compared to 2 percent across all states—but the state allows very few activity exemptions.

States with a more liberal population have, on the whole, more caretaking exemptions than conservative states (see table B.10). These results seem to be driven by the positive relationship between citizen ideology and exemptions for recipients who are pregnant or caring for young children. Furthermore, states with Democratic governors are more likely to exempt pregnant recipients from work requirements. This aligns with expectations of Democrats and those on the political left generally being in favor of a more expansive welfare state. It is particularly striking, however, that the percentage of women in the legislature has no significant relationship to the number of caregiving exemptions allowed by the state. Theories of descriptive representation would suggest that because female legislators are more likely to share with welfare recipients the experience of acting as caregivers that an increase in their presence would increase the likelihood of a state allowing for these exemptions. When it comes to representing the needs of welfare recipients as caregivers for young children, the results of the model suggest that interest groups and political parties are leading the charge.

Self-Care

In addition to incentivizing care for others, a state can promote self-care by expanding allowable activities to include counseling, life skills training, and other activities as determined on a case-by-case basis. Similarly, a state can exempt a recipient from work requirements in order to pursue self-care. These exemptions include those provided to recipients who are ill or disabled, elderly, survivors of domestic violence, or whose exemption is based on individual circumstances.

SELF-IMPROVEMENT ACTIVITIES

The likelihood of a state allowing a recipient to count counseling toward her work requirement increases as the proportion of African American organizations increases (see table B.7). A state is also more likely to offer counseling as a work activity when there is a Democratic legislature. A state is also more likely to count community service as a work activity as the proportion of socially conservative organizations in the state increases. Conservative organizations may support community service as work if it helps maintain the traditional family structure or if it is part of a religious tradition.

As the proportion of Chambers of Commerce in a state increases, a state is more likely to allow recipients to count life skills training and other activities as allowable activities. Promoting life skills training and other activities, such as rehabilitation services, could be in the interest of local service providers. In several states, the "other" work activity includes some type of rehabilitation, including physical therapy and drug or alcohol treatment. Allowing a recipient to count these activities toward the work requirement may be seen as a long-term investment, decreasing the likelihood that a recipient will need other government services.

SELF-CARE EXEMPTIONS

There are several exemptions available to recipients who are caring for themselves. Under the Family Violence Option, states can exempt recipients who have experienced domestic violence from activity requirements. Contrary to my theory, states with a domestic violence activity exemption do not have a greater proportion of domestic violence organizations than those without the exemption (see table B.11). Moreover, neither the percentage of women's organizations in a state nor the percentage of women in the legislature is significantly related to a state's propensity to provide an exemption for survivors of domestic violence. This is unexpected given that an overwhelming majority of those affected by domestic violence are women. The lack of a relationship provides evidence for Strolovitch's argument that interest groups are often representing the privileged among their members or constituents. Domestic violence organizations and women's groups may be focused on representing the interests of white, middle-class survivors, to the detriment of low-income women.

They do, however, have a greater share of social welfare organizations and a higher proportion of socially conservative groups than states without the domestic violence exemption. Providing an activity exemption to a recipient who has experienced abuse may enable them to focus more on the welfare of their family than on trying to meet requirements, thus preserving traditional family values. States with a greater share of industry groups are also more likely to provide activity exemptions for survivors of domestic violence. A recipient's personal circumstances are not independent of her working conditions, as Barbara Price from the New Jersey Coalition for Battered Women explained to the New Jersey Assembly Policy and Regulatory Oversight Committee. Leaving an abusive situation, Price argued, could impede a woman's entry into the labor force because women are sometimes "forced to leave their job because their batterer continues to harass them at work."[58] Without an activity exemption, a woman experiencing abuse may be forced back into an abusive situation in order to fulfill TANF's activity requirements. Industry interest groups may prefer providing exemptions to survivors of domestic violence than having to navigate the ramifications of domestic violence in the workplace.

Other activity exemptions are provided to recipients who need self-care because of their health or advanced age. States with an activity exemption for ill or disabled recipients have fewer health interest groups than those without the exemption. States with exemptions for elderly recipients have fewer groups representing those with disabilities than states without the exemptions. While this result would appear to show that these interest groups fail to represent their constituencies, they may be successful in a different sense. A state may not provide an activity exemption for disabled or elderly recipients because they move those recipients into a separate state-funded program or require them to pursue other forms of government assistance. Given that states can exempt only 20 percent of their caseload from the work participation rate calculation, states may choose to move recipients who face significant barrier to work to other programs without activity requirements. States may also approach illness and disability on a case-by-case basis. In Alaska, for example, recipients aged sixty and older may qualify as having "good cause" for noncompliance.

Finally, a state is less likely to offer exemptions for domestic violence survivors or for "other" reasons when neighboring states allow for more activity exemptions. This lends credence to the "welfare magnet" theory; states may be hesitant to allow exemptions for fear that they will draw potential recipients from other states. A state risks losing federal funding if it cannot meet its work participation rate because a large percentage of recipients are exempt from requirements. Moreover, recipients that are exempt from work requirements are often also exempt from time limits. Exempt recipients will need assistance for longer and may need to be covered using state funds.

Near Universal Support for (Postsecondary) Education

Similar to activities related to care work, I anticipated that women's organizations would be in favor of an expanded definition of work that encompasses educational activities because they provide women with greater control over their futures. I expect the same would hold true for populations who have traditionally been marginalized within the education system—including African American groups and Hispanic groups. Because educational activities are not paid employment, I expect that any resistance to counting education as work would come from businesses, economically conservative organizations, or Republicans in control of a state legislature or governor's seat.

A state with a Democratic governor is no more likely to allow education activities to count toward the work requirement than a state with a Republican governor (see tables B.6 and B.9); this runs counter to my expectations. Furthermore, a state with a Democratic-controlled legislature is no more likely than a state with a Republican-controlled legislature to consider educational activities as meeting a work requirement. States with a greater percentage of women in the legislature, however, are more likely to count basic education toward the work requirement.

Basic and High School Education

States with a greater proportion of civil rights organizations are more likely to count basic education classes or high school education as an allowable activity (see table B.6). These organizations may be working to ensure equal access to education; the negative relationship between the African American population in a state and education as an allowable activity suggests their work may be necessary. In states with greater African American populations, policymakers may assume that TANF recipients are overwhelmingly African American. Racial stereotypes around laziness or intelligence may lead policymakers to push for TANF recipients to engage in work rather than education. Similarly, states

with higher unemployment rates are less likely to count basic education or postsecondary education as an allowable activity. Policymakers
may assume that unemployment is higher because of the laziness of the
workers; the solution is to force welfare recipients into work rather than
allowing them to count education toward the work requirement. Policymakers in states with high unemployment may also decide that state
resources are better spent in job-related activities.

I do not find a statistically significant relationship between the proportion of women's groups in a state's interest group community and the
decision to count educational activities as work (see table B.6). Women's
interest groups are not absent from hearings about educational activities
for TANF recipients. Appearing before the Connecticut Human Services
Committee in 1999, Barbara Potopowitz from the Connecticut Permanent Commission on the Status of Women noted that "47% of the time
limited welfare recipients in Connecticut have not completed twelfth
grade." Citing research from the Center on Budget and Policy Priorities, she argued that providing education would help recipients receive
better-paying jobs that would ultimately help them achieve economic
self-sufficiency.[59] Natasha Pierre, another member of Connecticut's Permanent Commission on the Status of Women, appeared before the Senate Human Services Committee to express the commission's support for
SB 27 "because it would allow TANF recipients to obtain an education
beyond a high school diploma or certification program."[60] She explicitly
states that the commission supports the proposal because of the disproportionate impact it will have on women.

States with a greater proportion of industry groups are less likely to
count high school education toward the work requirement. Testimony
from a New Jersey Business and Industry Association representative appears to contradict those findings, however. Testifying before the state
assembly's labor committee, she said, "Time and again, employers tell
me they need workers with both the basic skills necessary to operate
in a workplace setting, as well as technical skills, such as the ability to
operate machinery."[61]

There is some indication that a state may allow educational activities to count toward the work requirement when there is greater need
among welfare recipients. As the percentage of adults with a high
school degree increases, the number of allowable educational activities

in a state decreases—states are less likely to offer basic education and high school education. If recipients already have this education, then policymakers may choose to focus on investing in other activities related to immediate employment. The availability of postsecondary education is negatively related to the unemployment rate in the state, however. In a state with high unemployment, education may provide recipients with the basic skills they need to be more marketable as they apply for jobs.

Carmen Cordero, a welfare rights activist from Connecticut, draws the connection between need and education. Testifying before the Connecticut Human Services Committee in 1997, Cordero pleads with the committee to "allow people on public assistance to attend college or learn training programs or long term training programs [. . .] so that they might also be able to find a living wage job just like everyone else behind over here. We all want a chance."[62] For her, the key to moving out of poverty is education.

English as a Second Language

In contrast to my expectations, the likelihood of a state counting ESL classes as work is negatively related to the proportion of Hispanic interest groups in the state (see table B.6). There is no significant relationship between ESL as a work activity and immigration interest groups, however. Advocates who testify on behalf of TANF recipients whose first language is not English often argue that these recipients should be exempt from activity requirements entirely. Shirley Berget from Connecticut Legal Services contended that many of the people she works with, including those who don't speak English, are not just "not job ready"—they are unable to work.[63]

While counting ESL classes may be viewed as additional flexibility for TANF recipients, the implementation of the policy could also have nativist undertones. If nonnative English speakers are forced to complete ESL classes, for example, then counting this educational activity as work is more akin to English-only policies in school or the workplace. Through this lens, an interest group representing Hispanics might advocate against such a policy. This would also explain why states with Democratic governors are less likely to count ESL classes as work.

Postsecondary Education

Postsecondary education may not be viewed as a divisive activity among interest groups; those who want welfare recipients to become economically independent may consider postsecondary education as valuable as job training in facilitating self-sufficiency. In 1999, a dean from the University of Wisconsin system told state legislators about the importance of providing access to higher education to recipients, arguing that recipients "who are able to pursue higher education will have higher earning power. Repeated research studies also predict higher success for their children."[64] Even in states that allow TANF recipients to count postsecondary education toward their work requirement, however, recipients often run up against restrictions. As mentioned previously, recipients may not be allowed to count postsecondary education as an allowable activity long enough to complete a program. South Dakota advocates told legislators in 1998 that extending the state's twelve-month time limit would increase self-sufficiency among TANF recipients. Cathy Bretchelsbauer from Bread for the World pointed out that allowing recipients to pursue education for longer would be especially beneficial for TANF recipients on South Dakota's reservations.[65]

Senator John Harms of Nebraska, himself the former president of Western Nebraska Community College, repeatedly introduced legislation to the Nebraska legislature to address this issue. Senator Harms explained his rationale in 2012:

> And so what this bill did was address that gap by allowing the participants to go through the core activities up to 36 months, gave them a length of time so they could successfully complete and finish the program. That allowed them to pursue that certificate or diploma or degree program. I think we all realize that any young person or adult who gets into a program like this carries a lot of burden. Many of them have families and are trying to work and do all these things, and we found that 12 months just didn't make it right for the family.[66]

Advocates also spoke favorably about Senator Harms's bill. Patricia Saldana from the Center for People in Need told legislators that, in her experience, recipients often gave up "because the barriers become too much and they don't have the time" to complete educational programs while working. Allowing recipients to count education toward their work requirement for thirty-six months would not only contribute to the economic success of these families, Saldana argued, but would also help employers who needed more highly trained workers.[67]

The percentage of industry groups in a state is negatively related to the probability of allowing postsecondary education to count as work, however (see table B.6). These industries typically pay low wages, often around the minimum wage. Promoting postsecondary education may decrease the number of workers willing to work for low wages, given the higher earning potential for those with advanced degrees.

What about Actual "Work"?

While states have the flexibility to introduce welfare recipients to educational opportunities and self-improvement activities, at the heart of activity requirements lies the goal of moving welfare recipients toward financial independence. Interest groups, aware that one of the four major goals of TANF is transitioning recipients to economic self-sufficiency, may be more interested in trying to influence the activities most directly related to work in the private sector.

One activity in which interest groups seem to have a significant influence is community work experience. As the proportions of civil rights and socially conservative groups increase in a state, the likelihood that a state will allow community work experience to count as an allowable activity increases (see table B.8). In contrast, states are less likely to allow community work experience to count toward the activity requirement as the proportion of labor groups in a state increases. While not explicitly calling out community work experience programs, Kevin Jarvis from the New Jersey AFL-CIO stressed the importance of paid work: "Minimum wage increases have been shown to most frequently affect single mothers and individuals trying to get off the welfare rolls and onto the employment rolls."[68] The American Federation of State, County and Municipal Employees (AFSCME) issued a resolution in 2002 condemning the use of community work experience, stating that "subsidized jobs programs have been significantly more successful than unpaid workfare in helping welfare recipients move into jobs with family-supporting wages" and "AFSCME supports wage-paying transitional jobs as an alternative to workfare."[69] Public labor unions may also oppose community work experience because often these placements are in clerical or janitorial positions that may otherwise be unionized.

States with a greater proportion of labor groups are also less likely to count on-the-job training as an allowable activity. AFSCME has also spoken out against the privatization of social safety net programs. Depending on how a state plans to implement training and work development activities, AFSCME may mobilize against the effort because it would take away jobs from public employees.[70]

The model predicting whether states will count job development programs as a work activity shows that states with more industry-related groups are less likely to include the activity in their count. Numerous advocates testified before the New Jersey Assembly Labor Committee on the importance of workforce development and training programs. Melanie Willoughby, president of the New Jersey Retail Merchants Association, stated that "workforce development is a very, very important [issue] to the retail industry."[71] This appears to contradict the results of the model, but testimony from another speaker sheds light on whom employers perceive as the most desirable employees:

And now we're seeing—I think it was last year that we saw $33 million being diverted from this training money for Welfare to Work—$44 million, I believe, this past session. Again a worthy cause, a worthy program, but every dollar that we're taking away from that fund is money that isn't going to support the kind of customized training that, we believe, has close to 100 percent placement.[72]

Underlying this testimony is an assumption that investing in welfare recipients is a bad investment. This reflects deeper stereotypes about welfare recipients—that they are lazy and perhaps incapable of becoming steady workers. The proportion of immigration groups in a state, however, is positively related to the state's counting job development programs toward the work requirement. Immigration groups may represent recipients with greater obstacles to employment—including citizenship status and language barriers—so the immediate connection to private sector employment may not be as crucial as gaining experience. These two types of interest groups—industry and immigration—both have potential interests in work requirements, but ultimately represent different constituents.

Unsubsidized work can both be counted as an allowable activity and used as the basis for an activity exemption. The activity requirement model suggests that unsubsidized work is more likely to count as an allowable activity in states with more conservative voters (see table B.8). More conservative citizens who are not supportive of expanding welfare programs may be supportive of counting unsubsidized work—the closest activity to not being on welfare. The way that most states have set up benefit levels, TANF recipients see a decline in their benefits as their net income increases. Benefits such as case management, transportation assistance, and childcare subsidies may still be available even if benefit levels are not high. It costs the state less money to have TANF recipients who are working unsubsidized jobs, which may make the program more palatable to fiscally conservative voters.

Many of the same trends apply when it come to providing an activity exemption for recipients engaged in unsubsidized work. The activity exemption for unsubsidized work is more likely in states with Republican governors (see table B. 11). The probability of allowing the exemption also increases as the proportion of economically conservative interest groups in the state increases. Regardless of whether unsubsidized work counts toward the activity requirement or qualifies as an activity exemption, it appears to be valued by conservative advocates and politicians.

Conclusion

Much of the impetus behind welfare reform came from the desire to increase employment among welfare recipients in the hopes that it would bring them to self-sufficiency. Under the first cash assistance program for low-income families in the first half of the twentieth century, aid was provided so that women raising children without a male head of household would not have to join the workforce. As norms changed and more women entered the working world, the expectation was that welfare recipients would follow suit. It was not until welfare reform, though, that recipients had to do more than meet the eligibility criteria to receive benefits.

Examining the allowable activities and activity exemptions under TANF provides insight into two questions: What is valued as work by the state? And who deserves to receive assistance even when they cannot complete the activities required by the state? The federal government provides general guidelines to the states as to what activities recipients may count toward meeting their work requirement (and the state's overall work participation rate), but states have the option of narrowing these options or including other activities that may benefit the recipient but do not contribute to the work participation rate. Similarly, the federal government allows states to exempt some of their recipients from these requirements without receiving a penalty, but it is up to the states to determine who receives these exemptions.

I have sought to explain how the interests of welfare recipients are expressed in these policies. I hypothesized that as part of a debate stretching back to the welfare rights movement, African American, civil rights, and women's organizations would support a more expansive definition of work that includes care work and a wider array of activity exemptions that acknowledges the burden placed on caregivers. I also expected business and industry groups to generally be supportive of policies that move recipients into the workforce.

Through both quantitative and qualitative analysis, I found that interest groups from a variety of perspectives—including pro-family, conservative groups, civil rights organizations, and African American groups—supported more expansive definitions of work. Contrary to my expectations, I find that the proportion of women's groups in a state is largely unrelated to the types of activities allowed to count as work. The legislative testimony suggests that for many interest groups ensuring all welfare recipients have access to a high school degree or postsecondary education is more important than job-specific training. As the proportion of industry and labor groups in a state increased, however, the number of educational activities and labor market–related activities decreased, respectively. No type of interest group was universally associated with an increased likelihood of expanding what counts as work, just as no interest group was consistently related to a decreased likelihood of allowing an activity to count toward the work requirement.

Given their stance toward social policies, I expected states with Democratic legislatures and governors to favor more allowable activities and activity exemptions. Democratic-controlled legislatures are significantly more likely to count a variety of activities, from counseling to community work experience, as allowable ways to fulfill work requirements. On the whole, states with Democratic-controlled legislatures also provide significantly more activity exemptions (see table B.11). Legislators can use both allowable activities and activity exemptions to manipulate the state's work participation rate and affect the TANF caseload; Democrats seem more willing to provide flexibility to recipients.

The relationship between governors and activity exemptions is less clear; under some circumstances, states with Democratic governors are more likely to provide activity exemptions, as in the case of pregnant recipients or survivors of domestic violence. In other cases, states led by Republican governors are statistically more likely to provide exemptions, such as to TANF recipients who are working in unsubsidized jobs, and more likely to count some activities as "work."

Finally, because female legislators are more likely to have shared common experiences with welfare recipients, who are largely women, I expected a state's work-related policies to become more flexible as the percentage of women in the legislature increased. Women's representation, however, has little statistical significance in predicting the allowable activities and activity exemptions in each state. An increase in women's representation is associated with an increased likelihood, however, that a state will count self-employment toward the work requirement. Self-employment provides a level of flexibility and independence; female legislators may feel that allowing this to count as an allowable work activity can be pivotal in enabling recipients to move toward self-sufficiency.

Some of the most important components of a state's TANF program concern the requirements regarding activity requirements; participation in these requirements is supposed to lead to financial self-sufficiency. Interacting with these work requirements is another critical element of a state's TANF program—the time limit, which places restraints on how long adult recipients can receive benefits.

5

Time's Up

Program Limits, Extensions, and Exemptions

Speaking before the Human Services Committee of the Connecticut legislature, TANF (and previously, AFDC) recipient Carmen Cordero expressed her frustration with the political process. "I will start, but out of respect to the people that are here that have been here all morning, there should be more representatives back here listening to the people's concerns."[1] In presenting the interests of welfare recipients, Ms. Cordero repeatedly hit on the central tenet of welfare reform: economic self-sufficiency for low-income families. She argued in favor of the education and training programs, support services, and transitional benefits that she believed would help those in need. Perhaps more importantly, she reasoned with lawmakers that these changes would break a cycle of dependency. "You want us off welfare," she noted. "You are saying that we are a nuisance." Would lawmakers consider her plea and create a more expansive welfare program—a carrot to entice self-sufficiency? Or would the state employ a stick to force recipients off the rolls?

The Perception of a Culture of Dependency

The dependency of welfare recipients did not always hold negative connotations. Virginia Sapiro argues that American public policy was set up to keep women dependent on either the state or male breadwinners. Early in the nation's history, women could not own property; even after they gained this right, women were frequently denied the educational and employment opportunities afforded to white men.[2] Mothers' pensions, the first type of government assistance available to women with children, provided support to widows and women who had been abandoned by their husbands, enabling them to continue with their work as caretakers and avoiding the breakup of families.[3] When ADC was originally passed under the Social Security Act of 1935, 85 percent of recipients qualified because of the death of a parent.[4] For a family struggling with the death of the male head of household, having a mother at home to care for her children was more important than being financially independent from the government. Public assistance for these families was also more palatable because assistance was technically provided for the children and not the female caretakers.[5] Moreover, even among families not receiving public assistance, the media suggested working women could cause problems for their children; thus, women were encouraged to remain dependent at least until their children were grown.[6]

Public opinion began to turn in the 1960s and 1970s. This change was driven by several factors. First, by the 1960s the racial demographics of the welfare rolls were changing. The percentage of minority women on the rolls increased as regulations prohibiting agricultural and domestic workers from receiving benefits were repealed. The structural changes that enabled women of color to receive assistance combined with the public narrative, spread by Daniel Patrick Moynihan and others, of the collapse of Black families. Policymakers expressed concerns that welfare recipients would never leave the rolls and would pass on a culture of dependency to younger generations.[7] Supreme Court justice Clarence Thomas spoke of this perceived culture of dependency when describing his sister: "She gets mad when the mailman is late with her welfare check. That's how dependent she is. What's worse is that now her kids feel entitled to the check too."[8]

Under AFDC, the needs of the caretaker were also included in the benefit calculation, thus making women direct recipients of government aid. The number of unmarried and divorced women receiving welfare increased, and the percentage of out-of-wedlock births was on the rise. Moreover, women were entering the labor force in larger numbers, but the percentage of AFDC families with outside income declined, creating the perception that recipients did not want to work.[9] These were not the deserving widows and abandoned mothers who originally received aid to care for their children. By the 1990s, a strong stigma was associated with welfare dependency.[10] Both print and television news overrepresented racial minorities in stories about poverty, and welfare recipients were often portrayed as uneducated and lazy.[11] In 1995, shortly before the passage of welfare reform, 79 percent of survey respondents believed most welfare recipients would remain dependent on the program, while only 15 percent believed welfare was used for a short period of time.[12]

This perception of dependency did not match the reality for many welfare recipients, however. In a survey of AFDC recipients in 1995, the Institute for Women's Policy Research found that half of the single mothers in their sample were working while receiving welfare benefits.[13] In their book, *Welfare Realities: From Rhetoric to Reform*, Bane and Ellwood discuss how the data on welfare recipients can be used by both sides to make their argument. Half of all welfare "spells" (the duration of time spent on the welfare rolls) lasted less than two years under AFDC, and only 14 percent of recipients had received welfare for ten years or more.[14] These statistics suggest that long-term welfare dependency was not as great a problem as conservative lawmakers made it out to be. At the same time, though, nearly a third of AFDC recipients who got off the rolls returned within six years, with 17 percent of recipients returning to AFDC within a year of leaving the rolls.[15] The return patterns of welfare recipients suggest that welfare dependency is a hard habit to kick.

Conservative lawmakers brought the issue of welfare dependency to the forefront of the welfare reform discussion; implementing strict time limits on receipt of benefits was seen as one way of cracking down on recipients who remained on the rolls for long periods of time. Proponents of time limits argue that time limits "compel recipients to cooperate with caseworkers" and push "poor mothers to be better role models for their children."[16] Dependency on the government is considered a personal moral failure with negative psychological consequences for the recipient's children.[17] Time limits fit into the broader policy goals of welfare reform: to increase self-sufficiency among low-income families.

The Rules

Time Limits

Under PRWORA, an adult TANF recipient can receive federal funding for only sixty months over his or her lifetime (children receiving assistance are not subject to a time limit). After that, any additional aid must be funded by the state.[18] States were given the option of adopting the federal sixty-month time limit, but they could also implement a shorter lifetime time limit. Many states took this option, with Connecticut having the shortest lifetime limit at twenty-one months. In 2005, Greg Kunz, an administrator in Idaho's Department of Health and Welfare, explained the rationale behind the state's twenty-four-month time limit:

> When we say that TAFI is a temporary program, it really is. Idaho has established in rule that no adult can receive more than 24 months of TAFI assistance in their lifetime. This creates a real sense of urgency and keeps this program as it was intended, a source of short-term temporary help.[19]

In addition to lifetime limits, some states have adopted periodic time limits, or benefit waiting periods. Periodic time limits allow the recipient to receive X months of assistance over Y months. A benefit waiting period forces a recipient to wait X months to receive assistance after having received Y months of assistance. In some ways the two are functionally equivalent. For example, take a state with a periodic time limit that allows recipients to receive six months of assistance over a twelve-month period. The recipient could choose to receive benefits every other month—January, March, May, and so on. Alternatively, the recipient could receive benefits from January through June, and then not be eligible to receive benefits again until the next year. In both cases the recipient receives six months' worth of benefits over the year.

A benefit waiting period operates similar to the second alternative for the recipient in a state with a periodic time limit. In Texas, a recipient can receive benefits for thirty-six months, but is then ineligible for sixty months. Those thirty-six months do not have to be consecutive, however. It would be possible for a recipient to receive thirty-six months of benefits over a five-year period, but then the recipient would be ineligible for another five years.

The problem with most measures of time limit stringency is the failure to incorporate non-lifetime time limits. Two states may both have a sixty-month lifetime limit, but a state with a periodic time limit or a benefit waiting period limits when a recipient can receive those benefits. To account for these time limits, I created an ordinal measure of time limit generosity. First, I calculated the total number of months a recipient is eligible for assistance in a sixty-month period. For states with only lifetime limits, this is simply the length of the lifetime limit. Take a state with a periodic time limit that limits recipients to receiving

Table 5.1. Months of Assistance over a 60-Month Period

Periodic (X)	Periodic (Y)	Ben. Wait (X)	Ben. Wait (Y)	Lifetime	In 60 Months
6	12	–	–	60	30
6	12	–	–	36	30
–	–	48	96	60	48
24	60	–	–	48	24
24	60	–	–	60	24
24	48	–	–	60	36
–	–	24	12	60	48
–	–	24	36	60	24
–	–	36	24	60	36
24	84	–	–	60	24
24	120	–	–	60	24
–	–	18	3	60	54
–	–	36	60	60	36
7	13	–	–	60	35
–	–	24	24	60	36

benefits in only six out of every twelve months. If the state has a lifetime limit of sixty months, in a sixty-month period the recipient can receive benefits for only thirty months. If a state has the periodic time limit and a lifetime limit of thirty-six months, those recipients can receive benefits for only thirty months as well. Thus, what looks like a more generous time limit is equivalent when evaluating the benefits received over a sixty-month period. Table 5.1 displays some of the other possible combinations.

This measure falls short, however, in distinguishing between states with a lifetime limit of only sixty months and states that have no lifetime limit. To account for that difference, I created an ordinal scale from the total months of assistance calculation. The scale ranges from 0 to 4, with higher numbers indicating a more stringent policy. States without a lifetime limit were coded "0." Table 5.2 provides the coding rules for the other states.

Figure 5.1 shows the change in time limit generosity over time. In 1997, twelve states had no time limits; by 2016 only two states had no time limits. The number of states in which a recipient could receive benefits in twenty-four months or fewer over a sixty-month period decreased

Table 5.2. Ordinal Scale of Time Limit Generosity

Max. Months of Assistance	Value
24 months or fewer	4
25–36 months	3
37–59 months	2
60 months	1
No time limit	0

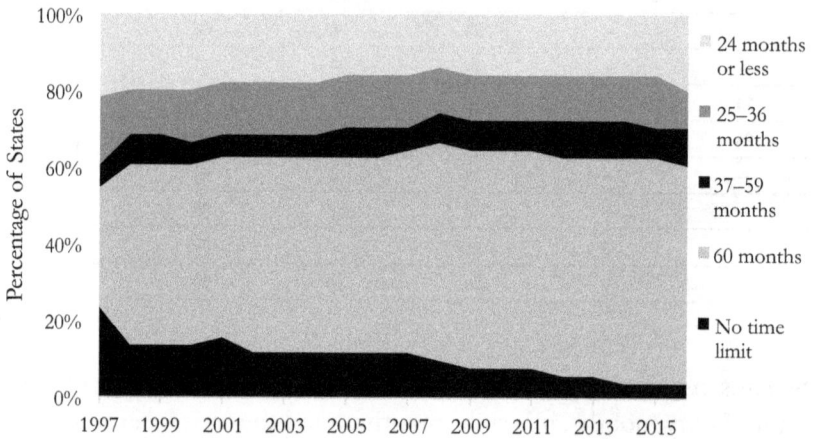

Figure 5.1. Time Limit Generosity over Time

slightly over time. The major area of growth was in the number of states that had adopted the federal sixty-month lifetime limit.

Time Limit Exemptions and Extensions

Time limit extensions and exemptions in many ways mirror activity exemptions. If a recipient is exempt from the time limit, then that month does not count toward their clock. By granting an exemption, the state recognizes that a recipient's current circumstances prevent her from participating in work activities.[20] For example, if a recipient was caring for an ill family member for two months, those two months would not be counted toward the lifetime limit of sixty months. Time limit extensions are given once a recipient has reached his or her time limit and acknowledge that some recipients need extra time to become self-sufficient.

Table 5.3 provides a list of the most common time limit exemptions and extensions, and the number of states that allowed the exemptions and extensions in 1997 and 2016. Between 1997 and 2016, the absolute number of states allowing time limit exemptions increased in a number of categories (recipient is caring for an ill or disabled family member, recipient is a survivor of domestic violence, and recipient is elderly) and remained stable in two other categories (recipient is caring for young child and recipient is receiving mental health or substance abuse treatment). In those twenty years, seventeen states added lifetime benefit limits; therefore, the percentage of states with lifetime limits allowing exemptions decreased in most categories.[21] The same was not true for time limit extensions. Not only did the absolute number of states allowing time limit extensions increase between 1997 and 2016, but the percentage of states allowing those extensions increased as well.

Similar to activity requirement exemptions, states frequently exempt recipients who may be seen as deserving of aid. By 2016, for example, twenty-one states granted time limit exemptions for survivors of domestic violence, and forty states granted time limit extensions for those recipients. Fewer states allow for time limit exemptions and extensions for elderly recipients; this could be because states encourage elderly recipients to apply for other assistance programs, such as Social Security. States prefer that recipients who qualify for Social Security or disability programs transfer to those programs because they will not count against their work participation rate.

Time limit extensions and exemptions for recipients who are cooperating with program requirements but are unable to find unemployment recognize that some recipients will have a more difficult time moving off of welfare than others. Depending on their backgrounds, some recipients may require more education or training before they can find employment. A majority of respondents in a 1993 survey indicated that a welfare recipient in a job training program but with a seventh-grade reading level should not be kicked off the rolls when the time limit expired.[22] By allowing extensions and exemptions for recipients who are cooperating but unable to find employment, the state is distinguishing between those who are "lazy" and do not want to work and those who are trying to be financially independent.

Moreover, as with activity exemptions, states grant time limit exemptions and extensions to recipients performing care work. The results of a 1993 poll suggests that Americans support granting exemptions to women providing care work—72 percent of respondents indicated that a mother with preschool children should be exempt from a time limit.[23] By 2010, thirty-three states granted time limit extensions to welfare recipients caring for an ill or disabled family member. Fewer states permit time limit extensions for recipients caring for small children.

Other time limit extensions and exemptions allow recipients to continue receiving aid if they are involved in activities that will ultimately lead to economic independence. Only a few states exempt from the time limit months in which a recipient is receiving mental health or substance abuse treatment. If the recipient is still receiving treatment once she reaches her time limit, however, there are several states that may grant a time limit extension. Also, a small number of states do not count months in which the recipient is working an unsubsidized job toward their time limit. As with providing an activity exemption to these recipients, granting a time limit exemption encourages recipients to continue working without losing the support of the welfare system.

Finally, some time limit exemptions and extensions appear to respond to real-world conditions. Several states grant time limit exemptions when support services, such as transportation and childcare, are not available. For recipients living in rural areas, a lack of transportation can be a major hurdle to finding a job—this exemption recognizes these challenges. The number of states permitting time limit extensions for recipients living in an area of high local unemployment experienced a sharp increase in 2001 (to eleven states, from seven states in 2000) and 2002 (to seventeen states). In states with a sixty-month time limit, the first TANF recipients would have been hitting their time limits in 2001 and 2002. Confronted with a number of welfare recipients about to be forced off the rolls, policymakers may have adopted more time limit extensions to lessen the blow.

In addition to capturing whether each state allowed for the time limit extension and/or exemption, I created an index summing up the ten reasons. The average number of time limit extensions increased from 1.1 in 1997 to 4.3 in 2016. The change in the average number of exemptions is much less dramatic. In 1997, the average number of exemptions

Table 5.3. Time Limit Exemptions and Extensions

Type of Exemption	States with Exemption in 1997 & 2016		States with Extension in 1997 & 2016	
Caring for ill/disabled family member	17	21	8	40
Caring for young child	9	9	2	10
Cooperating, but unable to find employment	3	2	11	19
Domestic violence survivor	12	21	8	40
High local unemployment	3	1	5	13
No support services available	6	5	6	14
Receiving mental health/substance abuse treatment	2	2	1	14
Recipient elderly	10	16	2	12
Recipient ill/disabled	20	19	11	42
Working unsubsidized job	3	2	4	13

is 1.7; in 2016, the average had risen only slightly to 1.9. The change in the total number of exemptions and extensions suggests that states exercise more leniency at the end of a recipient's time limit; it is not until the recipient has run out of time that the state decides to grant extra months of benefits.

Expectations

Many of the trends that I expect to find among time limits and time limit extensions and exemptions are similar to those I expected for activity requirements and activity exemptions. Generally speaking, I expect that the same forces that are associated with a broader definition of work and more generous activity exemptions will also be associated with a longer time limit and more time limit extensions and exemptions. I also expect that the factors associated with a stricter welfare program—more narrow activity requirements and fewer activity exemptions—will be associated with a more stringent time limit and fewer time limit extensions and exemptions.

Interest Groups

Given the history of welfare rights advocacy, I anticipate that feminist organizations, African American groups, and civil rights groups will all be in favor of a longer time limit and more exemptions and extensions. Specifically, I anticipate that feminist organizations will be in favor of time limit exemptions and extensions for recipients performing care work (caring for young children or other family members).

There are some interest groups that represent constituencies who may benefit from an extended time limit or from a time limit exemption or extension. These include groups representing the elderly, the disabled, and survivors of domestic violence. I anticipate that these groups will be in favor of a longer time limit and more exemptions and extensions.

I expect that organizations providing social services will be opposed to time limits and favor more expansive time limit exemptions and extensions. Catholic charities, for instance, advocated strongly against the federal time limit during the mid-1990s; the group argued that the policy did not account for the individual circumstances that may require some recipients to receive assistance for longer periods of time.[24] Moreover, advocacy organizations in Illinois lobbied for the governor to adopt a "stop the clock" measure that would allow recipients to pursue further education without having those months count against their time limit.[25]

Particular business sectors may be interested in seeing stricter TANF work requirements. Recipients living in states with shorter time limits must reenter the labor force sooner and may be forced to take the first job available to them. In contrast, in a state with a longer time limit, the recipient can focus on education and training, which will in turn set them up for a higher skilled job after getting off the rolls. Klarner et al. find that as the proportion of business interest groups in a state increases, the TANF time limit becomes shorter. The probability of a state having a sixty-month time limit decreases from 79.7 percent to 20.4 percent when levels of business power go from their highest to their lowest levels.[26] Former recipients typically made less than eight dollars an hour, and a significant portion made less than six dollars an hour, putting their earnings well below the poverty line.[27] I expect that, in states with a greater percentage of business organizations representing agriculture, construction, retail, and the food and beverage industry, there will be shorter time limits and fewer time limit exemptions.

Table 5.4. Expectations for Interest Groups

	Time Limit	Exemptions/Extensions
African American	+	+
Chamber of Commerce	−	−
Civil Rights	+	+
Disabled		+
Domestic Violence	+	+
Economic Conservative	−	−
Elderly		+
Women's	+	+
Industry	−	−
Social Conservative		+
Social Welfare	+	+

Note: Where + indicates the interest group favors a more generous policy, − indicates the interest group favors a more stringent policy, and blank indicates no expectations.

Social conservatives became involved in the national debate on welfare reform because of their concern about the moral decay in America. While they were primarily concerned with reducing out-of-wedlock births, these organizations were also concerned with issues of welfare dependency.[28] Therefore, I expect that socially conservative organizations will be in favor of time limits as a way to discourage dependency. At the same time, however, these organizations may support time limit exemptions/extensions for those who are deemed deserving of assistance. This may include the elderly, the ill or disabled, and those who have experienced domestic violence. Because of their views regarding traditional family values, socially conservative organizations may also favor exemptions for women who are caring for young children or other family members.

I anticipate that economically conservative organizations will take stances similar to social conservatives, though perhaps for different reasons. Roberts, for instance, argues that conservatives believe "reliance of the poor on welfare (rather than poverty itself) causes social problems."[29] This sentiment may be true for both economic and social conservatives, but economic conservatives may also be concerned about how welfare dependency affects the nation's budget and deficit, in addition to how it contributes to moral decline.

Political Environment

I would expect that states with Democratic governors and Democratic legislatures have more generous time limits than states under Republican control. It is important to note, however, that the time limit components passed under PRWORA had support from both Republicans and Democrats. Bill Clinton proposed during the 1992 presidential campaign that cash assistance be limited to two years.[30] Assuming that government is responsive to public opinion, I expect that states with a liberal citizen ideology will have more exemptions and extensions, as well as a longer time limit.

Also, because of their possible shared experience as mothers, I anticipate that states are more likely to adopt time limit exemptions and extensions for welfare recipients with small children when the legislature has a greater proportion of female legislators. I also expect that states with a greater proportion of women in the legislature will be more likely to adopt a time limit exemption or extension for recipients who have experienced domestic violence because it is an issue that predominantly affects women.

How Do the Rules Interact?

As with activity requirements and exemptions, state policymakers may make trade-offs between the lifetime limit in a state and the number of exemptions or extensions allowed. States with a strict time limit, for example, may offer a large number of time limit exemptions and extensions to the extent that many recipients never reach the time limit. Massachusetts provides a good example of this trade-off; the state's time limit exemption and extension policy is so flexible that the majority of the caseload is exempt from time limit requirements.[31] For those who are subject to the requirements, there is a periodic time limit restricting receipt of benefits to twenty-four out of every sixty months.

Figure 5.2 shows how these two rules interacted from 1997 to 2016. The vertical dashed line indicates the average number of months a recipient can receive benefits over a sixty-month period (49.7) and the horizontal dashed line represents the average number of time limit extensions (3.5). The states used in the qualitative analysis are labeled for reference. States in the upper right quadrant are, on average, more flexible on both the length of the time limit and the number of time limit extensions. Wisconsin, for instance, has a lifetime limit of sixty months—the same as the federal limit—and granted time limit extensions for recipients who are ill or disabled, caring for an ill or disabled family member, experiencing domestic violence, or living in an area with high local unemployment. States in the lower left quadrant are more stringent on both the time limit length and the number of extensions allowed than the average state. Idaho has a twenty-four-month lifetime limit and provides extensions only for recipients who are ill, disabled, or caring for an ill or disabled family member.

The states in the upper left and the lower right quadrants are strict in one measure and more lenient in the other. Texas has a benefit waiting period that means recipients can receive benefits for only thirty-six months in any sixty-month period. Once recipients have met their sixty-month lifetime limit, however, they may be eligible to receive an extension if they are ill or disabled, caring for someone who is ill or disabled, or experiencing domestic violence. They may also qualify for a time limit extension if support services, such as transportation or childcare, are not available, if they live in an area with high local unemployment, or if they have an unsubsidized job. Policymakers in Texas may

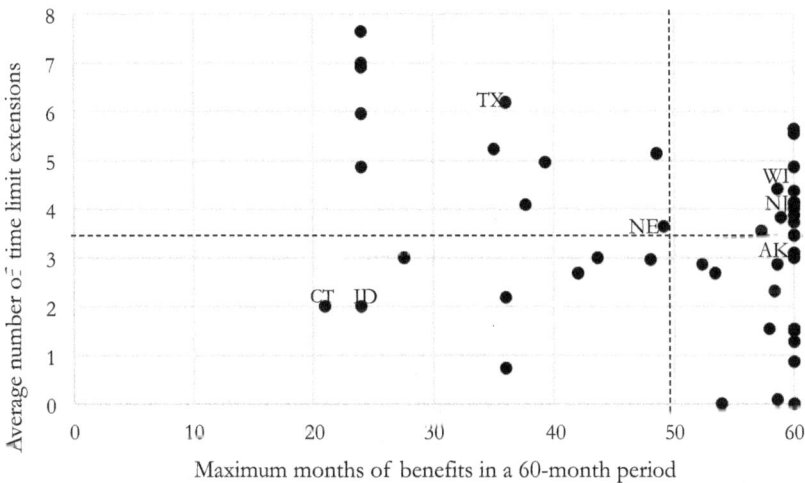

Figure 5.2. The Interaction between Time Limit Length and Extensions

feel that allowing for several extensions to the time limit makes up for the benefit waiting period; it allows them to argue that they are fighting against welfare dependency, while also recognizing that some recipients will need assistance for a longer period of time.

Results

To analyze the relationship between a state's interest group community and its time limit policy, I ran several models. First, I used two logistic regressions to examine the relationship between a state's interest group community and whether or not the state has a lifetime limit (coded as 1 if the state had a lifetime limit, and 0 otherwise) or a periodic time limit/benefit waiting period (also coded as 1 if the state had a limit, and 0 otherwise). Using the ordinal measure of time limit generosity, I ran an ordered logistic regression. I used logistic regressions when running models on individual time limit exemptions and extensions (coded as 1 when the state allowed the exemption or extension and 0 if it did not). Finally, I used OLS regression when running models on the total number of time limit exemptions or extensions allowed by the state.

Many of the results from the multivariate analysis run contrary to my expectations. In the next section I will review the results on the time limit models—the generosity of the time limit, the existence of a lifetime limit, and the existence of a periodic time limit or benefit waiting period. Following that, I will examine the results surrounding time limit extensions and exemptions.

Widespread Support for Time Limits

I anticipated that many interest groups would be in favor of a more generous time limit because of their general support for a more expansive welfare system, and specifically their belief that welfare recipients need to be given adequate time to gain the skills necessary to remain self-sufficient. In particular, I expected that African American groups, women's groups, civil rights groups, and social welfare groups would be in support of more flexible time limits. If these groups support more flexible time limits, then states should be less likely to adopt a time limit as the proportion of these groups in a state's interest group community increases. Similarly, a state should allow recipients to receive more benefits over a sixty-month period when the proportion of these groups increase. I largely find, however, that interest groups have no significant effect on whether a state adopts either a lifetime limit or a periodic time limit/benefit waiting period (see columns 1 and 2 of table B.14). The only significant relationship between a state's interest group community and time limits is a negative relationship between the total number of interest groups in a state and the existence of a lifetime limit.

On its face, adopting a periodic time limit appears restrictive—it places limits on how often a recipient can receive benefits in a given time period. What is not clear, however, is the alternative presented in these states. Consider, for instance, a state debating between a lifetime limit of twenty-four months and a periodic time limit in which the recipient can receive only twenty-four months of benefits in any sixty-month period. What is in the best interests of the welfare recipient—cutting the recipient off before she has reached the federal lifetime limit, or adopting a periodic time limit that forces her to ration her benefits? Advocates may find periodic time limits to be less severe than a strict lifetime limit because the recipient is not removed from the rolls permanently.

Such was the case when Nebraska debated replacing its periodic time limit, which allowed recipients to receive twenty-four months of benefits within a forty-eight-month period, with the federal sixty-month lifetime limit. In January 2007, Chris Peterson from the state's Health and Human Services System explained the rationale for the policy change:

> Current Nebraska statutes do not end or cap cash payments. If the state chooses not to adopt the federal 60-month lifetime limit, then state-only funds must be used for all payments after 60 months. Right now it's 24 out of 48 months you can receive cash. And then when that 48th month is over with, you start again. The 60 lifetime cap means you can receive ADC for five years for the whole lifetime. We believe that this may be an advantage for recipients with the federal requirements. With Nebraska's current program, many clients cycle on and off assistance because they can only receive benefits for 24 months within a continuous 48-month period. This proposal would allow continuous coverage up to 60 months, or for any 60 months over an extended period. [. . .] The estimated first year savings of adopting the federal 60-month lifetime limit is $1.72 million.[32]

According to Peterson, the policy change was intended to help welfare recipients who, under the periodic time limit, cycle on and off welfare. As an additional benefit to the state, implementing a lifetime limit would save the state money. Jen Hernandez, a lobbyist for Nebraska Appleseed, refuted Peterson's claims:

> Another justification for adopting a lifetime limit is that it will give incentives for family to move off public assistance quicker; however, there are already plenty of incentives built into the program to motivate families. Once a family goes on ADC, the parent must sign a contract and immediately engage in at least 30 hours a week of work activities. If the parent fails to comply with this requirement, a full family sanction is imposed that stops all ADC payments to the household, and it takes away the adults' Medicaid and reduces food stamps. Sanctions are a strong enough incentive to motivate families. The only impact of a lifetime limit on assistance is to force more children to live in poverty. Families that have received 60 months of assistance and still in need generally have very significant barriers preventing them from being successful in the work place. Taking away assistance will not eliminate the need—it will only leave the family without the ability to meet its basic needs.[33]

From Hernandez's perspective, families receiving assistance do not need the additional burden of a lifetime limit to seek self-sufficiency. The work requirements of the program, and the sanctions put in place if those requirements were not met, were incentive enough. Moreover, Hernandez argues that pushing families off the rolls does not take away their need. From this activist's perspective, a periodic time limit is more accommodating than a lifetime limit. By October 2007, the state had removed its periodic time limit.

The generosity of a state's time limit also appears to be largely unaffected by the state's interest group community. To measure the state's time limit stringency, I created an ordinal scale ranging from 0 to 4 indicating how many months a recipient would be eligible for benefits over a sixty-month period. I found states have a significantly less generous time limit policy as the proportion of women's groups increase in the state (see column 3 of table B.14); this result contradicts my expectations. For a robustness check, I ran an OLS regression using the number of months a recipient would be eligible for benefits over a sixty-month period as a continuous dependent variable; the results remain the same.

States with a Democratic governor are less likely to have lifetime limits; the same is true for states with a Democratic legislature and a more liberal voting population. The political environment variables are not significant in predicting the stringency of a state's time limit, though, or whether it will have a periodic or benefit waiting time limit. A state is more likely to have a lifetime limit as the African American proportion of the population increases; this aligns with previous research demonstrating how racialized stereotypes have translated into more stringent time limit policies.[34] Overall, the results suggest there is widespread support for some kind of time limit on welfare assistance; even those who favor government assistance may fear dependence.

State legislative testimony from several states demonstrates that legislators remain concerned about welfare recipients becoming dependent on the state. At a 2015 Senate Finance Committee hearing, Alaska senator Pete Kelly (R) expressed concern to Valerie Davidson, the commissioner of the Department of Health and Social Services, that the department was perpetuating a problem of dependency:

> I've had some experience, with some distant members of my family that were quite involved in the system, and it seemed like they were almost pursued by the department for services. [. . .] Do you have discussions on where there's a line where you become almost the creator of the [welfare] population by pursuing them so efficiently, by outreach? [. . .] There's a conundrum here; we don't want more and more people on welfare here, but you're required to—statutorily required—to distribute money to a certain segment of the population.[35]

Senator Kelly went on to ask Commissioner Davidson whether the goal of the Public Assistance Division was to promote self-sufficiency or provide basic living expenses. When the commissioner responded that the answer was both—to promote self-sufficiency by providing for basic living expenses—Senator Kelly asserted his belief that these two goals are in conflict.

Wisconsin legislators also expressed doubt that government assistance would lead to self-sufficiency. Wisconsin Assembly speaker Robin

Vos (R) reiterated Ronald Reagan's belief that "the best social program is a job" and that "public assistance was never intended to be permanent." Picking up on similar themes, Representative Chris Kapenga (R) described public assistance as "more of a web than a net, trapping people in the cycle of poverty."[36] For these Republican state legislators in Alaska and Wisconsin, the only solution to economic self-sufficiency is work; the longer someone is allowed to stay on public assistance, the more likely they are to fall into the "poverty trap."

Extensions for Which Kind of Work?

As with activity exemptions, time limit extensions and exemptions are granted to recipients who are taking care of other people (ill or disabled family members, young children) or who need to continue receiving assistance while they take care of themselves (domestic violence survivors, elderly). Time limit exemptions "stop the clock"—a month in which a recipient is exempt from the time limits does not count toward the lifetime limit. An extension is applied after the recipient has reached the lifetime limit.

I expect that business and industry groups would oppose time limit extensions and exemptions because they allow recipients to stay on the rolls for a longer period of time. In particular, I would expect them to be most strongly opposed to exemptions and extensions offered to able-bodied adults (i.e., business and industry groups may not be opposed to exemptions and extensions for the disabled or the elderly). Overall, the results conform to my expectations. Greater presence of Chambers of Commerce and industry groups is associated with fewer time limit extensions (see table B.16). In particular, as the percentage of Chambers of Commerce and industry groups increase, a state is less likely to provide an extension if the recipient is working an unsubsidized job. Representing employers, these organizations are probably more interested in transitioning employed welfare recipients off the rolls. As the density of industry groups and Chambers of Commerce increase in a state, however, the state is also less likely to provide a time limit extension to recipients receiving drug or alcohol treatment. The explanation for this relationship is not clear; it could be that in states with more business interests, there are simply fewer advocates for those struggling with drug and alcohol addiction.

On the other hand, I expect that several types of groups—including African American, feminist, civil rights, and social welfare groups— would be in favor of exemptions and extensions to accommodate the individual circumstances of recipients. States with a greater proportion of civil rights groups are less likely to adopt several exemptions and extensions. As the proportion of civil rights groups increases in a state, the likelihood that a state will allow an extension for recipients caring for an ill or disabled family member decreases. The likelihood of allowing extensions to survivors of domestic violence and in areas with high local unemployment also decreases as the proportion of civil rights groups increases. States with a greater proportion of civil rights groups are more likely, however, to offer a time limit exemption to recipients who do not have access to support services (see table B.18).

The proportion of women's interest groups in a state is not significantly related to the likelihood that a state will provide a time limit extension for recipients performing care work—taking care of an ill or disabled family member, or taking care of a child (see columns 1 and 2 in table B.16).[37] I expected women's organizations to advocate on behalf of survivors of domestic violence, but the logistic regression results actually show a negative relationship between the percentage of women's organizations in a state and the probability of allowing a time limit extension for survivors of domestic violence. These findings run against expectations that women's groups would advocate for a more expansive welfare policy and one that values care work.

It is also possible that the organizations I anticipated would lobby on behalf of welfare recipients are in fact doing that advocacy work, but are met with resistance by policymakers. The experience of Wisconsin advocates in 2002 demonstrates how this unfolds. Patti Seger, representing the Wisconsin Coalition Against Domestic Violence, made the case that survivors of domestic violence do not want to rely on government assistance:

> [W]ell over half of the women receiving welfare have experienced physical abuse by an intimate partner at some point during their adult lives, with as many as 30% of these women reporting abuse in a current relationship. A significant number of women receiving welfare also report physical and/or sexual abuse in childhood. We know from research and

experience that most battered women work or want to work *if they can do so safely* [emphasis in original]. Many use welfare and work as a way to escape an abusive relationship.[38]

Seger urged the Department of Workforce Development to adopt the Family Violence Option (FVO), which would provide time limit exemptions for survivors of domestic violence. The Wisconsin Coalition Against Sexual Assault also advised the department to adopt the FVO and find "ways to support these individuals rather than penalize them for being the victims of domestic and sexual violence." Responding to these suggestions, the Department of Workforce Development said:

> The department believes that accommodating and working with clients to overcome barriers and move toward self-sufficiency is preferable to merely exempting them from program requirements. [. . .] For example, allowable activities for participants in the W-2 Transitions placement include seeking and obtaining shelter to retain safety in a domestic abuse situation and activities needed to stabilize a family, such as making alternative school arrangements or obtaining mental health services.

The state's response to advocates may explain why the proportion of women's interest groups in a state increases the probability that a state will provide a time limit exemption in the event that support services are unavailable. This type of exemption can be individualized based on what support services are necessary for each recipient. One of these support services, for instance, is childcare. To exempt a TANF recipient from work requirements when they do not have available childcare is, in a roundabout way, providing an exemption for a recipient to perform care work. Policymakers may be more likely to adopt such exemptions because they are not blanket exemptions, and women's interest groups may advocate for these exemptions because women are disproportionately likely to be kept out of the workforce due to lack of childcare.[39]

In May 1997, the New Jersey Assembly convened a hearing specifically to discuss issues around childcare. Assemblywoman Diane Allen outlined the importance of this topic:

The need is ever more growing in light of the implementation of welfare reform and the need of single mothers to improve their education and their work opportunities while knowing that their children are safe and that they are being exposed to appropriate stimuli and that they are enjoying their stay at day care.[40]

Regina Purcell, director of the New Jersey Catholic Conference, provided the Church's perspective on childcare policy; she testified that Catholic bishops applauded the work exemption for welfare recipients when childcare is unavailable but also cautioned the legislature about how to interpret the broader childcare rule: "We believe that no parent should be pressured to accept child care that is less than adequate. In the rush to expand rapidly the amount of childcare to accommodate Work First New Jersey recipients, we must not sacrifice the safety or quality of care."[41] Similarly, Ceil Zalkind, representing the Association for Children in New Jersey, urged policymakers to be lenient in their interpretation of availability of support services:

> And interestingly, Georgia has said, "No child care, no work." If a parent is not able to access child care, the sanctions that would normally attach for not working would not attach. I think that's a provision that's in our Work First bill. It's left to the Department to describe what it means if a parent cannot access child care. I would urge you to look at that most liberally to ensure that someone who truly can't get child care is not penalized.[42]

As suggested by Zalkind, there is a lot of discretion in how exemptions and extensions are applied. The risk in using time limit exemptions or extensions to provide welfare recipients with access to benefits, rather than longer time limits, is that the choice is left to the individual caseworker. As with any case of bureaucratic discretion, the rules are likely to be applied unequally. For TANF recipients trying to prove that childcare or other support services are insufficient, this bureaucratic discretion takes on a paternalist tone, as a state employee determines what is best for the recipient rather than allowing the recipient to make that choice for themselves.

Finally, states are more likely to provide time limit extension for recipients with unsubsidized jobs as the proportion of women's organizations in the state increases. In many ways this encapsulates the problem that many welfare rights activists ran into when working with second-wave feminist groups during the 1960s and 1970s. For many women, moving into the labor force was a sign of progress, a move toward gender equality. Welfare rights activists, however, wanted their care work to be recognized as valuable labor and did not want to be forced into low-paying, low-skilled jobs. The time limit extension for recipients with unsubsidized employment demonstrates that work outside the home is still valued above the care work performed inside the home.

The Political Forces behind Extensions and Exemptions

Descriptive representation does not always have the predicted effect when it comes to a state's time limit extension and exemption policy. While I anticipated that states with a greater proportion of women in the legislature would offer more exemptions and extensions, the percentage of women in the legislature is not significantly related to whether a state offers any time limit exemption or extension (see tables B.16 and B.18). However, as shown through qualitative evidence (both above and in the section to follow), at least some female representatives appear to be aware of the barriers faced by welfare recipients. These representatives may not find more generous welfare policies to be the answer to addressing these barriers. In New Jersey, for instance, lawmakers seemed to focus on providing affordable childcare options for all families rather than honing in on particular solutions for welfare recipients. This may reflect a bias toward representing a larger, less stigmatized target population.

A Democratic legislature is more likely than a Republican legislature to offer a number of time limit exemptions, including to elderly recipients, ill or disabled recipients, and recipients who have experienced domestic violence (see table B.18). Democratic legislatures are also more likely to offer both time limit exemptions and extensions to recipients who are caring for a child or do not have support services (see tables B.16 and B.18). The wide array of exemptions and extensions that are more likely to be offered under a Democratic legislature may be a way of compromising with Republican lawmakers who insist on a time limit; if a recipient can easily be exempted from or extend their time limit, then is the severity of the time limit really felt?

The Curious Case of Connecticut

Given the predicted relationship between a state's political environment and the welfare policy of its neighbors, it would not be surprising if Connecticut adopted a generous time limit. The state, however, has the most restrictive lifetime limit in the country at twenty-one months and provides only four exemptions and two extensions to this limit. In this section, I delve into the debate between Connecticut's advocacy groups and its policymakers to try to understand why a "liberal" state would adopt such a restrictive policy.

With the exception of the office of governor, which was held by a Republican from 1997 to 2010, Connecticut is left-leaning; its citizen ideology was consistently more liberal than the national average, and both the upper and lower houses of Connecticut's legislature were controlled by the Democratic Party over that same period. Moreover, during that period, the percent of women in the legislature ranged from 28 to 32 percent, with an average of 29.6 percent (above the national average).

Connecticut is surrounded by neighbors with relatively generous time limit policies. Massachusetts is by far the most generous; the state effectively has no time limit because the majority of recipients receive a time limit exemption. New York has a lifetime limit of sixty months, and from 1997 to 2008 Rhode Island had a sixty-month lifetime limit until it imposed a forty-eight-month lifetime limit and periodic time limit in 2009. Given these policies, it seems unlikely that Connecticut would be considered a "welfare magnet."

In spite of this, Connecticut has the shortest lifetime limit in the country at twenty-one months. The state does allow for time limit exemptions if the recipient is elderly, ill or disabled, caring for an ill or disabled family member, or caring for a young child. Recipients who have experienced domestic violence, as well as those who are cooperating with program requirements but have not yet found employment, are also eligible for a time limit extension. Arguably, this last extension—for those who are cooperating but cannot find employment—can be applied to a large number of recipients when up to caseworkers' discretion. In fact, asked to explain the time limit before the Human Services Committee, Commissioner Joyce Thomas said:

Individuals who are looking for work, cannot find work, the twenty-one month period of time, there's a six-month extension that can be provided. And then there's an individual assessment, and then there is another extension. That's what the program really does. It focuses in on employment first, training secondary, and for those individuals that can't find employment, the time limit is extended.[43]

The state's focus on employment above all other goals is understandable when considering both the goals of TANF (economic self-sufficiency for recipients) and Connecticut's economy. A large proportion of Connecticut's economy (over 40 percent) comprises jobs in finance, insurance, and real estate or professional and business services. Given Connecticut's relatively small population (increasing from roughly 3.27 million in 1997 to 3.58 million in 2016), there are fewer able-bodied adults available to fill the jobs that are not in the dominant financial and professional sectors.[44] The state's emphasis on moving welfare recipients into low-paying jobs may reflect an attempt to fill employment gaps within the state and ensure a steady supply of low-wage labor.

Regardless of the motivation, advocates began speaking out against Connecticut's twenty-one-month lifetime limit before the first recipients were pushed off the rolls. In 1997, Sharon Langer, a staff attorney with Connecticut Legal Services, told lawmakers she was "very concerned about what's going to happen to families who are subject to the 21-month cutoff." She cautioned them against the strict measure: "We don't know what the ramifications are of the 21-month time limit."[45] Leslie

Table 5.5. Industry Percentage of State GDP, 1997–2016. Source: Bureau of Economic Analysis. https://www.bea.gov/regional/index.htm

	Connecticut	National Average
Agriculture*	0.21	1.22
Professional/business services	11.84	11.50
Construction*	3.43	4.67
Finance, insurance, and real estate*	26.72	19.19
Food/beverage*	1.76	2.12
Health care*	7.48	6.95
Retail*	5.50	6.10

* Connecticut's percentage is significantly different than the national average ($p < 0.01$).

Brett, executive director of the Permanent Commission of the Status of Women (a nonpartisan arm of Connecticut's General Assembly), advised lawmakers to start planning for the future. "We can't put our heads in the sand and hope that some magic will make all of the 55,000 recipients self-sufficient before the 21 months rolls around for each of them," Brett argued.[46]

Lawmakers also heard from advocates from Warriors for Real Welfare Reform, one of the few interest groups representing the interests of welfare recipients that is actually run by welfare recipients.[47] In addition to advocating for a more generous welfare program, these women also brought up issues of representations and feelings of marginalization. Carmen Cordero, the president of Warriors for Real Welfare Reform, told representatives she felt insulted that, after sitting in the committee hearing all morning, there was no one in attendance when it was her turn to speak. "If you want respect from us," she told them, "you will give us the same kind of respect that we want." In speaking against the twenty-one-month time limit, Cordero argued:

> No matter what you do to please the state you are still going to get eliminated in 21 months even though the federal government says five years, they put us on a time record. You have no idea of the amount of stress that puts on a woman when you sleep at night and you wonder how the hell you are going to support your children when all of this is happening.[48]

At the same hearing, Luz Lopez, assistant secretary of Warriors for Welfare Reform, told members of the committee that "nobody seems to care" about what would happen to the children affected by the twenty-one-month time limit. Lopez asked the lawmakers to "allow for more flexibility," especially among recipients who "are lacking jobs, child care, [and] transportation."[49] Lawmakers reassured her that children would not be left out in the cold, but made no mention of adjusting the time limits affecting their parents.

In spite of testimony against it, Connecticut went ahead with the twenty-one-month limit. Advocates have continued to lobby against the measure. In 2001, Lucy Potter, from Hartford Legal Assistants, argued that placing time limits on recipients was unfair when the state had not put in place the resources to help recipients become independent: "The long and short of it is that it's really unreasonable for the Governor to tell TFA recipients that as of October 2001 you should have been able to get your act together when the state has done nothing for these people despite having the resources to do it."[50] Leslie Brett again expressed her concern about Connecticut's time limit: "If you pick an arbitrary limit, and say it's two extensions, or it's 60 months, and persons have done everything they could and they have these barriers, what do we do next?"[51] Extensions such as those provided to recipients without access to support services ensure that recipients who have done everything they were supposed to do to succeed are not disconnected from the welfare system entirely.

Many of those who spoke out against the time limit also suggested that some recipients should be exempt from such a strict policy. Marcia Bok, from the Connecticut Chapter of the National Association of Social Workers, stressed the importance of providing flexibility to recipients with medical conditions:

> So this is a person who is showing a really good-faith effort to work as much as they possibly can, but their income is so low that they're below what they would get from cash assistance. And this provision says if they're working, and making a good-faith effort, and working as much as they can, according to their medical condition, they will be eligible for cash assistance up, at least, to the assistance level as long as they have the medical condition.[52]

Advocates also spoke in favor of exempting grandparents from the twenty-one-month time limit. Muriel Banquer, the coordinator for an elderly program at a mental health center, testified that the number of grandparents with custody of their grandchildren increased by over 50 percent in a decade.[53] Banquer argued that it was unfair to hold grandparents to the twenty-one-month time limit when they were "bravely struggling to keep families together." In her testimony, Banquer is arguing that because of the care work the grandparents are performing— taking custody of their grandchildren when their parents cannot care for them—they should be exempt from the time limits.

Several of the lawmakers empathized with the work it took to care for young children as an older adult. "And as a grandmother who looked after my two grandchildren for 48 hours and was exhausted for two days," Senator Mary Ann Handley expressed her respect for grandparents raising their grandchildren.[54] Representative Maria Kirkley-Bey recalled having custody of her granddaughter for a brief period of time: "And just the amount of energy it takes to deal with a child and work a full-time job—it's unbelievable." She went on to tell the story of a friend who was raising her four grandchildren because their mother had a drug problem. "I don't know where she gets the energy and God bless them."[55] The remarks from both of these lawmakers demonstrate how the shared experiences often found through descriptive representation (in this case, women sharing their experiences as grandmothers) can provide insight into the interests of the constituents most directly affected by the legislature's decisions.

The history of Connecticut's strict time limit demonstrates that even the most passionate activists, coupled with sympathetic policymakers, can fail to alter a state's welfare rules. Connecticut provides a rare case in which welfare recipients actually spoke for themselves and presented their cases to state legislators, and their testimony resonated with female legislators who themselves had been caretakers. Yet the state has not wavered in its twenty-one-month lifetime limit, suggesting that the economic conditions of a state (i.e., the need for low-wage labor) may outweigh the voice of welfare recipients. This is certainly not a new finding, but just another example of the unheavenly chorus singing without a lower-class accent.

Conclusion

The federal time limit established under PRWORA changed welfare from an entitlement, in which a recipient could receive assistance for as long as they met the requirements, into a temporary means of support for low-income families. The government would no longer endorse mothers' staying at home to care for their children if that care came at the government's expense. Women were encouraged to work outside the home to provide for their children, and those who could not earn enough money to make ends meet were labeled "lazy" and "dependent." As with other provisions of welfare reform, though, states were given discretion in the application of time limits. A state could choose to shorten a time limit, cutting a recipient off before the federal sixty-month limit, or use state funding to continue providing assistance after the recipient met the federal limit. States could also choose to exempt some recipients from the time limit and extend the time limit of others. I have sought to explain what drove some states to crack down on welfare dependency through a strict time limit while others offered a more lenient policy.

The quantitative analysis suggests that whether a state implements a lifetime limit or a periodic/benefit waiting time limit appears to be largely independent of the state's interest group community. In Nebraska, however, advocates fought against legislators' removing the periodic time limit in favor of a lifetime limit. This testimony suggests that the calculus for advocacy organizations is not always a straightforward choice between good or bad policy, but sometimes involves advocating for the least harmful option. Politically, states with a more liberal population and a Democratic-controlled government are less likely than more conservative states to have a lifetime limit, but partisan control has no significant effect on periodic time limits or benefit waiting periods. Testimony from Republican legislators suggests that the language of dependency that has surrounded welfare recipients remains common.

To some extent, the stringency of a time limit may be diluted by the types of exemptions and extensions allowed. While I expected that states with an increased density of organizations representing marginalized groups would have more time limit exemptions and extensions, that is not the case. In some instances, states are less likely to have exemptions or extensions as the percentage of these organizations in a state increases. There is evidence, however, that an increased presence of industry groups and Chambers of Commerce—organizations representing employers rather than potential TANF recipients—decreases the likelihood of various exemptions and extensions. These results suggest that a state's need for low-income labor may be influential in their time limit exemption and extension policies. This influence may be offset by the presence of sympathetic legislators, as states with Democratic-controlled legislatures are significantly more likely to offer time limit exemptions and extensions.

Connecticut provides a perfect illustration of a state that, on paper, should have a generous time limit policy; in reality, it has the shortest time limit in the country. Connecticut's legislature is consistently controlled by Democrats, the state's population is more liberal than the nation as a whole, and it is surrounded by states with relatively generous welfare policies. The testimony from state legislative hearings suggests that advocates, including welfare recipients themselves, were vocal in their opposition to the twenty-one-month time limit. Even the female legislators on the committees empathized with the burden of unpaid care work. Ultimately, though, the stringency of Connecticut's time limit is framed in terms of putting recipients to work. Together, activity requirements and time limits work hand-in-hand to move recipients quickly off the welfare rolls.

6

Benefit Boundaries

The Battle of Immigrant Eligibility

In 2013, before cutting to a commercial break during the CNN show *Lou Dobbs Tonight*, Lou Dobbs warned his viewers: "Americans are known for our charity and our generosity, but you may be shocked to find out how much money the federal government is spending on illegal immigrants." In the same episode, Dobbs interviewed Ann Coulter, who expressed her belief that "we should be taking immigrants who are better than us, not worse than us" and proclaimed that "we are scraping the bottom of the barrel [. . .] taking their terrorists, their losers, their poor people."[1]

Given this rhetoric, it should have come as no surprise that Republican presidential candidates would display similarly hostile attitudes toward immigrants. Donald Trump was most outspoken in his anti-immigrant sentiment with lines like, "We also have to be honest about the fact that not everyone who seeks to join our country will be able to successfully assimilate."[2] He also cited a Center for Immigration Studies report estimating that 62 percent of households headed by undocumented immigrants received some type of federal assistance. Other candidates followed suit; Ted Cruz proclaimed that, if he won the presidency, he would "end welfare benefits for those here illegally," even though in most instances undocumented immigrants are not eligible for federal assistance programs.[3] Marco Rubio stated, "In the 21st century, it [immigration] has to be more of a merit-based system," suggesting that immigrants who were not high-skilled need not apply for entry.[4] Even Jeb Bush, who arguably was more pro-immigration than many other Republican presidential candidates, said that legal status should be reserved for those who "pay a fine, learn English, don't commit crimes, work and pay taxes."[5] All of these sentiments reflect a belief that immigrants are an "other" who should not be afforded the same privileges as native-born Americans.

Noncitizens have had a long and complicated relationship with public benefits in the United States. In 1882, Congress passed legislation prohibiting entry to "any person unable to take care of himself or herself without becoming a public charge."[6] Social reformers saw immigrants as ill-prepared for American life; Jane Addams's description of immigrants from Southern Italy as representing "the pathetic stupidity of agricultural people crowded into city tenements" is but one example of this stereotype.[7] Many mothers' pensions program during the Progressive era had residency or citizenship requirements, and immigrant women had to conform to American cultural standards of "good" caretaking.[8] Prior to the 1996 welfare reform bill, legal immigrants and refugees were eligible for means-tested assistance programs on similar terms to citizens.[9] PRWORA greatly limited the eligibility of legal immigrants for assistance programs, though, as immigrants were summarily denied Supplemental Security Income (SSI) and nutrition assistance. In 1997 and 1998, some legal immigrants regained their access to Medicaid, SSI, and nutrition assistance, but most were left without support.[10] The same themes of personal responsibility and "the other" that shape welfare rules around work and behavioral requirements influence noncitizen eligibility.

Welfare recipients are made to abide by behavioral requirements to instill in them a strong moral ethic because there remains an underlying belief that one's poverty is the direct result of one's moral failings. Recipients are also required to participate in work-related activities so that they may move toward economic self-sufficiency and be productive members of society. And regardless of how well recipients follow these rules, most recipients are pushed off the rolls once they reach their time limit so as to discourage long-term dependency. But before they have the chance to get kicked off the rolls, noncitizen applicants face a series of eligibility rules designed to prevent them from receiving aid.

Freeloaders or Hard Workers?

Noncitizens have often been portrayed as freeloaders who came to the country to take advantage of the social services available. Chavez writes that opponents to immigrant rights believe extending the privileges enjoyed by citizens to immigrants "cheapens citizenship"—by virtue of their citizenship, native-born Americans are seen as more deserving of government aid.[11] At the same time, noncitizens are often recognized as hard workers willing to take the jobs Americans will not take, and historically immigration has increased productivity in the country.[12] This contradiction in perceptions means that in some respects noncitizens are seen as undeserving and cast in the same light as the stereotypical "welfare queen," while at other times noncitizen recipients are seen as deserving of aid because of their circumstances.

Some of this perception of freeloading comes from racial stereotyping. Neubeck and Cazenave argue that while many think of the underlying racism in welfare as white versus Black, it extends to all minorities that threaten white supremacy—including nonwhite immigrants.[13] The fear of the day that whites no longer make up a majority of the population combines with the belief that immigrants, similar to the stereotypes of Blacks, are unwilling to work and aim to be dependent on the government.[14] Some scholars and policymakers have feared—in a claim strikingly similar to the "culture of dependency" argument brought up in reference to African Americans—that the poverty and reliance on government aid of immigrant parents would be passed down to their children.[15] There has been some empirical support for this theory as well. Filindra finds that an increase in the size of a state's African American population and the percentage of the population living in poverty decreased the likelihood of the state's extending benefits to immigrants.[16]

The perception of whether an immigrant is freeloading is also related to the circumstances under which they entered the country. Historically, Americans have responded negatively to "illegal" immigrants; research has shown that increasing positive affect toward undocumented immigrants is related to increased support for welfare spending.[17] This finding is supported by an analysis of the discourse surrounding immigration in California and Arizona.[18] Brown finds that, in Arizona, anti-immigrant groups employ a racial frame to create an "us versus them" argument, with the racial majority falling on one side and all Hispanics becoming "them." In contrast, California advocates framed immigrants in terms of their legal status, which allowed legal permanent residents to be included in the same group as native-born citizens. While she cannot attribute these frames to the state's welfare policies, Arizona has adopted stringent welfare rules with respect to noncitizens, while California has one of the most expansive programs in the country.

Welfare Magnets: A Race to the Bottom

The race-to-the-bottom thesis, and the underlying motivations of both welfare recipients and policymakers, fuels a fiercely contested debate within the welfare literature. From the welfare recipient's perspective, the race-to-the-bottom thesis assumes that recipients will relocate to states offering the most generous welfare benefits. As a result, policymakers are motivated to make their policies less generous to avoid having their states become "magnets" for poor people. As it applies to noncitizens, Borjas asserts that noncitizens choose their location in the United States based on the benefit levels in the state. Immigrants are already incurring the costs of leaving their home countries, so assuming that the costs to move to all the states are the same, the immigrant welfare recipient should choose among the states with the most generous welfare policies. Native-born welfare recipients, however, typically do not have the resources to leave their home state in favor of a state with more generous welfare policies.[19]

Other research refutes the welfare magnet hypothesis promoted by Borjas. Van Hook and Bean find that less-educated immigrants (those with a high school degree or less) are no more likely than their native counterparts to receive AFDC.[20] Similarly, Capps, Fix, and Henderson find that low-income legal permanent residents used TANF (as well as food stamps and SSI) at lower rates than native families both before and after the passage of PRWORA.[21] Instead of supporting the stereotype of a state-dependent noncitizen, these findings support the idea of a hardworking noncitizen who has come to the United States in search of economic opportunity.

Research suggests that states decreased their AFDC benefit levels modestly when their neighbors decreased their benefit levels.[22] Berry, Fording, and Hanson, however, find no evidence that a state's poverty rate increases when their benefit level increases; that is, states do not become "welfare magnets."[23] In contrast, Bailey and Rom's results suggest that states engage in a "race to the bottom" by limiting access to welfare programs.[24]

The race-to-the-bottom theory can also be interpreted as involving states' desire to draw in the "right type" of immigrants—i.e., those who are highly educated and skilled workers. Policymakers who advocate for strict welfare policies may be representing those who fear immigrants' use of scarce resources.[25] Much of the responsibility for funding noncitizens has been transferred from the federal government to the states, so becoming a "welfare magnet" may create problems in a state economically. For the federal government, PRWORA's restriction on immigrant eligibility yielded a net economic gain: the Congressional Budget Office predicted in 1996 that half of welfare reform's budget savings would come from immigrant restrictions.[26] For states such as California, however, which began with generous programs, hard economic times may force them to reevaluate their program generosity.[27]

Policies Affecting Immigrant Eligibility

Many PRWORA provisions were designed to bring significant cost savings by reducing the number of noncitizens receiving assistance. The new eligibility rules did decrease the number of noncitizens receiving TANF. The percentage of immigrant-headed households receiving cash assistance dropped from 7.1 percent in 1994 to 3.2 percent in 1996.[28] More than removing children from the rolls, the noncitizen eligibility restrictions enacted under TANF made parents ineligible, thus creating a large number of child-only cases.

Categories of Eligibility

PRWORA created several classes of noncitizens (see figure 6.1). First, it distinguished between qualified and unqualified noncitizens. Unqualified noncitizens are not eligible for benefits and include tourists and students in the United States on a temporary basis, as well as undocumented immigrants. Secondly, under the broad category of qualified noncitizens, PRWORA makes a distinction between noncitizens who arrived in the United States prior to welfare reform, and those who have arrived after PRWORA was passed. The vast majority of states chose to continue providing access to TANF for eligible immigrants who entered the United States prior to PRWORA's passage.[29] Therefore, in

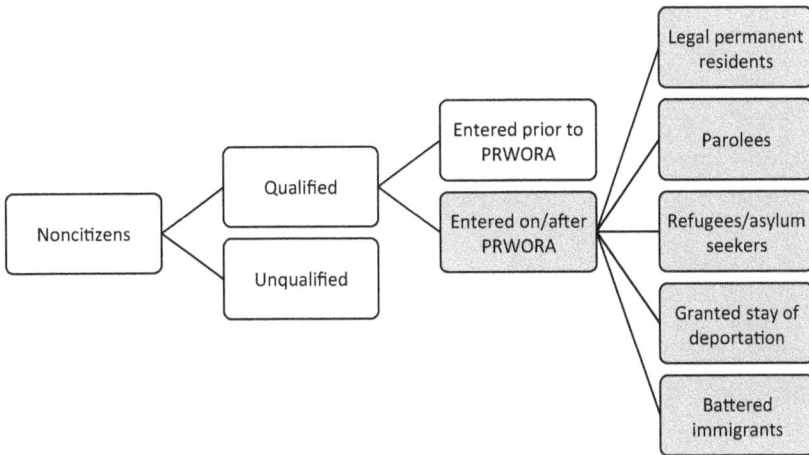

Figure 6.1. Classification of Noncitizens under PRWORA

this chapter I focus on eligibility for qualified noncitizens who arrived in the country after PRWORA was passed (in gray).

The third distinction is between different categories of noncitizens. Within this chapter, I will focus on five of these categories: legal permanent residents (LPRs), refugees and asylum seekers, noncitizens granted a stay of deportation, parolees, and battered noncitizens.[30] Finally, there is a distinction based on how long the noncitizen has been in the country. LPRs who have entered the country after the passage of PRWORA cannot receive federal benefits during their first five years in the country; after that five-year ban, the state can decide whether to extend eligibility. Refugees and asylum seekers, however, are not banned during the first five years in the country, but similar to LPRs, it becomes a state option after five years.[31] Like other victims of abuse, battered noncitizens may be afraid to leave their abusers because they depend upon them for financial support. They may also risk deportation if they separate from the partner who is often their sponsor. The Violence Against Women Act (VAWA) sought to alleviate these fears by making it easier for undocumented battered women to become legal permanent residents, but welfare reform made this process more difficult.[32]

As shown in figure 6.2, by 2016 almost all the states had extended eligibility to all five categories of noncitizens. In 2001, each category of noncitizens was eligible for TANF in forty states, though only thirty-five states allowed noncitizens in all categories to apply. This is a notable increase from 1997, when only ten states allowed noncitizens from each of the five categories to apply for benefits. By 2016, forty-two states allowed at least some noncitizens from each of the five categories to apply for benefits. Eligibility among the categories is highly correlated (see table 6.1

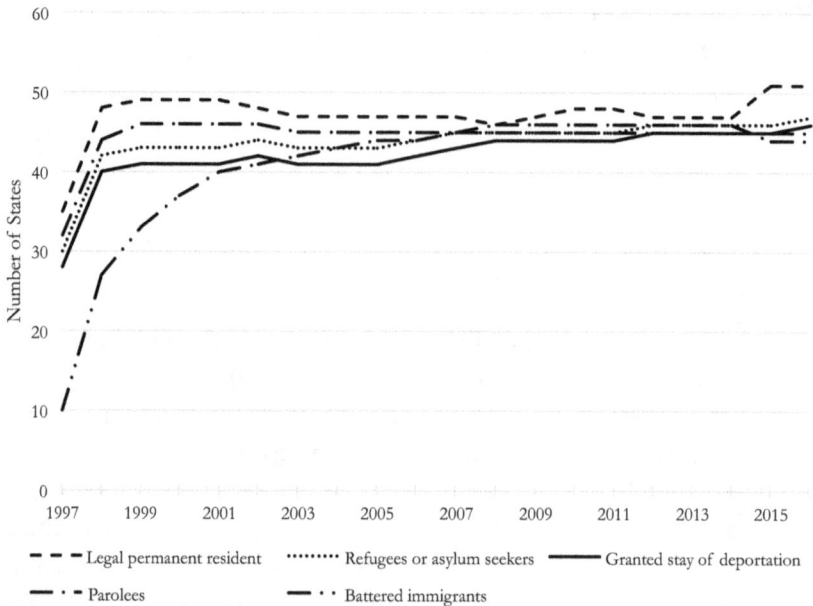

Figure 6.2. States Extending Eligibility to Different Types of Noncitizens, 1997–2016

Table 6.1. Correlation between Eligibility of Noncitizens, 1997–2016

	Legal permanent resident	Refugee	Stay of deportation	Parolee	Battered noncitizen
Legal perm. residents	1.00				
Refugees	0.22	1.00			
Stay of deportation	0.18	0.88	1.00		
Parolees	0.61	0.62	0.54	1.00	
Battered noncitizens	0.38	0.35	0.36	0.56	1.00

for correlations between measures of eligibility); when a state extends eligibility to one type of noncitizen, it does appear to be more likely to extend eligibility to other types of noncitizens.

Income Deeming

In addition to analyzing what types of noncitizens are eligible for assistance in the states, I consider the state's policy on income deeming. I measure two sources of income deeming; the first is a binary measure of whether a sponsor's income can be deemed available to the noncitizen. Most immigrants who enter the United States on the basis of family relationships (e.g., they are immediate relatives to citizens), as well as employment-based immigrants who come to the country to work for a relative, are required to have a sponsor sign an affidavit of support. According to the GAO, about 11 percent of sponsored noncitizens applied for TANF, Medicaid, or SNAP benefits in 2007.[33] Under PRWORA, when a noncitizen is eligible for state-funded benefits, the state has the option of holding the sponsor legally responsible for the noncitizen covered under the affidavit. For noncitizens applying for benefits, this means the sponsor's income and assets can be deemed available to the noncitizen; the amount deemed available varies by state. Often the result of this deeming is an increase in the applicant's income above the eligibility threshold, so that even categories of immigrants who are eligible may not be able to receive benefits.[34]

The deeming of sponsor income makes an adult noncitizen ineligible because of their resources rather than their immigration status. There are many adult noncitizens, however, who are ineligible because of their immigration or citizenship status, but whose children were born in the United States and thus are eligible for assistance. This setup—an eligible child with an ineligible immigrant parent—comprises about 25 percent of child-only cases, which make up about half of all TANF cases.[35] Some states, however, deem the ineligible parent's income available to the child. Just as the sponsor's income may make an otherwise eligible noncitizen ineligible for assistance, deeming an ineligible parent's income may make the child ineligible.

Table 6.2. States Requiring Income Deeming

	States with deeming, 1997	States with deeming, 2016
Undocumented parent's income	17	25
Sponsor's income	28	44

Expectations

Interest Groups

I anticipate that interest group attitudes about noncitizen TANF eligibility will closely follow their views on other welfare rules. Therefore, I expect that feminist organizations, civil rights groups, and social welfare groups will be in favor of more expansive welfare policies—allowing for a greater variety of noncitizens to receive assistance and opposing income deeming. Assuming that the majority of noncitizen TANF recipients are women, as is true for the overall TANF recipient population, I anticipate that feminist organizations will favor extending eligibility to noncitizens as a way to support vulnerable populations. Similarly, because battered immigrants are a (marginalized) subset of their constituency, I expect domestic violence organizations will support extending TANF eligibility to noncitizens who have experienced abuse.

I also assume that civil rights organizations will support extending eligibility to noncitizens. Previous research has shown that civil rights groups such as the NAACP are willing to work with Latino organizations such as the League of United Latin American Citizens and National Council of La Raza/UnidosUS to fight strict immigration policies in states such as Arizona.[36] The ACLU also has a history of advocating on behalf of immigrants' rights.[37] Finally, I anticipate that social welfare groups will be in favor of more generous welfare policies toward noncitizens, especially if they serve a largely noncitizen population. Many social welfare groups associated with organized religion, for example, provide social services to the poor and have expressed support for a more expansive welfare program that would serve a wider population. During the debate over welfare reform in Maryland, Catholic Charities came out in support of providing assistance for immigrants, and in Utah the Mormon Church has supported inclusive immigration policies.[38]

It is not clear whether the proportion of African American groups in a state will have a significant effect on the state's noncitizen welfare policies. Describing the relationship between minority groups, McClain lists three possible outcomes: coalition building, independence, and intra-minority competition.[39] Through coalition building, minority groups work together to increase both of their successes; examples of this include Latino politicians working to mobilize voters across many minority groups in order to win elections in non-Latino majority districts.[40] These coalitions are not ironclad, however.[41] When one group does not see itself as part of a larger minority collective, intra-minority competition may arise, in which the success of one group comes at the expense of another. Filindra writes that this competition often appears around issues of social policy, where one minority group believes that increasing resources to another group will decrease their slice of the pie.[42] Therefore, it's not unreasonable to expect that an increase in the proportion of African American groups may lead to more stringent welfare policies for noncitizens.

Noncitizens have more limited opportunity for political participation, given their citizenship status. Therefore, I anticipate that immigration groups will play an integral role in advocating for their interests. I expect that a state with a greater density of immigration interest groups will allow more categories of immigrants to apply for benefits and will be less likely to require income deeming of both undocumented parents and sponsors. There may be divisions within immigration interest groups as to which categories of immigrants are most deserving of representation. Immigration groups may find it easier to defend TANF eligibility for LPRs because of their connection to the workforce than for other noncitizens, for instance.

In much of the welfare literature, researchers use Hispanic/Latino and immigrant interchangeably. Of course, not all immigrants are Hispanic, and not all Hispanics are immigrants. Hispanics who have strong group-oriented values are more likely to identify with immigrants as an out-group and have an understanding of immigrants' relative position in society. They are also more likely than the general population to support pro-immigrant policies.[43] Thus, a state with a greater proportion of Hispanic interest groups may have less restrictive TANF eligibility policies for immigrants. More broadly, I anticipate that organizations representing immigrants will advocate for more expansive welfare policies for noncitizens.

Business and industry groups may be supportive of welfare rules that extend eligibility to noncitizens, especially if the industry is dependent on immigrant labor. For example, immigrants (both lawful and unauthorized) made up over 30 percent of the agricultural work force in 2014, although they constitute just over 17 percent of the US civilian labor force. Similarly, immigrants account for over 23 percent of the labor force in the construction industry in 2014.[44] These industries may support extending eligibility to categories of noncitizens because the recipients can be turned into workers. If this is the case, then the industries should be opposed to income deeming, both from undocumented parents to children and from sponsors to adults. Other business organizations that do not rely on immigrant labor may not favor extending eligibility to noncitizens. This may be true for umbrella organizations such as the Chamber of Commerce, which may represent multinational corporations that rely on human resources in multiple countries.[45]

State Demographics

I expect a state's policies toward noncitizens to vary depending on demographics. If nothing else, in a state with a large foreign-born population, noncitizen eligibility for social services is likely to be a more pressing issue on the political agenda than it would be for a state with a very small noncitizen population. Given that, at the national level, much of the impetus for reform of noncitizen eligibility came from the potential cost savings, a state with a large noncitizen population may be less likely to extend eligibility and more likely to require income deeming in order to rein in spending. At the same time, states with significant immigrant populations may adopt more lenient eligibility policies because they are dependent on immigrant labor. The changes under PRWORA and concurrent immigration reform in the mid-1990s did not discourage immigration completely; rather, immigrants are largely welcome to the country so long as they make economic contributions.[46] Graefe et al. find that being an immigrant destination state is associated with less stringent eligibility policies for legal immigrants and refugees.[47] It could be that states relying heavily on the economic contributions of immigrants see immigrants as more deserving of aid because of their contributions.

The racial and ethnic makeup of a state's immigrant population has been theorized to have an influence on the state's generosity toward noncitizens receiving welfare. Preuhs finds that as a state's Latino population increases, the state spends less on welfare per capita.[48] In contrast, Graefe et al. find that as the Hispanic proportion of the caseload increases, there is no noticeable change in welfare generosity.[49] Hero and Preuhs find that a state's Latino and immigrant population is not significantly related to whether the state extends welfare benefits to immigrants. States with a large Latino population, however, tend to have lower benefit levels.[50] Ybarra et al. examine state immigration policies more generally, and find that as the Hispanic population increases and the white population decreases, a state is more likely to enact punitive policies.[51]

The Black proportion of the population is traditionally related to more stringent welfare policies. With respect to welfare, Graefe et al. examine the relationship between the proportion of the caseload that is African American and eligibility for new and battered immigrants.[52] Their results suggest that, as African Americans make up a greater proportion of the caseload, eligibility stringency increases, which they argue supports the idea that racial animosity negatively affects all minorities.[53] Similarly, Filindra finds that as the size of the African American population in a state increases, states are less likely to extend TANF eligibility to legal permanent residents.[54]

Political Environment

Generally speaking, I expect that a more liberal government and citizen ideology will lead to more generous welfare policies. However, policymakers have to balance several objectives when adopting TANF rules. In addition to representing the interests of their constituents and promoting the values of their party, policymakers are also conscious of budgetary constraints. Eligibility rules for certain categories of noncitizens address questions of who deserves to receive welfare and thus may be more salient to voters. In contrast, income deeming can be used as a way of limiting eligibility (and thus controlling spending) without explicitly stating a noncitizen is ineligible. Policymakers in more conservative states may be unwilling to extend benefits to noncitizens for fear of their state's being seen as a "welfare magnet" and attracting noncitizens who might then take jobs away from US citizens.[55] Increased restrictions on noncitizen eligibility for TANF may also reflect the broader trend of states passing substantive immigration policy.[56]

As with other TANF rules, I expect that an increase in women's representation in the legislature will lead to more generous policies— broader eligibility guidelines and fewer types of income deeming. I also anticipate that an increase in Hispanic representation within the legislature will be associated with more flexible policies toward noncitizens. Wilson finds that Latino members of Congress are more likely than their non-Latino counterparts to sponsor Latino interest bills, and this effect is even more significant with bills that explicitly mention Latinos.[57] Similarly, Wallace finds that Latino representatives are more likely to take action on immigration, education, and labor legislation, but that ethnicity has no significant effect on roll call votes.[58] Ellis and Wilson examine whether having a Black or Latino committee or sub-committee chair affects which issues receive congressional hearings.[59] They find that the odds of having a hearing on a minority issue (civil rights, social welfare, or housing) increases more than threefold when the committee is chaired by a Black or Latino representative. An increase in Latino representation is also associated with more generous welfare benefits.[60]

Limiting Eligibility Explicitly vs. Implicitly

As with other types of welfare rules, states can make trade-offs when it comes to the rules surrounding noncitizen eligibility. A state can allow several categories of immigrants to be eligible for assistance, but also require income deeming from both sponsors and undocumented parents. I created a summary measure of the total number of categories of immigrants eligible for assistance, ranging from 0 to 5. The average across all state-years is 4.28; in 70 percent of state-years all five types of immigrants are eligible for assistance. In a comparison of means test, states that require sponsor income deeming extend eligibility to significantly more categories of immigrants than those that do not require income deeming. Similarly, states that deem undocumented parent's income to eligible children extend eligibility to significantly more categories of noncitizens than those that do not deem undocumented parental income.

I also created a variable capturing whether the state requires income deeming from sponsors, undocumented parents, neither, or both. In a majority of state-years, the state requires income deeming from at least one source; in an additional 40 percent of state-years, income is counted from both ineligible parents and sponsors. Figure 6.3 shows that, in over 60 percent of state-years in which none of the five categories of noncitizens are eligible for assistance, there is no income deeming.[61] Conversely, as more categories of noncitizens are eligible for benefits, the percentage of state-years without income deeming decreases significantly. The relationship is not perfect; in 29 percent of the state-years in which two categories of noncitizens are eligible for benefits there is both parent and sponsor income deeming in the state, while in 100 percent of state-years in which three categories of noncitizens are eligible there is at most one type of income deeming required by the state. The general trend, however, suggests that as states explicitly allow more noncitizens to apply for benefits, they may enact provisions that implicitly make it more difficult for them to receive assistance.

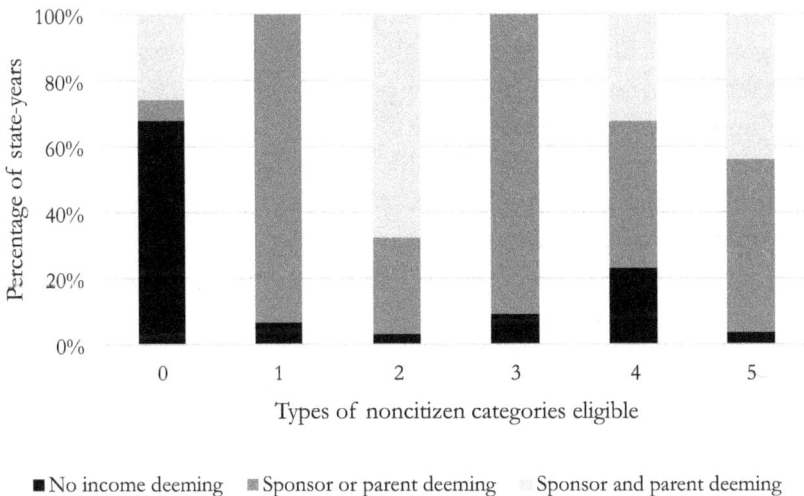

Figure 6.3. Relationship between Income Deeming and Eligibility of Noncitizens

Results

The eligibility rules for categories of immigrant are coded as 0 (the state does not extend eligibility to the category of immigrant), 1 (the state extends eligibility to some immigrants within the category), or 2 (the state extends eligibility to all immigrants within the category). The multivariate analyses are ordered logistic regressions. Two income deeming rules are coded as either 1 (the state requires the deeming) or 0 (the state does not require income deeming); the multivariate analyses of these variables are logistic regressions. I also created an ordinal variable to capture how long a state deems a sponsor's income to a noncitizen for the purposes of calculating eligibility. This variable takes on the value of 0 when the state does not deem sponsor income, the value of 1 when the state deems income for three years, and the value of 2 when the state deems income for ten years (or forty qualifying work quarters). All multivariate analyses include year indicator variables and state clustered standard errors.

As with other areas of TANF policy, I anticipated women's organizations and social welfare organizations would be in favor of more expansive welfare policies. Therefore, I expected that in states with a greater proportion of these types of organizations, more categories of noncitizens would be eligible for TANF. The analysis presents some support for this hypothesis. States with a greater proportion of women's organizations are more likely to extend eligibility to refugees or asylum seekers (see table B.21). States with a greater proportion of social welfare groups are more likely to extend eligibility to legal permanent residents. There is a positive association between the percentage of social welfare organizations and eligibility of other categories of noncitizens, but the relationships do not reach statistical significance.

Legal Permanent Residents: Us or Them?

In the "us versus them" debate, legal permanent residents (LPRs) are arguably the noncitizen category most similar to native-born Americans. It is perhaps not surprising then that very few states deny benefits to LPRs who have been in the country more than five years. In fact, there are only five states that have banned all LPRs from receiving

TANF benefits at some point between 1997 and 2016: Indiana (1998–2014), Mississippi (1997–2014), Montana (2002–2008), North Dakota (2003–2009), and South Carolina (2008–2014). States in which LPRs are eligible to receive benefits are significantly more likely to have Democratic governors. In nearly 75 percent of state-years in which LPRs were not eligible for TANF benefits, the state had a Republican governor, while in almost 55 percent of state-years where all LPRs were eligible for TANF, the state had a Republican governor. This aligns with a gradual shift among Democrats and Democrat-leaning independents toward supporting increased legal immigration.[62]

A common refrain among those opposing the extension of benefits to noncitizens is that immigrants do not pay taxes and thus should not have access to the same services as native-born Americans. Legal permanent residents are allowed to work and live permanently in the United States, however. Attorney General Richard Blumenthal, testifying before the Connecticut Human Services Committee in 2004, reminded the committee members that "legal aliens live among us, they are indistinguishable from our neighbors, co-workers, friends and indeed, in many instances they are our neighbors, co-workers and friends."[63]

Representatives from social welfare organizations repeatedly reminded legislators in both Alaska and Connecticut about the contributions of noncitizens. The executive director of Catholic Social Services in Alaska, Suzanne Goodrich, stressed that the immigrants losing welfare benefits "are in the country lawfully, they may have worked in the United States for many years, they may have families here, paid into social security and taxes."[64] Yasir Hamed, from the African Community Center for Educational and Social Services, told the Connecticut Human Services Committee that he was there to "bring a loud voice" for legal immigrants. He argued that immigrants are an integral part of American culture:

> The fact is legal immigrants are a major part of the American society. Legal immigrants are family members, they are students, workers, investors, business owners and they are clergymen. Legal immigrants also are members of the armed services. [. . .] Legal immigrants overall, and this is the most important part, pay taxes through which they help finance the cost of the schools, roads, Social Security, national defense, health

care and welfare payments. Accordingly, they deserve to also be users and beneficiaries of all these government programs.[65]

Goodrich and Hamed present a case for extending eligibility to noncitizens based on their contributions to American society. As Brown wrote in her analysis of immigration activists in Arizona and California, an "us versus them" mentality frequently arises when debating the rights of noncitizens.[66] This "us versus them" mentality may be harder to justify when noncitizens are permanent residents who are seen as contributing to the local community.

States are less likely to extend eligibility to LPRs as the unemployment rate increases, however. The probability of extending eligibility to LPRs also decreases as the density of interest groups representing industries that employ noncitizens increases. This suggests that, at least for some policymakers, there may be an economic motivation behind limiting noncitizen eligibility. For a state looking to decrease its caseload, limiting the eligibility of an entire category of applicants can provide those savings without having to make too many substantive changes to the state's overall TANF program. If states are in need of low-wage labor to work in industries such as agriculture, they may also choose to deny benefits to legal permanent residents.

Perceptions of Refugees

The "us versus them" mentality may break down when a noncitizen is seen as more deserving of aid, such as in the case of refugees or asylum seekers. The likelihood of a state extending eligibility to refugees and asylum seekers increases as the population becomes more liberal and when there is a Democratic governor. In contrast to my expectations, however, the percentage of women in the state legislature is negatively related to the probability of extending eligibility to refugees and asylum seekers. However, as the percentage of women's organizations in a state increases, a state is more likely to extend eligibility to these noncitizens. Testimony from Texas shows that women's organizations spoke in favor of extending eligibility to battered immigrants (see below), another category of noncitizen that is perceived as deserving of government assistance.

In 2017, Nebraska legislators considered a bill that would have required the Department of Health and Human Services to publish detailed information about resettled refugees and the amount of state and federal funding spend assisting those refugees. Numerous service organizations and advocates representing a variety of interest groups spoke against the bill, basing their opposition on the vulnerability and deservingness of the refugee population. Referencing his own military experience and representing Nebraskans for Peace, Ron Todd-Meyer told legislators:

> I am a Marine Corps veteran who spent a year in combat in Vietnam 50 years ago. Today's refugees are a result of a failed U.S. foreign policy similar to the failed policy that culminated in the 1975 defeat of U.S. aggression in southeast Asia and the ensuing refugees that fled. [. . .] Nebraskans pride themselves as being pro-life. In fact, they want us to issue a license plate. If we are . . . Nebraskans generally want a more just and livable world for our children, then we have a moral duty to welcome refugee families; men, women, and children who have been displaced and traumatized by war, disease, hunger, and the effects of man-made climate change.[67]

The sense that noncitizens who have come to America fleeing violence are deserving is certainly not universal, though. Speaking specifically about refugees, Doug Kagan from Nebraska Taxpayers for Freedom expressed his concern to state legislators:

> We believe that the state must determine how the influx of these refugees impacts area employment opportunities regarding the availability of jobs to our lawful citizens, affordable housing as we only have a finite number of affordable housing units currently in Nebraska, educational and healthcare resources, and likelihood that refugees will become self-sufficient and not dependent upon welfare.[68]

Other residents testifying before the legislature voiced similar concerns about the use of taxpayer funds. Moreover, some residents seemed to base their support for the bill—and their opposition to refugees—on misinformation. One resident told legislators he was worried about

Muslim immigrants with links to terrorism coming to Nebraska. Whether residents and policymakers view refugees as victims of violence and state repression or exploiting a loophole in the American immigration system likely has an impact on whether a state expands TANF eligibility to this group.

Hispanic Representation of Noncitizens

I also expected that states with a greater proportion of interest groups representing Hispanics and immigrants would be more likely to extend eligibility to a variety of categories of noncitizens. The ordered logistic regressions, however, show no significant relationship between the density of immigrant organizations in a state and noncitizen TANF eligibility. Contrary to my expectations, as the proportion of Hispanic organizations in a state increases, the state is less likely to extend eligibility to refugees or asylum seekers and noncitizens granted stays of deportation. This negative relationship may be because Hispanic organizations do not see themselves as representing refugees, asylum seekers, or noncitizens granted stays of deportation. When Fernando Betancourt from the Latino and Puerto Rican Affairs Commission testified before the Connecticut Human Services Committee in 2004, for example, he made mention only of legal permanent residents:

> The Latino and Puerto Rican Affairs Commission respectfully requests that the Connecticut Legislature restore equal access to public benefits to lawfully permanent residents. They, as well as their U.S. citizen counterparts, pay taxes used to pay for the cost of education, infrastructure and in many instances, help in the overall national defense in time of war and/ or peace.[69]

Legal permanent residents may be easy for Hispanic organizations to defend, precisely because their situation is like that of native-born Americans. Depending on public perception of noncitizens, however, an increase in the proportion of Hispanic interest groups might indicate that noncitizens are still separate from the native-born population; noncitizens are still considered "them" instead of "us."

We might assume that as people have more exposure to noncitizens, their tolerance will increase. They will see immigrants not just as noncitizens, but also "students, workers, investors, business owners." The quantitative analysis appears to support this theory. As the foreign-born population increases in a state, the likelihood of a state extending eligibility to all five categories of noncitizens increases significantly. There is also a negative relationship between the eligibility of several categories of noncitizens and the Hispanic proportion of the population (see table B.21). A large Hispanic population may prompt a backlash from native-born citizens who fear noncitizens will take their job or public resources. Nebraska resident Chip Smith verbalized this fear when he stated that noncitizens "who are a burden on our taxpayers, who take our entry-level jobs from lawful citizens, should not be welcomed."[70]

Another indicator of assimilation, or the perception of noncitizens more as "us" than "them," is participation in politics. Noncitizens, of course, cannot run for public office, but Latino citizens can. As the percentage of Latino legislators in a state increases, the state is significantly more likely to extend eligibility to noncitizens granted a stay of deportation (see table B.23). Latino representatives may feel responsible for representing the interests of all noncitizens, even if they themselves are not from immigrant backgrounds.

Income Deeming: Personal Responsibility and Labor Market Pressures

Under PRWORA, there is a general emphasis on personal responsibility; after all, one of the main program goals of TANF is for recipients to achieve economic self-sufficiency. When discussing responsibility for the welfare of noncitizens, though, the noncitizen's sponsor is also tasked with ensuring that the noncitizen does not need government assistance.

As the proportions of social welfare groups, Hispanic groups, and civil rights groups in the state increase, the state is more likely to require sponsor deeming (see table B.22). The proportion of civil rights groups and social welfare organizations is not significantly related, however, to how long a state deems a sponsor's income. More noncitizens become eligible for assistance when they do not have to include their sponsor's income. For social service providers, an immigrant with a supportive sponsor is one less person they have to care for; however, social welfare and immigration groups may see many who are still in need in spite of the support of their sponsors. Rick Tessandore, director of the Disability Law Center in Alaska, said that he assumes families are doing everything they can before they turn to welfare programs. In her testimony, Suzanne Goodrich agreed—extended families do as much as they can to support family members in the country.[71] Social welfare and Hispanic organizations may encourage policymakers to keep noncitizens on the rolls even when they have sponsors because it relieves the burden on outside groups.

Politically, the probability of sponsor income deeming decreases as the citizen ideology becomes more liberal. This comports with expectations that liberals favor a more expansive welfare state. When it comes to elected officials, however, states with Democratic legislatures are more likely to require sponsor deeming than legislatures controlled by Republicans. This is surprising given Republicans' strong belief in personal responsibility.

Representatives on the Alaska Health, Education, and Social Services Committee expressed concerns about personal responsibility during a 1997 meeting on welfare reform. Con Bunde (R), chairman of the committee, spoke fondly of work done by social welfare organizations such as Catholic Social Services (CSS). These organizations provided the social services that in a more expansive welfare state the government would provide. He also emphasized that the legislature encourages sponsors and families to take responsibility for noncitizens who may be in need. Similarly, Representative Al Vezey (R) asked whether it is the government's role to provide for noncitizens. He suggested that noncitizens with family capable of supporting them should not be eligible for public assistance and questioned the degree to which social service providers such as CSS work with the families of immigrants needing assistance.[72]

Sponsor income deeming generally applies to the whole family; states also have the option of deeming the income of undocumented parents to their children who are eligible to receive benefits. If a state counts the income of the undocumented parent in the calculation of a child's benefits, the child will be less likely to receive benefits. Such income deeming, however, raises questions as to whether children should be punished for the actions of their parents. Interest groups, including the Catholic Church, have raised concerns that some of the more punitive aspects of welfare reform end up harming the children in low-income families.[73] Concern over children's welfare might explain why the likelihood of deeming an undocumented parent's income decreases as the percentage of women in the legislature decreases. Aligning with traditional expectations about "women's issues," female legislators may be more concerned about the negative effects of welfare policies on children.

Deeming income from undocumented parents also raises the possibility of affecting a state's labor supply. As the proportion of industry groups in a state increases, the likelihood that a state will deem undocumented parent income decreases. The likelihood of a state deeming an undocumented parent's income also decreases if neighboring states deem the parent's income. Assuming that there is a "welfare magnet" effect and undocumented parents choose to move their families to states that do not deem their income when calculating their children's welfare benefits, industries that rely on undocumented labor may be in opposition to undocumented parent income deeming because it could reduce the labor force. When the top two industries for undocumented labor are included in the model separately, however, there is no significant relationship to the likelihood that a state will require undocumented parent deeming (see table B.24). That is, as a state has a greater proportion of agriculture and construction groups, the probability that it will require income deeming from an undocumented parent does not decrease significantly.

The probability that a state will deem undocumented parent income increases as the proportion of African American organizations in a state increases. This lends credence to the intra-minority competition theory. In a state with a limited number of jobs, minority candidates may compete for positions. Leaders of African American organizations may feel the need to protect those they represent by discouraging other workers from coming to the state. The state is less likely to require income deeming from parents to children as the Hispanic population in the state increases; this may be a sign of the Hispanic community's political power and resources, though it does not show up in measures of interest group influence.

A state's decision to require income deeming from either a noncitizen's sponsor or an undocumented parent reiterates the importance of personal responsibility under TANF. Organizations that work with low-income noncitizens push against these requirements, in part because of their experience with struggling families, and liberal states are less likely to adopt these requirements, presumably because they are less opposed to expanding the welfare state. The inclusion of income deeming in a state's noncitizen eligibility rules allows it to limit the noncitizen caseload without explicitly banning categories of immigrants.

Battered Immigrants

Finally, the question of personal responsibility becomes more complicated when considering the eligibility of battered immigrants. Battered immigrants represent a population marginalized along many axes. The majority of those affected are women, many of them may be racial minorities, they have been subject to abuse, and they are by definition noncitizens; battered immigrants would certainly be considered a disadvantaged subgroup.[74] For an intersectional group such as battered immigrants, does one part of their identity become more prominent? Are battered immigrants victims of abuse who are noncitizens or immigrants who have experienced abuse? Does the framing of their identity provide clues as to who will represent them politically?

If battered immigrants are judged along the same criteria as other noncitizens, there may be an expectation that they turn to their sponsor or family for assistance. As with other categories of noncitizens, I would expect that immigration and Hispanic interest groups would advocate on their behalf. The results support this; a state is more likely to extend eligibility to battered immigrants as the proportion of Hispanic groups in the state increases (see table B.21).

Battered immigrants are unlike other categories of noncitizens, though, in that their sponsors may also be their abusers. Because of this situation, battered immigrants may be seen as more deserving of government assistance than other welfare recipients. Women's and domestic violence organizations may also advocate on behalf of battered immigrants. In 2001, the Texas Human Services Committee held a hearing on the subject of an assistance program for battered immigrants. Among those testifying in support of the bill to extend benefits to noncitizens were representatives from the Texas Council on Family Violence, the National Training Center on Domestic and Sexual Violence, and the Texas National Organization for Women.[75] Jennifer Corrigan cited research about the importance of public benefits for battered immigrant women:

> Surveys of battered immigrant women have consistently shown that access to financial resources is the single greatest barrier to leaving an abusive relationship. In fact, the level of economic resources available to a battered woman is the best indicator of whether or not she will permanently separate from an abuser. National studies have shown the battered women often turn to public benefits to escape a violent relationship.

Corrigan spoke from the perspective of an advocate against domestic violence and the additional challenges faced by service providers who work with battered immigrants. Later testimony came from the perspective of an immigrant advocate. Laura Bachman from the Political Asylum Project of Austin explained to legislators:

> As you've already heard, there are many barriers that they [battered immigrants] face in addition to of course being victims of extreme cruelty and of battery. They also face barriers such as language and cultural isolation and complete economic deprivation. Although my clients in many instances I am their first point of contact because their immigration situation is of much importance to them, even with that, the first point they want to cover is their financial situation. In addition to their immigration status, they must have financial support.

It is not clear from Bachman's testimony how many of the noncitizens she works with are eligible for TANF, or how many would be classified as battered immigrants. Her testimony, along with Jennifer Corrigan's, does suggest, however, that interest groups are willing to advocate on behalf of some of the most marginalized people represented by their group.

In contrast, the New Jersey Assembly's Task Force on Domestic Violence heard testimony on two occasions in March 1998. In over 270

pages of transcripts from the hearings, there is no mention of noncitizens by any members of the task force or any of the fifteen people who
testified.[76] From these two examples, it appears that domestic violence
organizations will advocate for battered immigrants if they are the specific topic at hand, but they are likely not the top priority of these organizations. This may reflect the resources available to the organization or
to the population they serve. Texas domestic violence organizations, for
example, may see a greater proportion of noncitizens than organizations
in New Jersey.

Finally, as with other policies related to survivors of domestic violence, I anticipated that an increase in female legislators would increase
the likelihood of a state granting eligibility to battered immigrants. Contrary to these expectations, however, there is no significant relationship
between the percentage of women in a state's legislature and eligibility
for battered immigrants. Some of this might be explained by the role
of conservative female legislators. In Texas, for instance, Representative
Arlene Wohlgemuth (R) asked an advocate about the nature of abusive
relationships:

> Do you have statistics indicating the type of relationship that are the most
> likely to produce abuse? [. . .] I just have to make this point every now
> and then because there is so much misinformation out there. The point I
> would like to make is, less than 10% of the abuse cases are from the origi-
> nal husband and wife relationship. [. . .] The farther you move away from
> the husband-wife relationship, the husband-wife union, the more of this
> we are going to have. So anytime that this committee has the opportunity
> to bolster the two-parent family, the less that you have to deal with.[77]

Representative Wohlgemuth's comments shift focus from the needs
of those who have experienced abuse to the issue of the traditional
two-parent family. Her solution is not to extend TANF eligibility to
noncitizens, but to prevent abuse by strengthening two-parent families.
This also happens to be one of the goals of TANF. Policymakers may
choose to spend their time and financial resources addressing this goal
of TANF rather than extending eligibility to help noncitizens become
self-sufficient. The traditional family ethic of welfare policy wins out
over economic security.

Conclusion

Welfare recipients are at a representational disadvantage because of their intersectional identity; they are frequently marginalized along gender, class, and racial lines. Previous chapters have addressed how the peculiar representation of welfare recipients produces welfare rules surrounding morality, work ethic, and dependence. In this chapter, I have introduced a new axis of marginalization: citizenship. When a group cannot speak for themselves, either because they are not yet in the country when the rules that will affect them are formed or because they legally cannot participate in the political process, how are their interests represented?

I confront this question by analyzing two sets of welfare rules. One set, categories of eligibility, sets explicit limits on who may receive welfare benefits. The second set, income deeming, places implicit restrictions on eligibility. Both rules were changed under PRWORA, significantly decreasing the number of noncitizens eligible for TANF.

The debate over which categories of noncitizens should be eligible for assistance largely appears to center around an "us versus them" argument. Advocates testifying before committees in states from Alaska to Connecticut argued that noncitizens are part of the community and deserve to have access to the same services as native-born Americans. Those in the category of immigrant that is arguably most similar to American citizens—LPRs—are eligible for assistance in more states than those in any of the other categories. Compared to states in which LPRs are eligible for assistance, the states that do not extend eligibility to LPRs have higher unemployment rates and a greater percentage of interest groups representing low-wage industries. Thus, limiting eligibility for noncitizens may be one facet of a welfare program that is more restrictive in all areas, possibly because of financial concerns.

Income deeming does not explicitly limit eligibility, but it does move responsibility from the state to sponsors and families. A state that requires sponsor deeming sends a signal that welfare is a matter of one's own personal responsibility, rather than something to be taken care of by the state. Organizations that regularly work with low-income noncitizens frequently object to this policy. Families do provide support to the extent they are able, service providers argue, and when the family has nowhere else to turn that is when the noncitizen either turns to public assistance or relies on social service providers.

Finally, questions of responsibility and deservingness come to a head when addressing the concerns of battered immigrants. Marginalized in several ways, it would be easy for the interests of these noncitizens to be forgotten within larger interest groups. The qualitative evidence suggests that both immigrant and domestic violence groups will advocate on behalf of this subgroup, even though they do not constitute a large population, nor are they politically powerful. The quantitative evidence, meanwhile, shows a significant relationship between the proportion of Hispanic organizations in a state and eligibility for battered immigrants. There is no guarantee, however, that representation will represent the multiple layers of identity in one's life.

7

Expanding the Social Safety Net

The Future of Welfare

Exploring the political representation of welfare recipients—and how that representation translates into public policy—requires looking back at the history of public assistance in the United States and the slow transformation of unemployed mothers from sympathetic victims worthy of government aid to promiscuous women who placed a strain on the system. With such a negative public image surrounding welfare recipients, I find that the norms of political representation do not apply. Welfare recipients cannot count on descriptive representation from female or minority legislators; nor can they expect political parties to put their interests above those of the wealthy. Given their limited resources, welfare recipients are less likely to participate politically and there are few organizations specifically created to lobby on their behalf. In the absence of these traditional forms of political representation, welfare policy in the United States has instead been influenced by groups whose interests are only tangentially related to the well-being of welfare recipients.

Previously, I analyzed the relationship between a variety of TANF rules and these various channels of political representation. I examined how traditional gender norms influence a state's decision to both place requirements upon recipients and provide exemptions for those who are deemed deserving of such an exception. I considered what a state defines as "work" and how it evaluates the value of care work in a system focused on turning welfare recipients into workers. I found evidence that states with a greater proportion of labor unions allow fewer labor-market work activities but allow for more caretaker activity exemptions. Meanwhile, states with a greater proportion of interest groups representing industries that traditionally employ welfare recipients are less likely to count educational activities as work. Finally, I explained how strong beliefs in personal responsibility and a narrow view of deservingness limit who is eligible for assistance and how long they can stay on the rolls. I found both qualitative and quantitative evidence to suggest that Republicans remain concerned about dependency and little evidence that descriptive representation influences individual welfare rules.

However, what do these results mean for larger questions of descriptive representation, the centrality of political parties, and the influence of organized interests in public policy? With these larger questions in mind, I explore whether the individual TANF rules are less important than the type of recipient they affect. While I hesitate to return to measures that combine welfare rules, I evaluate whether in some circumstances an index of rules provides a better representation of interests. I present evidence that many of the rules underpinning TANF have spread to other social safety net programs. Finally, I explore the possibility that welfare as we know it is (once again) coming to an end, to be replaced by tax credits, guaranteed incomes, or other forms of government assistance.

What Drives Advocacy—Rule or Recipient?

The empirical analysis has largely focused on the extent to which advocacy organizations, political parties, and individual legislators respond to specific welfare rules. I have analyzed the rules individually, based on the argument that previous research that combines rules into indices has missed the competing interests at play. What if organized interests are less focused on the subset of rules, though, and more concerned with all of the rules that affect a particular recipient type? For example, domestic violence advocacy organizations may not advocate for specific rule changes, but may lobby state legislators to consider the importance of recognizing the unique circumstances of recipients who have experienced domestic violence. In response to the lobbying, policymakers take into account the bundle of rules that affect survivors of domestic violence when creating policy. If this is a more accurate representation of the advocacy process, then I would expect states to have a more generous bundle of policies that accommodate a certain kind of recipient as the proportion of advocacy groups representing that kind of recipient increases in the state. More generally, I would also expect that, as the proportion of feminist, African American, civil rights, and social welfare groups in a state increases, the state would adopt more of these policies.

To measure this effect, I created variables that capture whether a state includes an activity exemption, a time limit exemption, and a time limit extension for a particular recipient. These variables take a value ranging from 0 to 3, with 0 indicating that the state allows none of the exemptions/extensions, and 3 indicating that the state allows all of the exemptions/extensions. Variables were created for the following types of recipients: recipients with an illness or disability, elderly recipients, recipients caring for ill/disabled family members, recipients caring for young children, recipients who have experienced domestic violence, and recipients with an unsubsidized job. As shown in table 7.1, the generosity shown toward different kinds of recipients varies greatly. In more than 60 percent of state-years, there are neither activity exemptions nor time limit exemptions and extensions available to recipients working in unsubsidized jobs. For every other type of recipient, though, at least one policy accommodation is made in more than 50 percent of state-years. In over 10 percent of state-years, all three policy accommodations are available to recipients who either are caring for someone with an illness or disability or have an illness or disability themselves, and recipients who have experienced domestic violence (see table 7.1).

There does not appear to be any relationship between the proportion of advocacy groups in a state and the likelihood that it will adopt welfare rules favorable to a particular recipient type (see table B.25). There is no significant relationship between the proportion of disability rights groups in a state and its adopting more generous policies toward recipients with an illness or disability, or recipients caring for family with an illness or disability. Similarly, there is not a significant relationship between the proportion of groups representing the elderly in a state and the likelihood of its providing exemptions or extensions to elderly recipients. The number of policy accommodations for survivors of domestic violence is also not significantly affected by the proportion of domestic violence groups in a state. The only significant relationship between the proportions of advocacy organizations and policy accommodations for specific recipient types is a positive relationship between the proportion of social welfare organizations in a state and the number of policy accommodations for survivors of domestic violence.

Table 7.1. Percent of State-Years with Number of Policy Accommodations for a Given Recipient Type, 1997–2016

	0	1	2	3
Caring for ill/disabled recipient	5.78	33.24	47.25	13.73
Caring for young child	11.96	60.78	24.31	2.94
Domestic violence	12.65	45.49	30.20	11.67
Elderly recipient	40.10	27.06	25.78	7.06
Ill/disabled recipient	5.69	41.47	38.73	14.12
Working unsubsidized job	60.78	33.14	5.78	0.29

Aside from representation through interest groups, it is also possible that descriptive representatives and political parties focus more on creating a package of rules accommodating a type of recipient rather than each individual rule. For example, states with a Democratic legislature are significantly more likely to offer accommodations for recipients who are experiencing domestic violence or are caring for young children (see table B.25). Moreover, states with more liberal residents are more likely to adopt accommodations for recipients who are caring for young children or are elderly. Contrary to my expectations, an increase in the percentage of women in the state legislature is not related to an increase in the number of policy accommodations for any type of recipient. In fact, as women's representation increases, a state is significantly less likely to provide accommodations for recipients with an illness or disability.

To better understand the extent to which interest groups, political parties, and individual representatives conceive of welfare rules as bundles of rules meant to accommodate a particular type of welfare recipient, the measures would need to be more fully developed and include more rules. A measure of policies accommodating survivors of domestic violence, for instance, might also include whether a state exempts recipients from cooperating with child support enforcement. To fully grasp who represents the interest of elderly recipients, a more detailed measure may need to include rules that determine whether grandparents are eligible to receive benefits and if Social Security is counted as income when calculating eligibility. Including a more comprehensive list of rules will make it clearer whether advocacy is coming from groups generally in favor of a more expansive welfare state or those lobbying on behalf of a subgroup of welfare recipients.

Applying TANF Principles Elsewhere

States have learned from more than twenty years of welfare reform and applied many of TANF's core principles to other safety net programs. In 2018, the Wisconsin legislature introduced a package of bills during a special session to institute sweeping changes to the state's social safety net. Wisconsin's welfare reform package passed, with the help of a Republican legislature and Republican governor, and has been promoted as a model for a new wave of Republican welfare reform legislation.[1] While its package was perhaps the most comprehensive, Wisconsin was not the only state to pass reforms.

Drug Testing

Even though both the constitutionality and the effectiveness of drug testing public assistance recipients has been called into question, policymakers from a variety of states have proposed random drug testing as a condition of eligibility.[2] As part of Wisconsin Republicans' 2018 welfare reform package, public housing authorities are required to conduct drug testing as a condition of eligibility. Similar to arguments made when states introduced drug testing for TANF recipients, the Wisconsin Catholic Conference opposed the drug testing requirement because "these kinds of measures fail to recognize that drug abuse afflicts all income levels and that most of those in drug treatment programs relapse several times before achieving lasting recovery."[3]

As early as 2012, South Dakota legislators considered implementing random drug testing for Medicaid and SNAP recipients. Kim Malsam-Rysdon, secretary of South Dakota's Department of Social Services, testified that enacting such a bill would jeopardize the state's federal funding because it was against federal regulations. Several advocacy groups, including the South Dakota Coalition of Citizens with Disabilities, the American Civil Liberties Union of South Dakota, and South Dakota Voices for Children, opposed the bill. Advocates raised concerns that denying Medicaid would only perpetuate drug problems by making it more difficult for people to afford treatment; others noted that most Medicaid recipients are children.[4] The sponsor of the bill, Representative Mark Kirkeby, rebutted, "There was testimony that it is a humiliation and hardship to families. I don't think that really deems any rebuttal on my part. That's part of the deal."[5] Kirkeby's belief that families applying for public assistance should expect humiliation and hardship demonstrates that many of the long-standing stereotypes around welfare recipients are still prevalent today.

Child Support Cooperation

Building off the relationships established under cash assistance, state legislators have used eligibility for social safety net programs as leverage to force parents to cooperate with child support agencies. In 2017, the South Dakota legislature considered a bill that would require SNAP applicants to cooperate with the Division of Child Support. In 2019, a bill was introduced to the Alaska House that would have disqualified from the food stamp program anyone who refused to cooperate with child support services or who had past due child support payments.[6] Both of these bills were ultimately unsuccessful, but show a willingness to deny government services if parents do not work with child support agencies.

Part of Wisconsin's 2018 welfare reform package also required both SNAP and Medicaid recipients to comply with child support reporting requirements. Speaking in favor of the bill, Representative Joe Sanfelippo said:

> Assembly Bill 57 promotes personal responsibility and provides an incentive which promotes responsible parenting. Government should not encourage parents to abandon their responsibilities to provide for their children, yet that is exactly what we do when we do not hold parents accountable. A parent that knows they will still be responsible for their children even if they leave the family will be less inclined to leave.[7]

The assistant deputy secretary of Wisconsin's Department of Children and Families wrote that the bill reflects "the principle that parents are the natural providers for their children," but also acknowledged that "when parents fulfill their financial obligations to their children, families are less reliant on public benefit programs, [. . .] and generate savings for taxpayers."[8] For the state, these requirements serve two purposes: reinforcing the importance of individual responsibility and exercising fiscal restraint.

Advocates opposing the child support requirements called the provision "counterproductive and unnecessary" and pointed out that being unable to afford medical care would make it even more unlikely that noncustodial parents would pay child support.[9] Marsha Mansfield, director of the University of Wisconsin's Law School Family Law Clinic, also argued that these additional requirements add "stress to individuals already facing incredibly stressful situations, individuals who often also have extensive histories of trauma." This includes individuals recently released from prisons and those who are not native English speakers.[10] With such an emphasis on personal responsibility, policymakers do not need to consider how the individual circumstances of noncustodial parents might make it more difficult for them to pay child support. Their choices led them to their current situation, which does not negate their responsibility to care for their children.

Work Requirements

During the Trump administration, multiple states applied for waivers to institute work requirements for Medicaid recipients. Seema Verma, the Centers for Medicare and Medicaid Services administrator under Trump, framed her support for requirements in the language of dependency, personal responsibility, and deservingness that serves as the basis for TANF:

> The thought that a program designed for our most vulnerable citizens should be used as a vehicle to serve working age, able-bodied adults does not make sense [. . .] We owe our fellow citizens more than just giving them a Medicaid card, we owe a card with care, and more importantly a card with hope. Hope that they can achieve a better future for themselves and their families. Hope that they can one day break the chains of generational poverty and no longer need public assistance, and the hope that every American, no matter their race, creed, or origin can reach their highest potential.[11]

As of May 2022, thirteen states had work requirement waivers approved and nine additional states had submitted waiver requests to CMS. In addition, five states had their work requirements blocked in the courts.[12]

Idaho was one of the states to seek a Medicaid waiver to institute work requirements for able-bodied adults. An advocate from the League of Women Voters of Idaho noted that most Medicaid recipients were already working, making the work requirement "unnecessary" and "mean-spirited."[13] Speaking in favor of the bill, Fred Birnbaum from the Idaho Freedom Foundation said:

> Now there are some that consider reforms like work requirements as tantamount to making people jump through hoops, as if actually working was a barrier to success in life rather than a predictor of it. [. . .] We are at a crossroads in America. The ACA cannot stand as currently constructed. It either fails as a single-payer system modeled on Medicaid for All or we move toward an approach that begins with price transparency, accountability, and a choice for most, and a safety net only for the most vulnerable—a way station, not a hammock.[14]

The arguments that Medicaid should be reserved for only the "most vulnerable" or the "truly needy" echoes the arguments that drove welfare reform in the mid-1990s.

Kathy Garrett from the National Alliance for Mental Illness of Idaho pushed back against the stereotype that Medicaid recipients do not want to work. "Whenever possible," she said, "they will work. We sometimes put barriers up because often they need that healthcare and the services that Medicaid provides." She explained that people experiencing mental illness may be working at jobs that do not have healthcare benefits, and without those benefits, "they don't have access to their medications, they don't have access to treatment, and shortly fall into a crisis."[15] Advocates from several other health and disability rights interest groups, including Idaho's chapter of the American Lung Association, Disability Rights Idaho, and the Idaho Behavioral Health Alliance testified against the bill as well.[16]

Speaking about the possibility of work requirements for Alaskan Medicaid recipients in 2018, Senator Peter Micciche expressed his opinion that the state needed to "shift toward teaching a man to fish" rather than promoting dependency. Similarly, Jeremy Price from Americans for Prosperity wrote to legislators that government assistance should be a "hand up" and not a "hand out" and be reserved for those who "truly need the program."[17] Christie Herrera, from the Foundation for Government Accountability, told legislators:

> The reform would bring Medicaid in line with other welfare programs that require able-bodied adults to work in order to remain eligible, as required by federal law. The work requirement would not apply to the disabled, the elderly, or new mothers, among other groups. [. . .] The tax dollars saved by moving able-bodied Alaskans from welfare to work would be preserved for the truly needy.[18]

The bill introduced in 2018 was unsuccessful, but legislators reintroduced the legislation a year later. Senator Micciche reiterated his belief that the work requirement would "ensure that limited resources are prioritized toward those most in need" while encouraging "able-bodied Alaskans to reach their full potential."[19] Those opposed to the work requirement pointed out that most Medicaid recipients are working, but in low-wage positions that do not provide healthcare; others commented on the inefficient use of government resources in enforcing such a requirement. The advocacy from health interest groups demonstrates that there is opposition to work requirements from this sector, but they are selective in which program's work requirements to oppose.

Time Limits

Just as time limits were incorporated into TANF as a way of decreasing dependency, policymakers have added and enforced time limits to other social safety net programs to ensure that these programs remain temporary solutions. As part of its Medicaid reform, Idaho legislators proposed a five-year time limit for medical assistance. In introducing the bill, Representative Bryan Zollinger stated that anyone with a disability would be exempt from the time limit.[20] In addition, anyone who qualified for Medicare would also be exempt from the time limit. The intention of the bill was to target able-bodied adults. Jim Baugh, an advocate for Disability Rights Idaho, expressed concern over the ambiguity of who would be covered under the five-year time limit.

Under PRWORA, able-bodied adults without dependents (ABAWDs) are subject to a periodic time limit under SNAP; they may receive three months of assistance in a three-year period without meeting the work requirement. Recipients may be exempt from these requirements if they meet work requirements (twenty hours per week), are pregnant, or have an illness or disability that prevents them from participating in work requirements.[21] Policymakers justified the time limit as a way to promote employment among SNAP recipients; research has found the effects of the time limit on employment to be negligible. The time limit does decrease the number of ABAWDs who participate in SNAP.[22]

States have consistently used waivers to suspend the time limit during periods of high unemployment, and the 2009 Recovery Act suspended the time limit nationwide for part of 2009 and fiscal year 2010.[23] Several states began reinstating their time limit during the 2010s. New Jersey's SNAP waiver expired at the end of 2015; in response, the legislature held a hearing in January 2016. Democratic senators proposed applying for a waiver that would cover only counties with high unemployment. One senator described the expiration of the waiver as "blaming those receiving the benefit for not taking advantage of opportunities that either don't exist or, at the very least, are hard to find."[24] Raymond Castro, a senior policy analyst from New Jersey Policy Perspective, compared the time limit to TANF:

> [T]his requirement [is] very different than all the other programs that we have because, you know, in TANF, for example, if there is not work activity for you, to place you, you're allowed to continue—right?—which is only fair. But under this system, if the State is not able to provide the work activities that they need, they become ineligible for three years. So that's just very, very unfair.[25]

In March 2020, Congress passed the Family First Coronavirus Response Act, which suspended time limits for ABAWDs meeting work requirements for the length of the public health emergency.[26] As I will discuss in the next section, many of the assumptions about those receiving government assistance were challenged during the coronavirus pandemic.

Ending Welfare as We Know It, Again

While the personal responsibility narrative remains popular in much of American welfare policy, other policy proposals have taken a different approach to assisting low-income families. Some of this discussion was jump-started by the coronavirus pandemic.

Economic Impact Payments and Unemployment Insurance

Most households in the United States received three Economic Impact Payments (EIPs) during the course of the coronavirus pandemic. There was bipartisan support for these payments, even among those who traditionally do not support government assistance.[27] This support could be rationalized because people were not to blame for losing their jobs but were victims of a global pandemic and not going to work in the early days of the pandemic was seen as necessary to protecting public health. The impact was also widespread; over 40 percent of households reported that someone in their household had taken a pay cut or lost a job due to the pandemic.[28] For Americans who changed or lost jobs during the pandemic or had lower incomes, their EIPs were used to cover basic needs.[29] Whereas previously job loss might have been perceived as something that happened to other people, perhaps because of their own laziness or moral failings, the pandemic hit close to home for many Americans.

If the initial economic impact payment was a way to cover expenses while Americans stayed home from work for the sake of public health, later payments were presented as spurring economic growth and returning the country back to "normal." These EIPs differed from past stimulus measures, however. In contrast to stimulus payments issued during the Great Recession, for example, Americans who did not file taxes were also eligible for the rebates. Moreover, any child with a Social Security number was eligible to receive a payment under the 2021 American Rescue Plan.[30] These adjustments extended eligibility to an even greater number of low-income Americans.

Congress also expanded unemployment insurance (UI) during the pandemic in several ways. UI benefits were extended for an additional thirteen weeks beyond the maximum duration for regular UI benefits, and UI recipients received an additional $600 on top of the regular weekly benefit. Workers who did not qualify for UI under regular conditions were also eligible for expanded benefits.[31] Compared to those who applied for UI benefits but did not receive them, UI recipients in March through May 2020 reported fewer worries about paying rent or mortgage, utility bills, and medical costs.[32] As with TANF, critics of both the EIPs and expanded UI policies questioned whether increased assistance would promote dependency and discourage people from working.[33] In May 2021, an executive at the US Chamber of Commerce asserted that "paying people not to work is dampening what should be a stronger jobs market."[34] This rhetoric mirrors the language around welfare programs more generally.

Expanded Child Tax Credit

The American Rescue Plan expanded the Child Tax Credit and changed it to a monthly payment ($250 for children ages six through seventeen and $300 for children five and younger) rather than a lump sum at tax time. Notably, families who did not file income tax returns were also eligible for these tax credits.[35] The expanded CTC reduced child poverty dramatically by the end of 2021. Families reported spending the extra money on necessities, including food, housing, and utilities.[36] The stereotypes of parents misusing government assistance did not disappear, however. Senator Joe Manchin justified his opposition to continuing the CTC with concerns that parents would use the money for drugs.[37] As with the expanded unemployment insurance and EIPs, some economists expressed concerns that parents would be discouraged from working if the expanded CTC was made permanent. Supporters of the expanded CTC argued that it might increase labor force participation among parents because the additional money could be used to pay for childcare.[38]

In February 2021, Senator Mitt Romney released a plan for his Family Security Act, which combined elements of both PRWORA and the expanded CTC. Similar to the goals laid out in PRWORA, Romney's proposal seeks to promote marriage, this time by eliminating the marriage penalty in the Earned Income Tax Credit. As Samuel Hammond and Robert Orr write in "The Conservative Case for a Child Allowance," Romney's plan may also decrease abortion by making the child allowance available to expectant mothers during their third trimester.[39] To pay for monthly payments similar to the expanded CTC—$350 for each child under the age of six, and $250 for each child aged six to seventeen—Romney proposes eliminating TANF.[40] Romney's original proposal did not include work requirements, but in February 2022 he indicated he was open to adding requirements.[41]

Is it possible that the United States could move toward a permanent monthly benefit for families? Both Democrats and Republicans may find reasons to support such a proposal. For Democrats, the expanded Child Tax Credit is the closest the United States has ever come to instituting a universal basic income.[42] For Republicans, such a monthly benefit may encourage a return to the traditional nuclear family with a single (male) breadwinner.

Areas of Future Research

Previously, I have focused on the portion of TANF that provides direct cash assistance to welfare recipients. In most states, though, the majority of state and federal TANF funding is not used to provide cash assistance, but rather covers administrative costs and funds non-cash benefits such as childcare subsidies and family formation programs.[43] The TANF block grant structure gives states flexibility on how they spend federal money, but what drives states to spend more money on cash assistance versus non-cash assistance? How do states determine which non-cash assistance programs will receive funding? Research suggests that racial stereotyping may drive states to spend less of their block grant on cash assistance.[44] Future research should explore the extent to which interest groups, political parties, and descriptive representation influence these other components of welfare policy. I would expect, for instance, that states with a Republican controlled statehouse and socially conservative interest groups would be more likely to fund family formation programs. Examining in greater detail how the two political parties envision the use of block grants will become more relevant as more programs are devolved to the states.

I have also made assumptions about the interests of welfare recipients. I assume, for instance, that it is in the best interests of welfare recipients to not have requirements related to attending parenting classes or seeking child support from absent fathers. I also assume that it is preferable to have more activities to choose from to meet activity requirements. These assumptions originate from the idea that welfare recipients do not need the government providing guidance on how to live one's life.

Proponents of paternalism, however, would argue that it *is* in recipients' best interests to have the government involved in the details of their personal lives, and some recipients may prefer it. Apart from Carmen Cordero's appearance before the Connecticut state legislature, very little of the legislative testimony related to state welfare rules has actually come from welfare recipients.

Moving forward, when discussing how the interests of welfare recipients are represented, it would be informative to hear about these interests from welfare recipients themselves. Do welfare recipients feel well-represented by their local representatives? Do they see female or minority legislators as better representatives of their interests than white, male legislators? Are welfare recipients trying to mobilize, or as Skocpol alluded to, are they too busy with the business of living to worry about what is happening within government?[45] Scholars may also be completely missing the issues that are of most concern to welfare recipients—while much of the political science literature on welfare policy has focused on the work requirements of TANF, perhaps this isn't the central focus of those receiving benefits. Listening to those who are most directly affected by these policies may move the literature in a new direction.

Finally, I argue that a state's TANF policy poorly represents the interests of those it most directly affects because welfare recipients lack the resources to speak for themselves and are stereotyped as undeserving. Some of these challenges affect all low-income citizens—regardless of whether someone is receiving government assistance, she may still not have the time to create an interest group to advocate on issues important to her or to contribute to politicians who best align with her interests. What happens, though, when citizens who have internalized a feeling of being overlooked receive attention? After this population is mobilized, to what extent do political parties and individual politicians feel compelled to represent these interests? One recent example of this includes Donald Trump's constituency.

Donald Trump ran a campaign promising to speak for those who had been silenced. He promised to represent the interests of low-income families that had been forgotten by those in Washington—the coal miners, the factory workers, and all blue-collar Americans. To Trump, these people were worthy of attention—indeed, they were a constituency large enough to create a pathway to the presidency. How do we reconcile the attention paid to this marginalized population and the policies the Trump administration actually proposed? Following the release of Trump's first budget, analysts warned that many of the budget cuts would be felt hardest by those in rural communities, and the first Republican attempt to repeal the Affordable Care Act was estimated to increase the uninsured population by twenty-four million people.[46] In spite of their support, his policy proposals do not provide relief for those who are hurting. The case of low-income Trump voters raises questions as to whether having a voice—and seemingly being represented—leads to more favorable policy outcomes.

Welfare reform passed with bipartisan support more than twenty-five years ago. Given the unique situation of welfare recipients—low-income women who are often racial or ethnic minorities—their voices have been overlooked, and yet there is no clear indication of who—political parties, politicians, or interest groups—is behind the policies that influence them most directly. As trust in government wavers and voters feel ever more alienated by "Washington elites," it is imperative that we continue to scrutinize the connection between political representation and public policy.

ACKNOWLEDGMENTS

So many people provided support to get the book to this point and I am so grateful for all of them. First, NYU Press has shepherded me through the whole book publishing process. The anonymous reviewers provided excellent suggestions that have made the book better, and Sonia, my editor, has been so kind in answering all my questions, regardless of how obvious the answers may be.

I would be remiss if I didn't thank two of my undergraduate mentors who made academia seem worthwhile: Claudia Leeb and Heath Brown. Claudia introduced me to feminist theory, which changed my life. Heath worked with me on my earliest research as an undergraduate and continues to provide me with advice and support.

At Penn State, Michael Berkman, Lee Ann Banaszak, David Lowery, and Eric Plutzer provided great mentorship and feedback on the earliest drafts of what would become this book. At Miami University, I have wonderful colleagues who embody the teacher-scholar model and make for excellent trivia teammates. Within the political science department, Monica Schneider provides the best mentoring. Miami's College of Arts and Science gave me time to work on revisions of this book and provided me with funding to hire Malena Dailey, who as an undergraduate provided critical research assistance.

I have great friends throughout the country who provided feedback on drafts, answered my questions, and listened to my complaints. I'm so glad that I have Christopher Ojeda to go to when I need to talk TANF. Lee Hannah and Michael Kenwick keep me going on a day-to-day basis in our group chat. Clare Brock has been a super-supportive co-author as we both work on our first books. And I have the best friend I could ever ask for in Kim Seufer. I don't know how I got so lucky to find a friend that can provide fashion advice, talk political science research, and quote *Parks and Recreation*. There is no comparison.

My family has always supported my academic endeavors, and I don't thank them enough. My parents and my sister are my biggest cheerleaders. Finally, Kevin Reuning has been by my side throughout the whole process. He answered my methods questions without being condescending, reminded me that I needed to take breaks, and always made sure we had plenty of ice cream in the house. And JoJo and Frida provide comic relief and unconditional love that only dogs can provide.

APPENDIX A

Methods

The standard practice when analyzing state welfare policy is to draw upon welfare rules. Rules are preferred over legislation because the legislation is not what directly affects the recipients; in many cases, the policy passed by the legislature is then interpreted by state bureaucrats. Furthermore, using rules to measure policy change allows for a more fine-grained analysis due to the data available through the Urban Institute's Welfare Rules Database (WRD). The WRD is an online database that contains more than one thousand variables for the fifty states and the District of Columbia since 1996 (though my analysis is limited to rules from 1997 to 2016). The policies are taken from caseworker manuals and are continually updated; each year, the Urban Institute reaches out to welfare division managers and other state government officials to verify the accuracy of the rules. The WRD is the go-to data source for state welfare policy and has been used by many scholars conducting research on welfare policy.[1] Research on welfare policy that does not include data from the WRD usually covers a timespan that includes both AFDC and TANF or focuses on a limit number of rules that can be gathered from other sources, such as the US Government Accountability Office or other reports issued by the Urban Institute.[2]

Fellowes and Rowe created perhaps the most frequently used indices to measure two broad dimensions of welfare policy: initial eligibility of applicants and flexibility of work requirements.[3] These scales are problematic, though, if there is not one overarching interest influencing welfare policy. As an example, the eligibility scale includes a binary variable for whether the state has a family cap, as well as several variables capturing whether certain groups of recipients are eligible for time limit extensions (e.g., elderly recipients, ill or disabled recipients).

De Jong and his colleagues used factor analysis to identify three underlying dimensions of welfare policy: rules regarding eligibility requirements, behavioral requirements to maintain eligibility, and rules regarding time limits and exemptions.[4] These dimensions run into problems similar to the Fellowes and Rowe scales. For example, the eligibility requirement for groups dimension includes both activity requirements and noncitizen eligibility. Activity requirements are considered more stringent when states accept only work; more lenient policies accept activities that expand beyond paid employment. Noncitizen eligibility is considered more lenient when different types of noncitizens are eligible to receive assistance. Industries have an interest in more stringent activity requirements, which force recipients into the labor market, while also increasing leniency for noncitizens, because it increases the low-wage labor pool available through welfare work programs. Using dimensions built from factor analyses assumes that an interest group always favors more lenient or more stringent policies.

I improve upon previous measures of welfare rules by disaggregating rules according to how they situate welfare recipients as the other (see table A.1). My measurement strategy assumes neither that interest groups take positions on all welfare rules nor that they always advocate for a more lenient or stringent policy. With these new measures, I expect that organizations will take an interest in TANF policy to the extent that it helps them achieve their goals.

Moreover, this project covers a wide array of welfare rules to capture the diverse population of interest groups that take interest in a state's welfare program. The welfare rules examined in the first empirical chapter (chapter 3) include those related to regulating a recipient's morality, such as the family cap policy. In contrast to previous research that has examined the motivation behind a state adopting a family cap policy, I not only take into account whether the policy exists, but also whether there are any exemptions to the policy. Included in this chapter is also a measure of how much the state requires from a recipient in cooperating with child support enforcement. This variable is a scale comprising all the possible requirements a state may impose on a recipient. Other rules included in this chapter capture whether recipients are subject to random drug test screening, and whether recipients are required to take

Table A.1. TANF Rules Covered in the Empirical Chapters

Chapter 3	
Family Cap	Does the policy exist, and are there exemptions? (Ordinal)
Drug Screening Requirement	Does the requirement exist? (Binary)
Immunization Requirement	Does the requirement exist? (Binary)
Parenting Class Requirement	Does the requirement exist? (Binary)
School Attendance Requirement	Does the requirement exist? (Binary)
Child Support Reporting Requirements	How many requirements does the state place on the recipient? (Scale ranging from X to Y)
Chapter 4	
Allowable Activities	Does the state count [activity] as an allowable activity? (Binary) How many activities may a recipient choose from to meet activity requirements? (Scale ranging from X to Y) How many education-related activities may the recipient count toward the activity requirement? (Scale ranging from X to Y) How many labor force-related activities may the recipient count toward the activity requirement? (Scale ranging from X to Y) How many self-improvement-related activities may the recipient count toward the activity requirement? (Scale ranging from X to Y)
Activity Exemptions	How many exemptions does the state allow? (Scale ranging from X to Y) Does the state count [exemption] as an activity exemption? (Binary)
Chapter 5	
Existence of Time Limit	Is there a lifetime time limit? (Binary) Is there a periodic time limit or benefit waiting period? (Binary)
Generosity of Time Limit	In how many months may a recipient receive benefits over a 60-month period? (Ordinal)
Time Limit Exemptions and Extensions	Does the state allow for a time limit exemption in the case of [circumstance]? (Binary) Does the state allow for a time limit extension in the case of [circumstance]? (Binary)
Chapter 6	
Sponsor Deeming	Is the sponsor's income deemed to the noncitizen? (Binary)
Parental Income Deeming to Child	Is an ineligible parent's income deemed to a child eligible for aid? (Binary)
Immigrant Category Eligibility	Is [immigrant category] eligible for benefits after five years in the country? (Binary)

parenting classes or attend parent-teacher conferences. These are coded as binary variables (does the requirement exist or not).

The second empirical chapter (chapter 4) covers policies designed to turn welfare recipients into workers. I focus on the types of activities that a recipient may count toward her work requirement and the exemptions given to those work requirements. To capture the flexibility in allowable activities, I create three scales measuring three different dimensions of work (employment-related, education, and self-improvement). I also analyze the relationship between a state's interest group community and each allowable activity individually. Finally, I create a scale summing up the number of activity-related exemptions permitted by the state.

The third empirical chapter (chapter 5) looks at rules that are designed to keep TANF temporary through four types of rules. First, I focus on whether the state institutes a time limit—either over the course of a lifetime, or through a periodic time limit or benefit waiting period. Second, I create an ordinal measure designed to capture the generosity of a state's time limit over a sixty-month period. Third, I examine the time limit extensions provided to recipients after they have reached the state and/or federal lifetime limit. Fourth, I analyze the time limit exemptions allowed by the state.

Finally, the fourth empirical chapter (chapter 6) investigates the rules related to noncitizen eligibility. Similar to previous research on welfare and immigration, I take into account which categories of immigrants who arrived in the United States after the passage of welfare reform are eligible to receive assistance following their first five years in the country. In a departure from previous research, however, I also consider how sponsor income deeming (declaring the sponsor's income available to the noncitizen when determining eligibility) and ineligible parent income deeming (declaring the parent's income available to an otherwise eligible child when determining eligibility) limit the eligibility of noncitizens.

INDEPENDENT VARIABLES: INTEREST GROUPS

I compiled a dataset of more than twenty thousand state and local interest groups from a wide variety of interests using Associations Unlimited, an online database maintained by the Gale Group. I collected my sample of interest groups from this source rather than lobbying reports or campaign contributions because Associations Unlimited includes grassroots groups that may not register to lobby or regularly participate in political campaigns, but still have a presence in the state. The founding date provided with the information about the groups allows me to adjust for changes in the state's interest group population over time. Because the

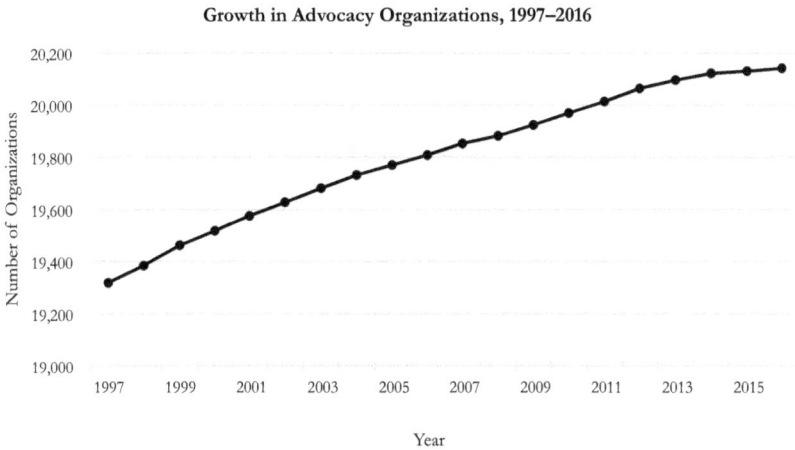

Figure A.1. Total Number of Organizations

database receives frequent updates, though, using this approach risks not capturing groups that fell apart prior to data collection. The total number of groups in the dataset increased from over 19,200 in 1997 to just above 20,100 in 2016 (see figure A.1 for the trend over time).

The groups fall into one of twenty different categories (see table A.3 for categories and number of organizations in each category). In some cases, the categories represent industries (such as agriculture and construction), others represent policy areas (such as civil rights or immigration), and still others represent groups of people (such as Hispanics or the elderly). The organizations within each group category were selected based on keywords (table A.2 provides a list of the keywords used for each category and examples of organizations that fall within each category). The group categories are theoretically driven based on the intersectional identity of the stereotypical welfare queen (low-income, African American, woman) and which types of organizations have historically been involved in welfare policy. I draw from Skocpol's *Protecting Soldiers and Mothers* to gather information on groups that were involved in public assistance prior to the New Deal. I also referred to Reese's *Backlash against Welfare Mothers*; her book identifies groups that were in support of and opposed to AFDC. For an account of the activism of welfare recipients and their allies during the welfare rights

Table A.2. Keywords Used in Organization Search

Organization Type	Keywords	Organization Examples
African American	"African American" OR "Racism"	Black Alliance for Educational Options–Ohio Chapter; Concerned Black Men of Philadelphia
Agriculture	"Agriculture" OR "Fruits and Vegetables" OR "Organic Farming"	Arkansas Farm Bureau; Florida Watermelon Association
Chambers of Commerce	"Chambers of Commerce"	Birmingham Business Alliance; Albany Chamber of Commerce
Civil rights organizations	"Civil Rights and Liberties" OR "Human Rights" OR "Social Justice"	Urban League of Greater Chattanooga; American Civil Liberties Union of Utah
Construction	"Construction"	Home Builders Association of Georgia; Dakota Asphalt Pavement Association
Disabled	"Disability" OR "Disabled" OR "Disabled Veterans" OR "Disabilities" OR "Handicapped"	California Disability Services Association; Aloha Independent Living Hawaii
Domestic violence	"Domestic Violence" OR "Trauma" OR "Victims"	Alaska Network on Domestic Violence and Sexual Assault; Kentucky Domestic Violence Association
Economically conservative	"Libertarian" OR "Small Government" OR "Tea Party"	Libertarian Party of New Hampshire; Washington Conservative Union
Elderly	"Elder Abuse" OR "Retirees" OR "Retirement" OR "Social Security"	AARP–Arizona; Wisconsin Alliance for Retired Americans
Feminist	"Feminism" OR "Reproductive Rights" OR "Women's Rights"	National Organization for Women–Des Moines; Women's Action for New Directions–Arkansas
Food and beverage	"Restaurant" OR "Food service" OR "Restaurant Workers"	Colorado Restaurant Association; Kansas Restaurant and Hospitality Association (KRHA)
Health	"Health" OR "Health Professionals" OR "Health Services" OR "Health Care" OR "Hospital" OR "Medical Care" OR "Medical Reform" OR "Pediatrics"	Community Health Network of Connecticut, Inc.; Physicians for Social Responsibility–Greater Boston
Hispanic	"Hispanic" OR "Latin American" OR "Cuban" OR "Dominican Republic"	Casa De Esperanza; Dallas Concilio of Hispanic Service Organizations
Immigration	"Immigrant" OR "Refugees" OR "Immigration"	Illinois Coalition for Immigrant and Refugee Rights; American Immigration Lawyers Association–Oregon Chapter
Other ethnic and racial minorities	"Minorities" OR "Arab" OR "Muslim" OR "Asian American"	Muslim American Society–Maryland; Indiana Association of Chinese Americans
Miscellaneous business	"Business" OR "Business and Commerce" OR "Employers"	Vermont Business Roundtable; Nevada Association of Employers
Retail	"Retailing"	Retail Association of Maine; Michigan Association of Convenience Stores
Social welfare	"Child Welfare" OR "Homeless" OR "Social Welfare" OR "Social Work" OR "Poverty"	Community Action Partnership–Idaho; Central Louisiana Homeless Coalition
Socially conservative	"Conservative Traditionalists" OR "Pro-Life" OR "Right to Life" OR "Christian Right"	Delaware Citizens for Life; Christian Coalition of North Carolina

Table A.3. Interest Group Categories

Business Interests	Number of Organizations
Agriculture	531
Chambers of Commerce	4,686
Construction	357
Food and Beverage	149
Misc. Business (representing executives)	2,515
Retail	111
Labor	2,409
Policy-Based Interests	
Civil Rights	460
Domestic Violence	145
Economically Conservative	99
Health	2,967
Immigration	42
Socially Conservative	167
Social Welfare	1,536
Identity-Based Interests	
African American	477
Disabled	2,456
Elderly	437
Women	364
Hispanic/Latino	111
Other Racial/Ethnic Minority	133
Total Groups	**20,152**

movement, I turned to Nadasen's *Welfare Warriors*. Finally, much of the categories are drawn from Winston's book *Welfare Policymaking in the States*, which examines the types of interest groups that lobbied at the national level prior to the passage of welfare reform. All of these sources highlight groups that have supported a more expansive welfare state and groups that have opposed a more generous welfare state.

CONTROL VARIABLES

Several sets of control variables are included in the model. These control variables account for the level of need in the state, the political environment, and the greater welfare context. The first set of control variables concern the demographics of a state. The Black percentage of the population is included, as well as the Hispanic and foreign-born percentages of the population. Previous welfare research consistently shows that states with a greater Black population have more stringent welfare policies.[5] Schneider and Ingram's theory of social construction argues that policymakers create policy in response to the citizens it will affect.[6] Therefore, if a state has a greater Black population and the stereotype of Black welfare recipients suggest that they are dependent on the state and unwilling to work, state policies will reflect these stereotypes. The Hispanic and foreign-born population plays a greater role when considering a state's welfare rules toward immigrants.[7]

The poverty rate is included to measure the potential caseload in the state. Several states (seven in 2019) use the federal poverty level as an income threshold for determining welfare eligibility.[8] States with a higher poverty rate will have more citizens eligible for TANF. Where the poverty rate provides a measure of those who are in need of services, the population receiving TANF measures how many are actually receiving assistance. The two measures have a low correlation (0.02), which suggests that in some states with a great level of need there are barriers to receiving assistance. Some of these barriers may include the strict behavioral and work requirements and eligibility requirements that I explore in the pertinent chapters.

In addition to being (by definition) low-income, many welfare recipients lack a high school diploma or GED.[9] In a state with a highly educated population, there may be less need for welfare, as unemployment is generally lower among those with more education. On the other hand, the education level of recipients matters when a state is creating training and education opportunities. A state with a large adult population without a high school degree may decide to place an emphasis on education and allow education to count as a core activity, whereas states with a more educated population may choose to focus solely on employment. To account for these factors, I include the percentage of the adult population with a high school degree as a control. This measure is highly correlated with several other control variables, including the Black percentage of the population and the percentage of the population living in poverty. However, dropping this variable would lead to biased results if states do in fact create welfare policy based on the skills their population already possesses.

Table A.4. Correlation between Control Variables

	Pct. population Black	Pct. population Hispanic	Pct. population foreign born	Poverty rate	Unmarried births	Pct. population receiving TANF	Citizen ideology	Pct. legislature female	Max. TANF benefit
Pct. population Black	1.00								
Pct. population Hispanic	0.06	1.00							
Pct. population foreign born	0.16	0.86	1.00						
Poverty rate	0.30	0.07	-0.14	1.00					
Unmarried births	0.51	0.12	0.05	0.61	1.00				
Pct. population receiving TANF	-0.07	-0.19	0.01	-0.05	-0.16	1.00			
Citizen ideology	-0.07	0.09	0.37	-0.27	0.02	0.33	1.00		
Pct. legislature female	-0.34	0.40	0.50	-0.31	-0.14	0.08	0.43	1.00	
Max. TANF benefit	-0.53	0.13	0.32	-0.52	-0.38	0.22	0.55	0.50	1.00

Note: Because there are both continuous and ordinal control variables, I use Spearman's rank correlation coefficient. Democratic governor and Democratic legislature are not included in the table because they are binary variables. Measures of neighboring state policy are not included because they differ for each welfare rule.

Finally, the percentage of births to unmarried women is also included because one of TANF's stated purposes is to reduce out-of-wedlock births. Therefore, states with higher incidence of unmarried births may adopt more stringent welfare policies. As shown in table 4, the percentage of unmarried births is moderately correlated with the Black population (0.51) and the percentage of the population in poverty (0.61). This is not entirely unexpected given that the stereotype of a welfare recipient is a poor, unmarried Black woman. The political environment of the state may also affect its welfare policy. If policymakers are responding to the preferences of citizens, then I would anticipate that states with a more liberal population would have more generous welfare policies. I include Berry et al.'s measure of citizen ideology to control for this; the measure ranges from 0 to 100, with higher scores indicating more liberal ideologies.

I also include variables capturing the partisan interests of policymakers. Party control is measured as two separate variables; the first is a dichotomous variable indicating whether the governor is a Democrat. The second variable is coded for the partisan makeup of the legislature—if neither house is Democratic, the variable takes on the value of 0; if the legislature is divided, the variable takes on the value of 0.5; and if both houses are Democratic, the variable takes on the value of 1. As I argue in chapter 2, descriptive representation literature argues that the interests of citizens are best represented by those who share characteristics or experiences with them. The vast majority of welfare recipients are women and previous research on the subject has found that welfare benefits are more generous when women's representation is higher.[10] To measure women's representation I include the percentage of the legislature that is female. If interest groups are truly driving state welfare policies, the percentage of women in the legislature and Democratic control of state government should have no effect on policy outcomes.

The welfare context control variables consist of a measure of program flexibility and a measure of policy diffusion. As a general measure of a state's welfare generosity, I include the maximum monthly benefit for a family of three, adjusted for the state cost of living. AFDC and TANF benefits are a common measure of welfare generosity; previous research has shown a relationship between benefit levels and descriptive representation, business interest group power, party control, among other concepts.[11] The correlation among control variables also testifies

Table A.5. Data Sources

Variable	Source
Welfare rules	Welfare Rules Database, Urban Institute. http://anfdata.urban.org/wrd/query/query.cfm
Percentage Black; percentage Hispanic; percentage foreign born	US Census Bureau, "Estimates of the Population by Race and Hispanic or Latino Origin for the United States and States." http://www.census.gov/popest/archives/
Unmarried births percentage	US Department of Health and Human Services, Centers for Disease Control and Prevention. "Demographic Characteristics of Mother by State/County." http://205.207.175.93/VitalStats/ReportFolders/ReportFolders.aspx
Percentage living in poverty; population receiving TANF; maximum TANF benefit	University of Kentucky Center for Poverty Research. http://www.ukcpr.org/data
Democratic governor; Democratic legislature	Klarner, Carl. 2003. "The Measurement of the Partisan Balance of State Government." *State Politics & Policy Quarterly* 3(3): 309–319.
Women in legislature	Center for American Women and Politics. http://www.cawp.rutgers.edu/facts/levels_of_office/state_legislature

to these relationships; maximum TANF benefit is positively correlated with citizen ideology and the percentage of women in the legislature. For each model, I also include a measure of the mean of the neighboring states' policies. According to the "race to the bottom" theory, states create stricter policies in order to compete with their neighbors; it is assumed that states with the most lenient policies will attract more welfare recipients looking for the most lenient program with the greatest benefits. Even if states are not "racing to the bottom," they do learn best practices from their neighbors, or from professional associations that bring together policymakers and bureaucrats from different states.

QUALITATIVE DATA

To supplement the quantitative data coded from the Welfare Rules Database and state interest group populations, I examined the extent to which interest groups are mentioned in reference to TANF policies in state legislature committee hearings. Winston collected information on interest group testimony in case studies on Texas, Maryland, and North Dakota before, during, and immediately after the passage of PRWORA.[12] She makes notes of which type of interest groups (professional associations, intergovernmental groups, etc.) were involved in the hearings, but does not focus on the specific welfare rule that each group testified about.

I improve upon Winston's method by compiling a larger sample, from more states and over a longer time frame. I collect information on which interest groups testify in front of the legislative committees and their positions on specific welfare rules. I also take note of how they frame welfare recipients (e.g., Are TANF recipients deserving of assistance?). Finally, I analyze how the legislators respond to this testimony to look for evidence of descriptive and substantive representation. This information is then used to expand upon the quantitative results and provide further insight into unique cases. This additional data provides specific examples of interest groups with defined constituencies lobbying on a limited number of welfare rules rather than becoming involved in the broader administration of the program. Moreover, by collecting data past the initial transition period from AFDC to TANF I am able to demonstrate that interest groups continued to lobby on welfare after the large federal policy change. The time period encompasses when a state's recipients hit the federally mandated sixty-month time limit, as well as when the federal government issued new regulations under the Deficit Reduction Act of 2005.

To select cases, I first searched state legislative websites for committee testimony, witness lists, or minutes from committee meetings. I could not find any of this information for thirteen states; in eight states, material was available beginning in 2010 or later.[13] After determining which states had that information publicly available, I selected states based on four variables, to the extent that variation was available: foreign-born population, Black population, party control, and change in welfare policy. The material covers the years 1996 (the year welfare reform was passed) to 2016 (the last year of the quantitative data analysis), though not all states have information for all years. Table A.6 provides the years of available data for each state.

I selected states with varying levels of foreign-born residents because previous work has shown mixed results in the relationship between immigration population and welfare policy. Some scholars have found that states with high immigrant populations have more flexible welfare policies because noncitizens have gained political clout; others find states have more stringent policies as a result of backlash from the white majority.[14] I expect that states with higher levels of immigration will have more interest groups representing immigrants, which may lead to more favorable welfare policies. The average foreign-born population for the time period (1997 to 2016) was 8.46 percent; as shown in table A.6, Connecticut, New Jersey, and Texas are significantly above that percentage, while other states, such as Idaho and South Dakota, are much lower than the average. Because welfare policy is so highly racialized in the United States, I also selected states with varying levels of Black population. The average Black percentage of the population from 1997 to 2018 was 10.77 percent. Similar to the foreign-born population statistics, New Jersey and Texas are above this average while Idaho and South Dakota fall far below it. Other states, such as Connecticut and Wisconsin, are below the average but still have a significant Black population. As mentioned above, previous research has shown that states have more restrictive policies when Blacks make up more of the population or a greater proportion of the caseload. According to the Racial Classification Model, policymakers create policy based on the stereotypes they hold of the policy's target group.[15] Therefore, in states where

Table A.6. States Used in Qualitative Analysis

State	Name of TANF program	Time period of qual. data available	Percent Foreign-born population (1997–2016)	Percent Black population (1997–2016)	Years of Dem. leg. control (1997–2016)	Number of policy changes (1997–2016)
Alaska	ATAP (Alaska Temporary Assistance Program)	1996–2020	6.79	3.96	0	3
Connecticut	TFA (Temporary Family Assistance)	1999–2020	12.99	10.25	20	2
Idaho	TAFI (Temporary Assistance for Families in Idaho)	2003–2020	5.69	0.71	0	3
Nebraska	ADC (Aid to Dependent Children)	1996–2020	5.56	4.52	NA	8
New Jersey	WFNJ (Work First New Jersey)	1996–2020	20.83	14.29	14	2
South Dakota	TANF	1997–2020	2.44	1.17	0	6
Texas	TANF	1997–2020	16.06	11.99	2	5
Wisconsin	W-2 (Wisconsin Works)	1999–2020	4.28	6.15	2	4
US Average			**8.46**	**10.76**	**8**	**5**

Blacks make up a large proportion of the caseload, we may expect more restrictive policy proposals; more restrictive proposals would shape the types of interest groups that come before the legislature to testify in favor of or against a policy change. I also expect that states with higher minority populations will have more interest groups representing those groups and lobbying on their behalf.

My qualitative sample includes both traditionally Republican and Democratic states. Connecticut's legislature was solidly Democratic during the entire time period, while Alaska, Idaho, and South Dakota had Republican-dominated legislatures. Other states switched party control, and in Wisconsin for much of the time period the legislature was divided. The majority party has control over the legislative agenda (both adding items to the agenda and keeping items off the agenda), so whether there even are hearings on proposed welfare policy changes may be dependent on the party in control. Moreover, conservative governments have been found to implement more stringent policies in general and more severe sanctions in particular.[16] Therefore, I anticipate that states with conservative legislatures will see more restrictive proposals than states with more liberal legislatures, which will in turn influence the interest groups called to testify before the legislature.

Finally, it is important to select both states in the sample that saw change in their welfare policy, and states that did not see a change. Table A.6 shows in how many of the following seven categories the state changed its policy at least once: family caps, behavioral requirements, allowable activities, activity exemptions, time limits, time limits exemptions and extensions, and immigrant eligibility.[17] On average, a state made changes to about five of these policy areas. Within my sample five states are below the mean, with Connecticut and New Jersey seeing the fewest policy changes. Two states are above the mean, with Nebraska changing its policy in every one of the areas counted, and one state, Texas, had exactly five policy changes.

Either the presence or absence of interest groups may explain why a state did not change its welfare rules. We may see no policy change because there was no interest group advocating for a change in policy. However, a state's unchanging welfare policy may also be the result of a fight between interest groups lobbying for and against the status quo, in which interest groups in favor of the status quo are successful. Interest group research has shown that factors of the policy process, such as the limited amount of time to cover a multitude of issues, provide advantages to defenders of the status quo.[18] California provides an example of this bias toward the status quo. In 2015, a wide array of organized interests, from Planned Parenthood to the US Catholic bishops, fought unsuccessfully to repeal the state's family cap policy.[19] A lack of policy change may indicate an absence of interest group advocacy, but it may also indicate an unsuccessful attempt at policy change.

APPENDIX B

Full Models

CHAPTER 3

Table B.1/A3.1. Behavioral Requirements: Interest Group Models

	Drug Screening	Immunization	Parenting Class	School Attendance	Total
Interest Groups					
Total interest groups	0.00	0.00	0.00	0.00	0.00
Feminist groups (% of total)	0.11	0.17	−0.16	0.06	−0.02
African American groups (% of total)	0.19	0.07	0.06	0.07	0.09
Civil rights groups (% of total)	−0.04	−0.10	−0.40	−0.38	−0.21
Social welfare groups (% of total)	−0.11	−0.01	0.03	0.08	−0.02
Social conservative groups (% of total)	−0.58	−0.08	−0.38	−0.01	−0.19
Econ. conservative groups (% of total)	−0.03	0.04	−0.54	0.28	−0.06
Health groups (% of total)	−0.02	0.00	–	–	0.00
Constant	−0.36	−0.54	0.33	0.18	2.07*
N	990	1020	1000	1020	1020

Note: Year dummy variables not shown; standard errors are clustered by state.

* $p < 0.05$; ** $p < 0.01$; *** $p < 0.001$

Table B.2/A3.2. Family Cap & Child Support Reporting: Interest Group Models

	Family Cap	Child Support Reporting Requirements
Total interest groups	0.00	−0.01
Feminist groups (% of total)	−0.18	0.02
African American groups (% of total)	0.33	0.09
Civil rights groups (% of total)	−0.07	0.04
Pro-life groups (% of total)	−0.36	−
Social conservative groups (% of total)	−0.55	0.49
Econ. conservative groups (% of total)	0.37	−0.04
Social welfare groups (% of total)	−0.20	−0.20*
Constant	−	7.46***
N	1020	1020

Note: Year dummy variables not shown; standard errors are clustered by state.

$* \ p < 0.05; \ ** \ p < 0.01; \ *** \ p < 0.001$

Table B.3/A3.3. Behavioral Requirements: Full Models, No Lags

	Drug Screening	Immuni-zation	Parenting Class	School Attendance	Total
Interest Groups					
Total interest groups	-0.01	-0.01	0.01	-0.02**	0.00
Feminist groups (% of total)	0.27	0.52	-0.19	1.14*	-0.38
African American groups (% of total)	0.06	-0.23	0.17	0.33	-0.17
Civil rights groups (% of total)	0.26	0.13	-0.31	-1.12***	0.11
Social welfare groups (% of total)	-0.06	-0.02	-0.02	0.67**	0.06
Social conservative groups (% of total)	-0.54	-0.05	0.63	2.77	1.51
Econ. conservative groups (% of total)	-0.10	-0.12	-1.11	0.06	-0.08
Health groups (% of total)	0.04	0.01	–	–	0.09
State Need					
Black population (%)	0.09	0.08	-0.11	-0.01	0.01
Hispanic population (%)	0.01	0.12*	-0.17*	0.32***	0.06
Population living in poverty (%)	0.09	0.11	-0.13	-0.29*	0.19
Unmarried births (%)	0.02	-0.02	0.28*	-0.11	-0.04
Population receiving TANF (%)	0.03	0.07	-0.61	-0.98*	-0.27
Political Environment					
Citizen ideology	-0.01	0.00	-0.01	-0.07*	-0.01
Women in legislature (%)	0.00	-0.02	0.14*	-0.34***	-0.02
Democratic governor	0.52	-0.48*	-0.75*	0.83	0.85
Democratic legislature	-0.70	0.71	0.22	-0.12	-0.72
Greater Welfare Context					
Maximum TANF benefit	0.00	0.00	0.00	0.00	0.01
Other behavioral requirements	0.73*	1.00*	1.20**	2.94***	–
Neighboring state policy	-0.48	-3.66*	-2.51	-8.90***	0.98
Constant	-5.42	-0.50	-8.57	21.11***	-2.75
N	906	936	916	936	936

Note: Year dummy variables not shown; standard errors are clustered by state.

* p < 0.05; ** p < 0.01; *** p < 0.001

Table B.4/A3.4. Family Cap & Child Support Reporting: Full Models, No Lags

	Family Cap	Child Support Reporting Requirements
Interest Groups		
Total interest groups	0.00	−0.01*
Feminist groups (% of total)	−0.43	0.08
African American groups (% of total)	0.19	0.19
Civil rights groups (% of total)	0.26	0.00
Pro-life groups (% of total)	−1.01*	−
Social conservative groups (% of total)	0.17	1.10*
Econ. conservative groups (% of total)	−0.01	0.08
Social welfare groups (% of total)	−0.13	−0.18*
State Need		
Black population (%)	0.13**	0.00
Hispanic population (%)	0.06	−0.01
Population living in poverty (%)	−0.16	0.00
Unmarried births (%)	0.05	0.11*
Population receiving TANF (%)	−0.08	0.06
Political Environment		
Citizen ideology	0.04	−0.03
Women in legislature (%)	−0.01	−0.02
Democratic legislature	0.57	−0.01
Democratic governor	0.00	0.28
Greater Welfare Context		
Maximum TANF benefit	−0.01*	0.01***
Other behavioral requirements	−0.15	−0.13
Neighboring state policy	−1.68**	0.22
Constant	−	1.18
N	936	976

Note: Year dummy variables not shown; standard errors are clustered by state.

* $p < 0.05$; ** $p < 0.01$; *** $p < 0.001$

CHAPTER 4

Table B.5/A4.1. Types of Welfare Recipients

	Age	Education	Child	Description
1	< 20	HS	< 6	Younger than 20 with a HS diploma and a child under six years old
2	< 20	HS	>= 6	Younger than 20 with a HS diploma and a child at least six years old
3	< 20	no HS	< 6	Younger than 20 without a HS diploma and a child under six years old
4	< 20	no HS	>= 6	Younger than 20 without a HS diploma and a child at least six years old
5	>= 20	HS	< 6	At least 20 with a HS diploma and a child under six years old
6	>= 20	HS	>= 6	At least 20 with a HS diploma and a child at least six years old
7	>= 20	no HS	< 6	At least 20 without a HS diploma and a child under six years old
8	>= 20	no HS	>= 6	At least 20 without a HS diploma and a child at least six years old

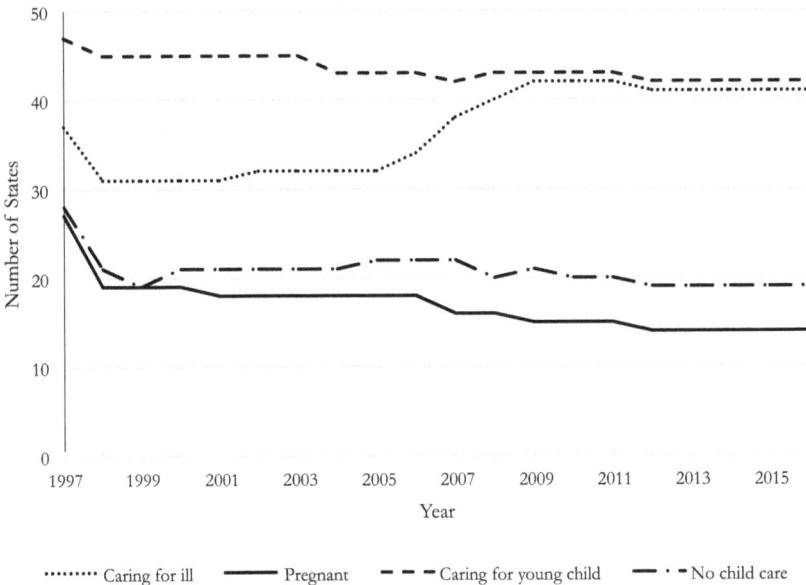

Figure B.1/A4.1. Caretaking Activity Exemptions over Time

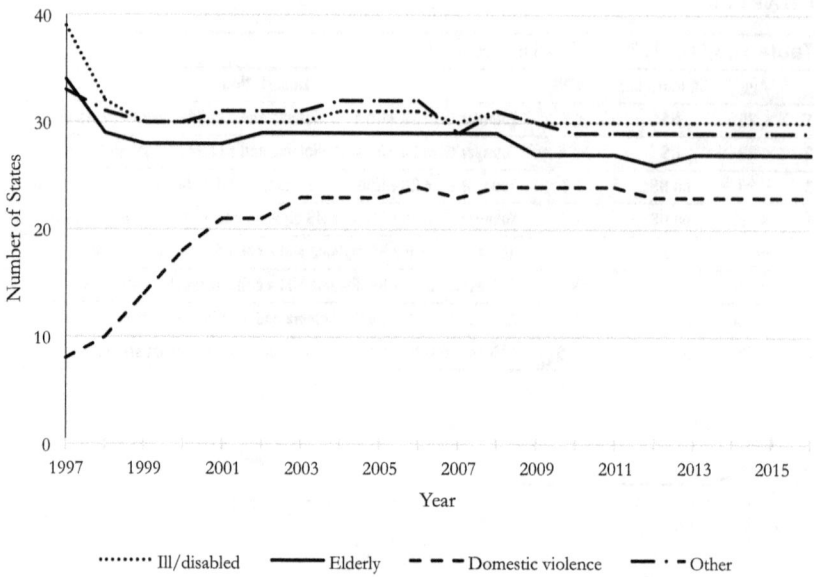

Figure B.2/A4.2. Self-Care Exemptions over Time

Table B.6/A4.2. Allowable Education Activities

	Basic Education	ESL Classes	High School Education	Postsecondary Education
Interest Groups				
Total interest groups	−0.01	0.00	−0.03***	0.01
Women's groups (% of total)	0.10	−0.36	−0.21	0.30
African American groups (% of total)	−0.12	0.36	−0.25	−0.32
Civil rights groups (% of total)	1.87***	0.54	0.98*	−0.10
Social welfare groups (% of total)	−0.20	−0.07	0.29	0.05
Pro-family groups (% of total)	0.59	0.69*	0.10	0.16
Econ. conservative groups (% of total)	0.16	0.89	−0.30	−0.29
Chambers of Commerce (% of total)	0.11	0.00	0.12	0.00
Industry groups (% of total)	−0.16	−0.20	−0.39*	−0.36*
Immigration groups (% of total)	–	0.34	–	–
Hispanic groups (% of total)	–	-1.11*	–	–
State Need				
Black population (%)	−0.13*	−0.10*	−0.16*	−0.09
Hispanic population (%)	−0.08	0.08	0.26*	−0.05
Foreign born population (%)	–	−0.03	–	–
Unemployment rate (%)	−0.61***	−0.46	−0.17	−0.52**
High school graduates (%)	−0.56**	−0.07	−0.39*	−0.15
Population receiving TANF (%)	0.27	0.06	0.66	0.08
Political Environment				
Citizen ideology	0.03	0.04	0.02	0.02
Women in legislature (%)	0.16*	0.06	−0.05	−0.11
Democratic governor	−0.76	−0.91*	0.07	0.24
Democratic legislature	0.23	−0.25	−0.10	−0.26
Greater Welfare Context				
Monthly TANF benefit	0.00	0.00	0.01	0.01
Neighboring state policy	−7.23**	−1.89	−21.03**	−5.07**
Constant	48.14**	10.19	52.53**	23.08*
N	936	936	936	934

Note: Year dummy variables not shown; standard errors are clustered by state.

* p < 0.05, ** p < 0.01, *** p < 0.001

Table B.7/A4.3. Allowable Self-Improvement Activities

	Providing Childcare	Counseling	Life Skills Training	Community Service	Other
Interest Groups					
Total interest groups	0.00	−0.01	−0.01	0.00	0.00
Women's groups (% of total)	−0.22	−0.16	0.09	0.39	−0.16
African American groups (% of total)	0.01	0.55*	0.07	0.09	0.20
Civil rights groups (% of total)	0.01	−0.11	−0.38	0.28	0.25
Social welfare groups (% of total)	−0.17	0.11	0.04	−0.08	0.18
Pro-family groups (% of total)	1.30**	0.47	0.42	0.78*	0.11
Econ. conservative groups (% of total)	−0.12	0.26	0.29	−0.82	0.48
Chambers of Commerce (% of total)	0.06	0.12	0.18*	0.10	0.22**
Industry groups (% of total)	0.12	−0.04	−0.24	0.06	−0.20
Immigration groups (% of total)	0.37	0.23	−0.38	0.30	0.35
Domestic violence groups (% of total)	−	−0.34	−	−	0.61
State Need					
Black population (%)	0.13	−0.08	−0.07	0.09	0.04
Hispanic population (%)	0.12*	0.02	−0.05	−0.09	0.00
Unemployment rate (%)	−0.31	−0.15	0.37	0.00	0.09
High school graduates (%)	0.10	0.11	0.06	−0.11	0.00
Population receiving TANF (%)	−0.05	0.59	0.42	−0.52	0.16
Political Environment					
Citizen ideology	0.05*	−0.01	0.01	−0.05	0.04
Women in legislature (%)	0.02	−0.03	0.02	0.04	0.05
Democratic governor	−0.34	−0.08	−0.18	−0.69*	−0.39
Democratic legislature	0.93*	0.83*	0.08	0.90	0.04
Greater Welfare Context					
Monthly TANF benefit	0.00	0.00	0.00	0.00	0.00
Neighboring state policy	1.78	−0.57	−1.86	−3.39**	−0.32
Constant	−17.16	−15.35	−10.57	5.47	−17.14
N	936	936	936	936	936

Note: Year dummy variables not shown; standard errors are clustered by state.

* $p < 0.05$, ** $p < 0.01$, *** $p < 0.001$

Table B.8/A4.4. Allowable Labor Market Activities

	Job Development Program	On-the-Job Training	Unsubsidized Job	Subsidized Job	Community Work Experience	Self-Employed
Interest Groups						
Total interest groups	0.00	0.00	−0.01	0.00	−0.01	0.01
Women's groups (% of total)	−0.59	−0.85*	−0.15	−0.07	0.26	0.21
African American groups (% of total)	−0.21	0.18	0.09	0.01	0.03	0.02
Civil rights groups (% of total)	−0.15	−0.08	0.89*	0.37	0.87**	0.24
Social welfare groups (% of total)	−0.33	−0.07	−0.74**	−0.08	0.25	−0.06
Pro-family groups (% of total)	0.20	0.10	1.46	0.49	1.62***	0.05
Econ. conservative groups (% of total)	0.17	1.14	0.38	−0.34	−0.54	0.03
Chambers of Commerce (% of total)	−0.09	−0.01	−0.06	0.03	0.05	0.03
Industry groups (% of total)	−0.46**	−0.15	0.31	0.11	−0.04	0.10
Immigration groups (% of total)	3.10**	1.43	0.26	0.00	−0.37	−1.13
Labor groups (% of total)	−0.21	−0.28*	−0.14	−0.12	−0.96***	−0.02
State Need						
Black population (%)	−0.12	−0.01	0.10	0.01	0.04	−0.03
Hispanic population (%)	−0.09	0.08	0.01	0.02	0.18*	−0.15**
Unemployment rate (%)	0.48	−0.08	−0.68**	−0.09	−0.22	−0.23
High school graduates (%)	0.07	0.16	0.09	0.07	0.14	−0.28*
Population receiving TANF (%)	0.42	0.77	1.08**	0.17	1.01*	0.33
Political Environment						
Citizen ideology	0.03	0.02	−0.06*	0.02	0.07**	−0.04
Women in legislature (%)	−0.02	−0.09	0.00	−0.02	−0.02	0.17***
Democratic governor	−0.95	0.13	−0.60	−0.47	0.80	−0.56
Democratic legislature	0.08	0.69	2.00***	1.23*	0.87*	0.21
Greater Welfare Context						
Monthly TANF benefit	0.00	0.01	0.00	0.00	0.00	0.00
Neighboring state policy	−0.66	−0.21	0.84	−1.84	1.01	−0.03
Constant	3.98	−8.67	−3.36	−5.22	−16.20	16.99
N	936	936	936	936	936	936

Note: Year dummy variables not shown; standard errors are clustered by state.

* $p < 0.05$, ** $p < 0.01$, *** $p < 0.001$

Table B.9/A4.5. Allowable Activity Scales

	Education	Labor Market	Self-Improvement
Interest Groups			
Total interest groups	0.00	0.00	−0.02
Civil rights groups (% of total)	0.69	0.69	0.68
Chambers of Commerce (% of total)	0.00	0.24	0.60*
Women's groups (% of total)	0.33	−1.07	0.78
Econ. conservative groups (% of total)	0.87	0.01	0.38
Pro-family groups (% of total)	0.78	2.27	3.89**
Immigration groups (% of total)	0.52	–	–
Labor groups (% of total)	−0.48	−1.32*	–
Industry groups (% of total)	−0.58*	−0.15	−0.20
Social welfare groups (% of total)	0.52	0.66	0.47
Domestic violence groups (% of total)	–	–	0.10
State Need			
Black population (%)	−0.35**	−0.09	0.13
Hispanic population (%)	0.00	0.14	−0.06
Foreign born population (%)	−0.12	–	–
Unemployment rate (%)	−1.47**	−1.07	−0.54
High school graduates (%)	−0.39	0.13	−0.09
Population receiving TANF (%)	0.48	1.62	−0.46
Political Environment			
Citizen ideology	0.14**	0.16	0.13
Women in legislature (%)	−0.04	−0.23	0.08
Democratic governor	−0.87	−2.69	−2.04
Democratic legislature	−0.69	3.50	3.11
Greater Welfare Context			
Monthly TANF benefit	0.00	0.00	0.01
Neighboring state policy	−6.92***	−1.51	−2.65*
Constant	–	–	–
N	936	936	936

Note: Year dummy variables not shown; standard errors are clustered by state.

* $p < 0.05$, ** $p < 0.01$, *** $p < 0.001$

Table B.10/A4.6. Caretaker Activity Exemptions

	Caring for Family with Illness or Disability	Caring for Young Child	No Childcare Available	Recipient Is Pregnant	Total Caretaking Exemptions
Interest Groups					
Total interest groups	−0.01	0.03***	0.00	−0.01	0.00
Women's groups (% of total)	−0.20	−0.51	0.41	−0.20	−0.01
African American groups (% of total)	−0.37	−0.39	−0.23	−0.85**	−0.15
Social welfare groups (% of total)	0.03	0.05	0.14	−0.07	−0.04
Civil rights groups (% of total)	0.34	0.45	0.56	0.57	0.10
Pro-family groups (% of total)	−0.20	0.85	0.75*	0.24	0.15
Econ. conservative groups (% of total)	−0.03	1.06	−0.46	0.28	0.02
Chambers of Commerce (% of total)	−0.13	0.04	0.02	−0.11	0.01
Industry groups (% of total)	−0.04	0.62**	−0.11	0.07	0.01
Labor groups (% of total)	0.08	0.64	0.11	0.71**	0.20**
Health groups (% of total)	−0.14	–	–	−0.17	−0.06
Disability rights groups (% of total)	−0.35	–	–	–	0.02
State Need					
Black population (%)	0.10	0.32**	−0.07	0.04	0.02
Hispanic population (%)	0.03	−0.01	−0.03	0.16**	0.02
Unemployment rate (%)	−0.01	0.15	0.70***	0.15	0.08
Population receiving TANF (%)	0.97**	2.40***	−0.33	−0.18	0.00
Unmarried birthrate	–	–	–	−0.04	0.02
Political Environment					
Citizen ideology	0.04	0.06*	0.02	0.08*	0.02*
Women in legislature (%)	−0.03	−0.03	−0.02	−0.06	−0.02
Democratic governor	−0.02	0.64	0.14	0.91*	0.12
Democratic legislature	0.51	0.34	0.03	0.91	0.15
Greater Welfare Context					
Monthly TANF benefit	0.00	0.00	0.00	−0.01*	0.00
Neighboring state policy	1.59	−8.32**	−7.06***	−3.85**	−0.04
Constant	4.02	−18.77*	−1.95	3.19	−0.20
N	936	936	928	936	976

Note: Year dummy variables not shown; standard errors are clustered by state.

* p < 0.05, ** p < 0.01, *** p < 0.001

Table B.11/A4.7. Other Activity Exemptions

	Recipient with Illness or Disability	Recipient Elderly	Domestic Violence	Recipient Working	Other Exemptions	Total Exemptions
Interest Groups						
Total interest groups	0.00	0.00	0.00	0.01	0.02***	0.00
Women's groups (% of total)	−0.04	−0.44	−0.29	−0.12	0.34	−0.09
African American groups (% of total)	−0.21	−0.51	−0.92**	0.57*	−0.48	−0.40
Social welfare groups (% of total)	−0.06	−0.10	0.57**	0.16	−0.04	0.03
Civil rights groups (% of total)	0.06	−0.19	0.42	−0.41	−0.44	0.06
Pro-family groups (% of total)	0.09	−0.54	1.57***	0.77*	0.17	0.42
Econ. conservative groups (% of total)	0.12	0.17	0.22	0.90*	0.61	0.31
Chambers of Commerce (% of total)	−0.18	−0.05	0.01	−0.11	−0.07	−0.03
Industry groups (% of total)	−0.10	−0.02	0.28*	−0.02	0.18	0.09
Labor groups (% of total)	0.08	0.22	0.03	−0.23	−0.01	0.26*
Health groups (% of total)	−0.32**	−0.04	–	–	0.02	−0.10
Disability rights groups (% of total)	−0.10	−0.36*	–	–	–	−0.05
Senior citizen groups (% of total)	–	0.19	–	–	–	0.24
Domestic violence groups (% of total)	–	–	−0.69	–	–	−0.14
State Need						
Black population (%)	0.09	0.05	0.23***	−0.10	0.00	0.07
Hispanic population (%)	0.02	0.06	0.10	−0.05	−0.06	0.03
Unemployment rate (%)	−0.34	0.10	0.57*	0.54***	−0.15	0.10
Population receiving TANF (%)	0.88*	0.29	−0.04	−0.19	−0.38	0.09
Unmarried birthrate	–	–	–	–	–	0.02
Political Environment						
Citizen ideology	0.04	0.03	0.07*	0.06	0.02	0.06**
Women in legislature (%)	−0.10*	−0.04	−0.02	−0.05	0.09	−0.03
Democratic governor	0.31	0.20	0.84*	−0.91*	−1.19***	−0.01
Democratic legislature	0.51	0.39	1.05	−0.96	1.61**	0.74*
Greater Welfare Context						
Monthly TANF benefit	0.00	0.00	0.00	0.01	−0.01*	0.00
Neighboring state policy	1.55	0.27	−5.42***	−4.33*	−2.65*	−0.14
Constant	8.59	4.07	−18.25*	0.12	2.83	1.04
N	936	936	936	936	936	936

Note: Year dummy variables not shown; standard errors are clustered by state.

* p < 0.05, ** p < 0.01, *** p < 0.001

Table B.12/A4.8. Alternate Model Specifications

	Length (Months) of Caring for a Young Child Exemption	Month Pregnancy Exemption Begins
Interest Groups		
Total interest groups	0.01	−0.02
Women's groups (% of total)	−0.72	−0.30
African American groups (% of total)	1.41**	−1.08
Social welfare groups (% of total)	0.05	−0.57
Civil rights groups (% of total)	−2.90***	0.47
Pro-family groups (% of total)	−0.81	0.93
Econ. conservative groups (% of total)	3.29***	3.38**
Chambers of Commerce (% of total)	0.12	−0.34**
Industry groups (% of total)	−0.08	0.11
Labor groups (% of total)	0.24	0.47**
Health groups (% of total)	−	−0.53
State Need		
Black population (%)	−0.19	0.03
Hispanic population (%)	0.16	0.09
Unemployment rate (%)	−0.61	−0.29
Population receiving TANF (%)	1.00	0.44
Unmarried birthrate	−	−0.21
Political Environment		
Citizen ideology	0.11	0.03
Women in legislature (%)	−0.08	0.09
Democratic governor	1.43**	0.16
Democratic legislature	−0.92	−0.75
Greater Welfare Context		
Monthly TANF benefit	0.01	−0.01
Neighboring state policy	11.71	−1.12
Constant	3.17	−
N	787	297

Note: Year dummy variables not shown; standard errors are clustered by state.
* $p < 0.05$, ** $p < 0.01$, *** $p < 0.001$

CHAPTER 5

(a) Recipient is ill/disabled

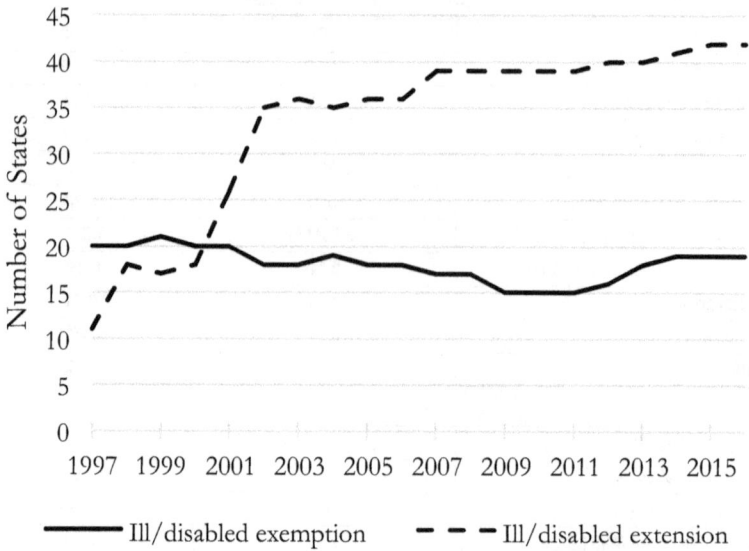

(b) Recipient caring for ill/disabled relative

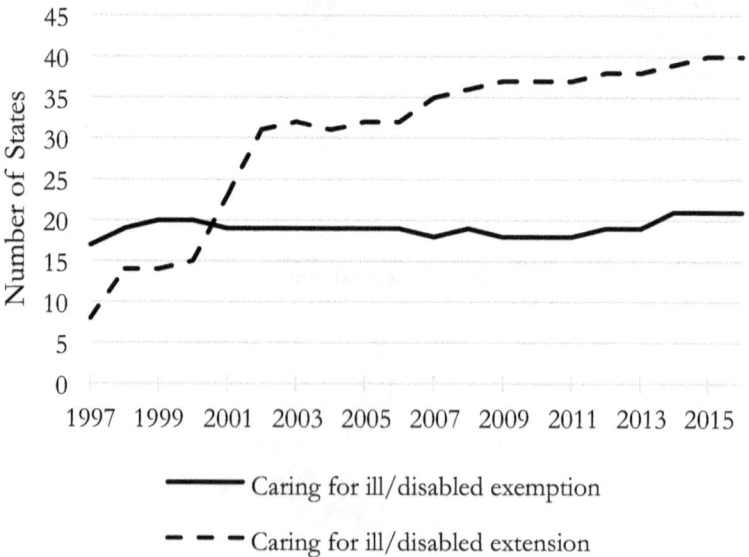

Figures B.3a–j/A5.1a–j. Time Limit Extensions and Exemptions over Time

(c) Recipient is elderly

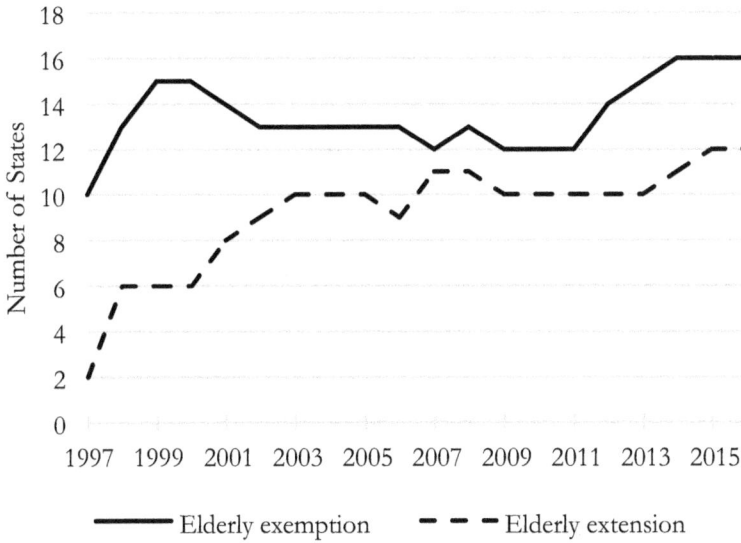

Elderly exemption — — — Elderly extension

(d) Recipient is receiving treatment

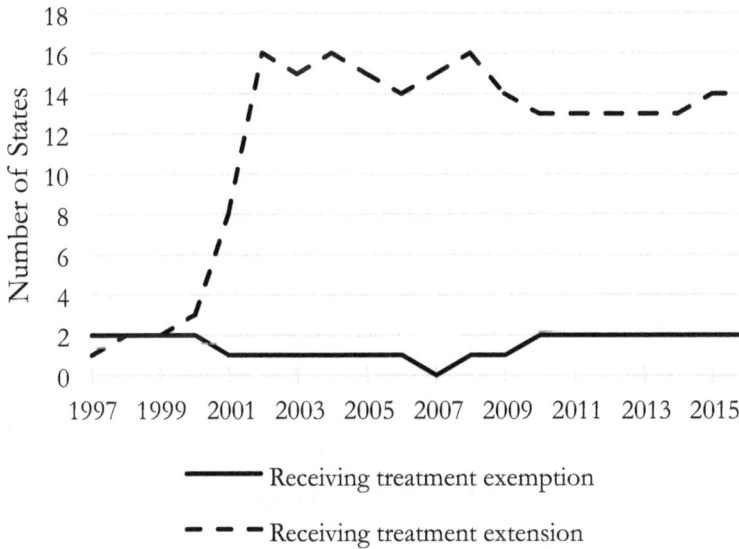

Receiving treatment exemption

— — — Receiving treatment extension

Figures B.3a–j/A5.1a–j. (*continued*)

(e) Recipient is caring for young child

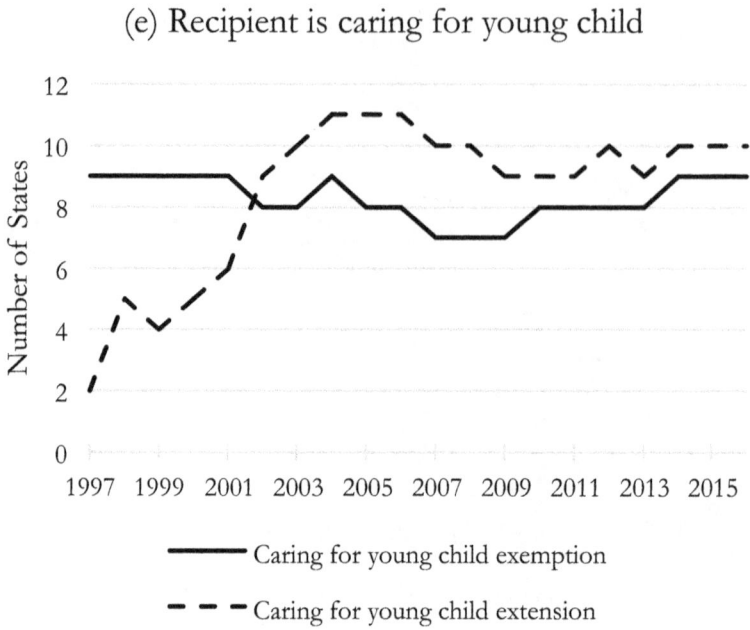

Caring for young child exemption

Caring for young child extension

(f) Recipient experienced domestic violence

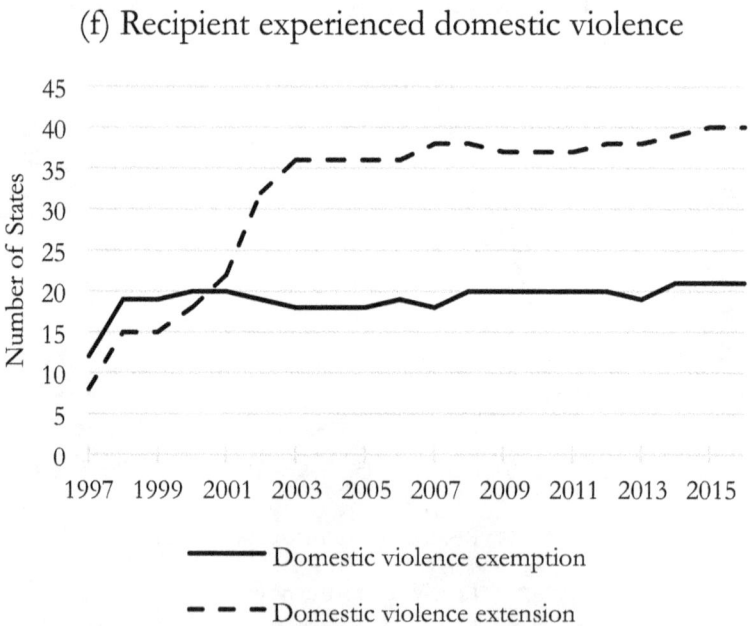

Domestic violence exemption

Domestic violence extension

Figures B.3a–j/A5.1a–j. (*continued*)

(g) Recipient lacks support services

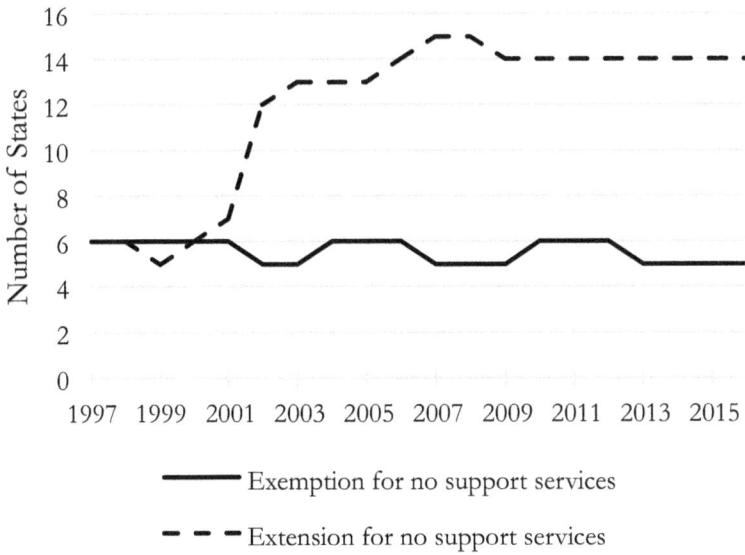

Exemption for no support services

Extension for no support services

(h) Recipient lives in area with high unemployment

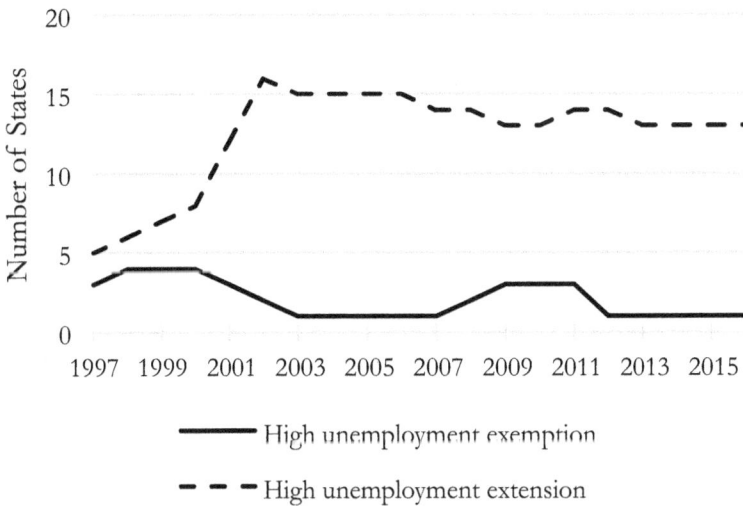

High unemployment exemption

High unemployment extension

Figures B.3a–j/A5.1a–j. (*continued*)

(i) Recipient works in unsubsidized job

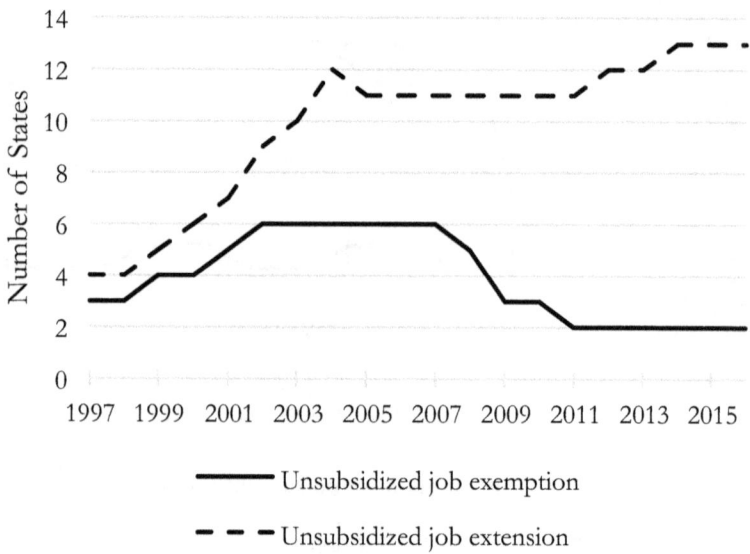

Unsubsidized job exemption

Unsubsidized job extension

(j) Recipient is cooperating

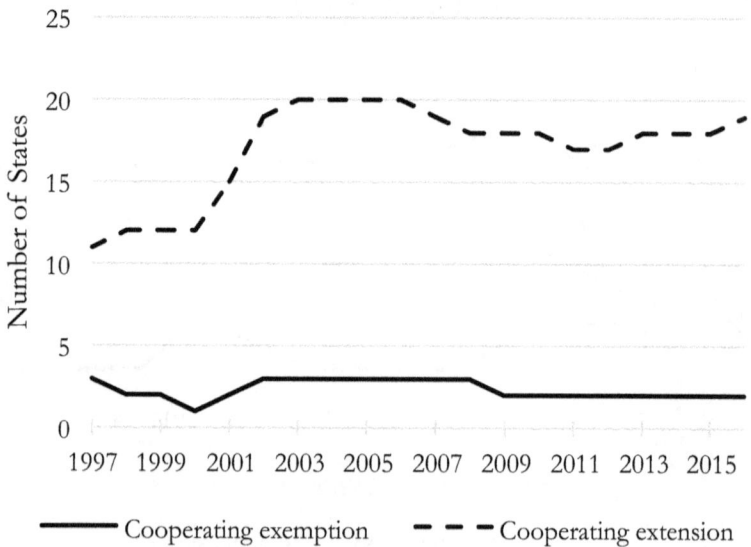

Cooperating exemption

Cooperating extension

Figures B.3a–j/A5.1a–j. (*continued*)

Table B.13/A5.1. Time Limits: Interest Groups Model

Interest Groups	Lifetime Limit	Other Time Limit	Benefits over 60-Month Period
Total interest groups	−0.01	0.01	0.00
Social welfare groups (% of total)	0.03	0.53*	0.37*
Civil rights groups (% of total)	0.29	0.07	0.25
African American groups (% of total)	0.69*	0.13	0.55*
Women's groups (% of total)	0.41	0.45*	0.56**
Domestic violence groups (% of total)	−0.02	0.09	0.02
Disability rights groups (% of total)	0.29	0.17	0.34**
Senior citizen groups (% of total)	0.01	0.06	0.06
Health groups (% of total)	0.01	0.25	0.25*
Pro-family groups (% of total)	0.66	−0.34	0.20
Econ. conservative groups (% of total)	0.71	0.18	0.16
Chambers of Commerce (% of total)	0.22**	0.10	0.26***
Industry groups (% of total)	0.21	0.03	0.22*
Constant	−14.71	−14.74	–
N	1020	1020	1020

Note: Year dummy variables not shown; standard errors are clustered by state.

* $p < 0.05$, ** $p < 0.01$, *** $p < 0.001$

Table B.14/A5.2. Time Limits

	Lifetime Limit	Other Time Limit	Stringency over 60-Month Period
Interest Groups			
Total interest groups	−0.03***	0.02	0.00
Social welfare groups (% of total)	−0.16	0.46	0.30
Civil rights groups (% of total)	−0.66	0.23	0.39
African American groups (% of total)	0.29	−0.13	0.30
Women's groups (% of total)	−0.07	0.70	0.59**
Domestic violence groups (% of total)	−0.54	−0.09	−0.17
Disability rights groups (% of total)	0.39	−0.05	0.26
Senior citizen groups (% of total)	−0.91	0.36	0.14
Health groups (% of total)	−0.39	0.36	0.16
Pro-family groups (% of total)	−0.53	−0.97	0.13
Econ. conservative groups (% of total)	0.18	0.34	−0.14
Chambers of Commerce (% of total)	0.16	−0.16	0.13
Industry groups (% of total)	0.04	−0.09	0.15
State Need			
Black population (%)	0.40*	−0.10	−0.01
Hispanic population (%)	0.13	−0.13	−0.01
Unemployment rate (%)	−0.27	−0.09	0.25
Population receiving TANF (%)	0.03	−0.27	−1.24***
Political Environment			
Citizen ideology	−0.13***	0.03	0.01
Women in legislature (%)	−0.16	−0.08	0.01
Democratic governor	−1.02*	0.06	−0.17
Democratic legislature	−1.81*	−0.06	−0.19
Greater Welfare Context			
Monthly TANF benefit	0.00	−0.01**	−0.01
Neighboring state policy	−5.28**	5.39**	0.27
Constant	17.88	−0.74	−
N	936	936	936

Note: Year dummy variables not shown; standard errors are clustered by state.
* p < 0.05, ** p < 0.01, *** p < 0.001

Table B.15/A5.3. Time Limit Extensions: Interest Groups Model

	Caring for Family with Illness or Disability	Caring for Child	Elderly	Recipient with Illness or Disability	Domestic Violence	No Support Services	Receiving Treatment	High Local Unemployment	Unsubsidized Job	Cooperating
	(1)	(2)	(3)	(4)	(5)	(6)	(7)	(8)	(9)	(10)
Interest Groups										
Total interest groups	0.00	0.00	0.01	0.00	0.00	0.00	0.00	0.00	0.00	0.00
Social welfare groups (% of total)	−0.09	0.33	0.21	0.06	0.07	−0.23	−0.09	−0.26	−0.40	−0.13
Civil rights groups (% of total)	−0.46*	0.05	−0.47	−0.25	−0.22	−0.58	−0.55	−0.69**	0.19	−0.40*
African American groups (% of total)	−0.30	0.02	−0.46	−0.14	−0.09	0.15	−0.17	0.09	−0.13	0.21
Women's groups (% of total)	−0.13	−0.16	−0.15	−0.12	−0.15	−0.35	−0.72*	−0.44*	0.17	−0.19
Pro-family groups (% of total)	−0.48	−0.10	−0.61	−0.48	−0.12	−0.22	−1.16**	−0.71	−0.69	−0.69
Econ. conservative groups (% of total)	0.55	0.35	1.16**	0.53	−0.01	0.29	0.55	0.40	0.49	0.12
Chambers of Commerce (% of total)	−0.06	0.01	−0.06	0.00	0.04	−0.11	−0.11	−0.06	−0.10	−0.01
Industry groups (% of total)	−0.02	0.00	−0.06	0.04	−0.06	−0.29	−0.24	−0.25*	−0.21	−0.28*
Health groups (% of total)	−0.10	−0.10	−0.10	−0.01	−	−	−0.05	−	−	−
Disability rights groups (% of total)	−0.19	−	0.01	−0.06	−	−	−0.19	−	−	−
Elderly groups (% of total)	−	−	0.31	−	−	−	−	−	−	−
Domestic violence groups (% of total)	−	−	−	−	−0.11	−	−	−	−	−
Constant	6.47	−4.26	−0.64	0.40	−1.65	7.51	9.17	6.70	4.20	4.30
N	952	941	925	943	944	940	915	935	934	934

Note: Year dummy variables not shown; standard errors are clustered by state.

* $p < 0.05$, ** $p < 0.01$, *** $p < 0.001$

Table B.16/A5.4. Time Limit Extensions: Full Model

	Caring for Family with Illness or Disability	Caring for Child	Elderly	Recipient with Illness or Disability	Domestic Violence	No Support Services	Receiving Treatment	High Local Unemployment	Unsubsidized Job	Cooperating
	(1)	(2)	(3)	(4)	(5)	(6)	(7)	(8)	(9)	(10)
Interest Groups										
Total interest groups	−0.01*	0.00	0.00	−0.01	0.00	0.00	0.00	0.01	0.01	0.00
Social welfare groups (% of total)	−0.07	0.54*	0.08	−0.02	0.01	−0.29	−0.49	−0.31*	−0.89**	−0.28
Civil rights groups (% of total)	−0.69**	0.30	−0.24	−0.34	−0.53*	−0.23	−0.50	−0.75**	−0.31	−0.50
African American groups (% of total)	−0.44	0.13	−1.27*	−0.41	0.32	−0.23	−0.84	−0.04	0.42	0.26
Women's groups (% of total)	−0.25	0.31	−0.59	−0.28	−0.65**	−0.10	−0.93	−0.17	0.34	−0.01
Pro-family groups (% of total)	−0.88*	−0.50	−1.31	−0.71	−0.28	−0.04	−1.56**	−0.68	−2.37***	−0.92
Econ. conservative groups (% of total)	0.03	0.80	0.82	−0.21	0.19	0.05	0.51	0.53	1.19*	0.43
Chambers of Commerce (% of total)	0.00	−0.04	−0.05	−0.02	0.04	−0.21	−0.36*	−0.11	−0.40***	−0.16
Industry groups (% of total)	−0.03	0.09	0.02	−0.01	−0.05	−0.36	−0.36*	−0.28*	−0.67**	−0.36*
Health groups (% of total)	−0.11	0.06	−0.25	−0.08	−	−	−0.19	−	−	−
Disability rights groups (% of total)	−0.19		−0.04	−0.12	−	−	−0.57	−	−	−
Elderly groups (% of total)	−	−	−0.42	−	−	−	−	−	−	−
Domestic violence groups (% of total)	−	−	−	−	−0.43	−	−	−	−	−
State Need										
Black population (%)	0.05	−0.09	0.07	0.08	−0.08	0.05	0.14	0.01	−0.25**	−0.05
Hispanic population (%)	0.20*	−0.12	0.11	0.23*	0.09	−0.01	−0.05	−0.04	−0.17**	−0.09*
Unemployment rate (%)	−0.04	0.45	−0.11	0.02	0.41	−0.48*	0.48	−0.16	0.12	0.22
Population receiving TANF (%)	−0.15	−0.59	1.42***	−0.28	0.25	−0.86	0.33	−0.49	−0.56	−0.59
Political Environment										
Citizen ideology	−0.06*	0.08**	0.06	−0.04	−0.05	0.01	−0.04	0.02	−0.04	−0.01
Women in legislature (%)	−0.01	−0.06	0.10	−0.03	−0.03	0.06	0.05	−0.03	−0.08	−0.04
Democratic governor	0.45	0.34	−0.46	0.42	−0.20	−0.48	0.44	−0.10	−0.04	0.00
Democratic legislature	0.33	1.67**	0.63	0.27	−0.25	1.11*	0.69	−0.10	0.17	0.83
Greater Welfare Context										
TANF benefit	0.01	−0.01	−0.01	0.00	0.00	−0.01*	0.00	0.00	0.00	0.00
Neighboring state policy	−6.05***	−9.55**	−1.23	−3.69*	−3.82*	−2.04	−1.61	0.03	−1.24	−0.89
Constant	7.95	−9.53	−1.12	7.14	0.77	16.03	24.44	10.71	30.44***	14.17*
N	882	870	852	873	887	882	865	885	874	874

Note: Year dummy variables not shown; standard errors are clustered by state.

* $p < 0.05$, ** $p < 0.01$, *** $p < 0.001$

Table B.17/A5.5. Time Limit Exemptions: Interest Groups Model

	Caring for Family with Illness or Disability	Caring for Child	Elderly	Recipient with Illness or Disability	Domestic Violence	No Support Services	Unsubsidized Job
	(1)	(2)	(3)	(4)	(5)	(6)	(7)
Interest Groups							
Total interest groups	0.01	0.00	0.00	0.00	0.00	0.01*	0.01
Social welfare groups (% of total)	−0.13	−0.33	−0.28	−0.14	0.04	0.53	0.26
Civil rights groups (% of total)	−0.01	−0.06	0.11	−0.18	−0.14	0.00	−0.41
African American groups (% of total)	0.22	0.16	0.08	0.37	0.04	0.67*	0.20
Women's groups (% of total)	0.01	0.03	−0.08	0.08	−0.07	0.02	0.62
Pro-family groups (% of total)	−0.05	−0.35	−0.06	−0.32	−0.13	−1.67	0.55
Econ. conservative groups (% of total)	0.28	−0.33	0.27	−0.20	−0.09	0.77*	−1.25
Chambers of Commerce (% of total)	0.01	0.04	−0.10	0.06	−0.06	0.35	0.01
Industry groups (% of total)	0.06	−0.17	−0.01	0.04	0.01	0.22	−0.27
Health groups (% of total)	0.14	−0.04	−0.07	0.28*	–	–	–
Disability rights groups (% of total)	0.21	–	0.08	0.22	–	–	–
Elderly groups (% of total)	–	–	−0.20	–	–	–	–
Domestic violence groups (% of total)	–	–	–	–	−0.15	–	–
Constant	−5.16	1.58	3.64	−6.81	1.53	−21.11	−4.91
N	948	916	909	907	952	939	943

Note: Year dummy variables not shown; standard errors are clustered by state.
* $p < 0.05$, ** $p < 0.01$, *** $p < 0.001$

Table B.18/A5.6. Time Limit Exemptions: Full Models

	Caring for Family with Illness or Disability	Caring for Child	Elderly	Recipient with Illness or Disability	Domestic Violence	No Support Services	Unsubsidized Job
	(1)	(2)	(3)	(4)	(5)	(6)	(7)
Interest Groups							
Total interest groups	0.01**	0.04***	0.01	0.01*	0.01	0.12***	0.03**
Social welfare groups (% of total)	−0.21	−0.67*	−0.40	−0.10	−0.02	1.31**	0.35
Civil rights groups (% of total)	0.16	0.50	0.20	0.01	0.03	2.80**	−1.64**
African American groups (% of total)	0.15	0.93*	0.09	0.37	−0.21	−0.95	−0.43
Women's groups (% of total)	−0.09	−1.02	−0.39	0.28	0.29	1.36*	1.89***
Pro-family groups (% of total)	−0.32	−0.39	−0.36	−0.37	−0.24	−2.81***	0.11
Econ. conservative groups (% of total)	0.30	1.23	0.46	−0.19	−0.25	−1.49	−2.49*
Chambers of Commerce (% of total)	−0.01	0.53	−0.07	0.08	−0.10	0.81***	−0.25
Industry groups (% of total)	0.12	−0.37	0.07	0.14	0.03	1.97***	−0.66*
Health groups (% of total)	0.15	−0.30	0.00	0.36**	−	−	−
Disability rights groups (% of total)	0.18	−	−0.07	0.24	−	−	−
Elderly groups (% of total)	−	−	−0.48	−	−	−	−
Domestic violence groups (% of total)	−	−	−	−	0.11	−	−
State Need							
Black population (%)	−0.05	−0.09	−0.08	−0.04	0.02	0.41**	0.03
Hispanic population (%)	−0.03	−0.11	−0.01	−0.05	−0.10*	−0.44*	−0.19**
Unemployment rate (%)	0.10	0.11	−0.29	−0.04	0.06	0.92**	0.38
Population receiving TANF (%)	−0.18	0.20	0.68*	0.07	−0.26	−2.07*	−1.57***
Political Environment							
Citizen ideology	0.08*	0.08	0.08**	0.03	0.03	−0.05	0.07
Women in legislature (%)	0.04	0.09	0.01	−0.01	0.04	0.05	−0.09
Democratic governor	0.26	−0.51	−1.14***	0.39	0.26	−0.36	−1.76
Democratic legislature	0.99	2.14***	1.75**	1.17*	1.32**	1.75**	−0.01
Greater Welfare Context							
TANF benefit	−0.01*	−0.01*	−0.01**	−0.01	0.00	−0.04**	−0.01
Neighboring state policy	−1.13	−17.22**	−1.66	−0.66	−1.07	2.59	−5.33
Constant	−4.77	−15.03	3.27	−9.91	0.53	−70.61***	−5.51
N	877	849	843	840	881	881	870

Note: Year dummy variables not shown; standard errors are clustered by state.

* p < 0.05, ** p < 0.01, *** p < 0.001

CHAPTER 6

Table B.19/A6.1. Type of Noncitizens Allowed: Interest Group Models

	Legal Perma-nent Resident	Refugee/ Asy-lum Seeker	Granted Stay of Deportation	Parolee	Battered Immigrant
Interest Groups					
Total interest groups	−0.01	0.00	−0.01	−0.01	0.00
Women's groups (% of total)	0.22	0.50*	0.24	0.79**	−0.05
African American groups (% of total)	−0.48	−0.02	−0.22	−0.15	−0.17
Civil rights groups (% of total)	0.24	0.28	0.30	0.52	0.09
Social welfare groups (% of total)	0.49	0.01	0.08	0.36	0.15
Pro-family groups (% of total)	0.06	0.32	−0.07	0.03	0.19
Hispanic groups (% of total)	0.38	−1.20***	−0.60	−0.19	0.60
Immigration groups (% of total)	0.90	0.95	2.10	0.57	0.17
Econ. conservative groups (% of total)	−0.71	−0.32	−0.37	−0.92*	−0.38
Chambers of Commerce (% of total)	0.06	−0.14	−0.09	0.05	−0.04
Industry groups (% of total)	−0.09	−0.04	−0.16	0.13	0.09
Domestic violence groups (% of total)	–	–	–	–	−0.02
N	1106	1106	1106	1106	1097

Note: Year dummy variables not shown; standard errors are clustered by state.

* $p < 0.05$, ** $p < 0.01$, *** $p < 0.001$

Table B.20/A6.2. Income Deeming: Interest Group Models

	Undocumented Parent	Sponsor
Total interest groups	0.01*	0.00
Women's groups (% of total)	0.24	0.56
African American groups (% of total)	0.46*	−0.37
Civil rights groups (% of total)	0.05	0.36
Social welfare groups (% of total)	−0.23	0.51**
Pro-family groups (% of total)	−0.22	0.29
Hispanic groups (% of total)	−1.19*	0.40
Immigration groups (% of total)	0.30	−0.61
Econ. conservative groups (% of total)	0.80	−0.65
Chambers of Commerce (% of total)	−0.12	0.13*
Industry groups (% of total)	−0.38*	−0.12
Constant	4.29	−7.64*
N	918	918

Note: Year dummy variables not shown; standard errors are clustered by state.

* $p < 0.05$, ** $p < 0.01$, *** $p < 0.001$

Table B.21/A6.3. Types of Noncitizens Allowed: Full Models

	Legal Permanent Resident	Refugee/ Asylum Seeker	Granted Stay of Deportation	Parolee	Battered Immigrant
Total interest groups	−0.05**	0.00	−0.02**	−0.04	−0.01*
Women's groups (% of total)	0.24	1.09**	0.79	2.22	−0.35
African American groups (% of total)	−0.22	0.65	0.77*	2.20*	0.08
Civil rights groups (% of total)	−1.64**	−0.40	−0.76	−1.56*	−0.45
Social welfare groups (% of total)	0.84***	0.08	0.26	0.26	0.13
Pro-family groups (% of total)	−0.26	1.20*	0.09	−0.68	0.19
Hispanic groups (% of total)	0.55	−3.64***	−1.85***	−2.18	1.65*
Immigration groups (% of total)	−0.58	−1.05	1.11	−3.14	−0.83
Econ. conservative groups (% of total)	−0.34	−0.37	−0.56	0.36	−0.37
Chambers of Commerce (% of total)	0.39***	0.06	0.15	0.47**	0.09
Industry groups (% of total)	−0.48*	0.00	−0.23	0.34	0.00
Domestic violence groups (% of total)	–	–	–	–	0.06
State Need					
Black population (%)	−0.18	−0.08	−0.19**	−0.34*	−0.07
Hispanic population (%)	−0.44*	−0.10	−0.18*	−.55*	−0.14*
Foreign-born population (%)	1.91**	0.90***	0.64***	1.58*	0.28**
Unemployment rate (%)	−0.70*	−0.09	−0.68**	0.20	0.30
Population receiving TANF (%)	0.82	1.12*	1.14**	2.91*	0.67*
Political Environment					
Citizen ideology	0.00	0.06*	0.05	−0.04	−0.02
Women in legislature (%)	−0.37**	−0.19**	−0.09	0.04	0.01
Democratic governor	2.11***	1.85***	1.34***	1.77	0.26
Democratic legislature	0.57	−0.09	0.24	−1.60	−0.43
Greater Welfare Context					
Monthly TANF benefit	0.03**	0.01***	0.01	0.04**	0.01*
Neighboring state policy	−3.87*	−4.16***	−6.12***	−4.97**	−1.65**
N	923	923	923	923	914

Note: Year dummy variables not shown; standard errors are clustered by state.

* $p < 0.05$, ** $p < 0.01$, *** $p < 0.001$

Table B.22/A6.4. Income Deeming: Full Models

	Undocumented Parent	Sponsor	Time for Sponsor Deeming
Total interest groups	0.01	−0.04*	−0.02*
Women's groups (% of total)	0.29	−0.06	0.30
African American groups (% of total)	0.89**	−0.75	−0.86**
Civil rights groups (% of total)	−0.73	1.12**	0.48
Social welfare groups (% of total)	−0.35	0.83**	0.38
Pro-family groups (% of total)	−0.33	0.59	0.40
Hispanic groups (% of total)	−0.90	3.99*	1.85**
Immigration groups (% of total)	−0.54	0.57	0.94
Econ. conservative groups (% of total)	0.49	−1.38	−1.14**
Chambers of Commerce (% of total)	−0.04	0.06	0.14
Industry groups (% of total)	−0.64**	−0.34*	−0.03
State Need			
Black population (%)	−0.01	0.03	0.13*
Hispanic population (%)	−0.36***	−0.04	−0.01
Foreign-born population (%)	0.58***	0.18	0.03
Unemployment rate (%)	−0.26	0.16	0.23
Population receiving TANF (%)	−0.17	0.79	−0.30
Political Environment			
Citizen ideology	0.05	−0.11**	−0.05*
Women in legislature (%)	−0.16**	0.01	−0.02
Democratic governor	−0.73	−0.65	−0.41
Democratic legislature	−0.76	1.11*	1.04*
Greater Welfare Context			
Monthly TANF benefit	0.00	0.00	0.01*
Neighboring state policy	−5.59**	1.28	1.88
Constant	10.56	−4.94	−
N	842	842	807

Note: Year dummy variables not shown; standard errors are clustered by state.

* p < 0.05, ** p < 0.01, *** p < 0.001

Table B.23/A6.5. Types of Noncitizens Allowed: Latino Legislative Representation

	Legal Permanent Resident	Refugee/ Asylum Seeker	Granted Stay of Deportation	Parolee	Battered Immigrant
Total interest groups	−0.05**	0.00	−0.02**	−0.04	−0.01
Women's groups (% of total)	0.24	0.96*	0.71	2.24	−0.36
African American groups (% of total)	−0.22	0.64	0.81*	2.17*	0.10
Civil rights groups (% of total)	−1.64***	−0.37	−0.83*	−1.54*	−0.46
Social welfare groups (% of total)	0.84***	0.10	0.27	0.26	0.13
Pro-family groups (% of total)	−0.26	1.17*	−0.09	−0.70	0.15
Hispanic groups (% of total)	0.55	−3.59***	−1.69**	−2.24	1.68*
Immigration groups (% of total)	−0.58	−1.02	0.87	−3.27	−0.87
Econ. conservative groups (% of total)	−0.34	−0.40	−0.53	0.37	−0.33
Chambers of Commerce (% of total)	0.39***	0.07	0.16*	0.47*	0.09
Industry groups (% of total)	−0.48*	0.02	−0.22	0.37	0.00
Domestic violence groups (% of total)	–	–	–	–	0.07
State Need					
Black population (%)	−0.18	−0.10	−0.24***	−0.35	−0.08
Hispanic population (%)	−0.44	−0.36*	−0.58**	−0.62	−0.22
Foreign-born population (%)	1.91***	1.11***	0.95***	1.67	0.32*
Unemployment rate (%)	−0.70*	−0.05	−0.69**	0.22	0.32
Population receiving TANF (%)	0.82	1.02*	1.19**	2.93**	0.59
Political Environment					
Citizen ideology	0.00	0.05	0.03	−0.04	−0.02
Latinx in legislature (%)	0.00	0.25	0.36**	0.06	0.08
Women in legislature (%)	−0.37*	−0.18**	−0.08	0.04	0.02
Democratic governor	2.11***	1.79***	1.19**	1.78	0.24
Democratic legislature	0.57	−0.21	0.01	−1.59	−0.42
Greater Welfare Context					
Monthly TANF benefit	0.03**	0.01**	0.00	0.04*	0.01*
Neighboring state policy	−3.86*	−4.25***	6.37***	−4.97**	−1.60**
N	923	923	923	923	914

Note: Year dummy variables not shown; standard errors are clustered by state.

* $p < 0.05$, ** $p < 0.01$, *** $p < 0.001$

Table B.24/A6.6. Income Deeming: Agriculture & Construction

	Undocumented Parent	Sponsor	Time of Sponsor Deeming
Total interest groups	0.02*	−0.04*	−0.01*
Women's groups (% of total)	0.53	0.13	0.18
African American groups (% of total)	0.88**	−0.77	−0.77*
Civil rights groups (% of total)	−0.62	1.12**	0.45
Social welfare groups (% of total)	−0.22	0.83**	0.36
Pro-family groups (% of total)	−0.22	0.77	0.38
Hispanic groups (% of total)	−1.17*	4.25	1.93**
Immigration groups (% of total)	−0.74	0.42	0.91
Econ. conservative groups (% of total)	0.89	−1.17	−1.03*
Chambers of Commerce (% of total)	−0.06	0.03	0.11
Agriculture groups (% of total)	−0.36	−0.28	−0.02
Construction groups (% of total)	−0.98*	−0.82	−0.29
State Need			
Black population (%)	−0.02	0.04	0.12*
Hispanic population (%)	−0.35***	−0.04	−0.02
Foreign-born population (%)	0.58***	0.19	0.02
Unemployment rate (%)	−0.49*	−0.01	0.13
Population receiving TANF (%)	−0.17	0.63	−0.10
Political Environment			
Citizen ideology	0.07*	−0.10*	−0.06*
Women in legislature (%)	−0.14**	0.01	−0.04
Democratic governor	−0.64	−0.73*	−0.48
Democratic legislature	−0.47	1.17*	1.04*
Greater Welfare Context			
Monthly TANF benefit	0.00	0.00	0.01*
Neighboring state policy	−4.94**	1.41	1.52
Constant	7.33	−4.16	−
N	842	842	807

Note: Year dummy variables not shown; standard errors are clustered by state.

* p < 0.05, ** p < 0.01, *** p < 0.001

CHAPTER 7

Table B.25/A7.1. Policy Accommodations for Given Recipients

	Working Unsubsidized Job	Elderly	Recipient with Illness or Disability	Caring for Family with Illness or Disability	Caring for Young Child	Domestic Violence
Total interest groups	0.00	0.00	0.00	0.00	0.00	0.00
Social welfare (% of total)	−0.01	−0.02	−0.02	−0.01	0.00	0.09**
Civil rights groups (% of total)	−0.02	0.01	−0.02	0.03	0.08	0.02
African American groups (% of total)	0.10	−0.09	0.02	−0.03	0.05	−0.10
Women's groups (% of total)	0.08	−0.01	0.03	−0.02	−0.03	−0.05
Pro-family groups (% of total)	−0.03	−0.09	0.00	−0.06	0.00	0.13
Econ. conservative groups (% of total)	0.12	0.17	0.08	0.16	0.14	−0.09
Chambers of Commerce (% of total)	−0.03	0.00	−0.02	−0.01	0.01	0.01
Industry groups (% of total)	−0.03	0.02	−0.02	0.00	0.02	0.02
Elderly groups (% of total)	–	0.00	0.05	0.13	–	–
Disability rights groups (% of total)	–	–	0.02	−0.03	–	–
Health groups (% of total)	–	–	0.00	0.02	–	–
Domestic violence groups (% of total)	–	–	–	–	–	−0.11
State Need						
Black population (%)	−0.02	0.00	0.01	0.00	0.00	0.02*
Hispanic population (%)	−0.02**	0.02	0.01	0.01	−0.01	0.01
Unemployment rate (%)	0.01	−0.02	−0.02	0.04	0.03	0.12**
Population receiving TANF (%)	−0.13	0.18	0.02	0.01	−0.03	−0.09
Political Environment						
Citizen ideology	0.01	0.02*	0.00	0.01	0.02***	0.00
Women in legislature (%)	−0.01	−0.01	−0.03*	−0.02	−0.02	0.00
Democratic governor	−0.03	−0.09	0.17	0.08	0.03	0.12
Democratic legislature	−0.08	0.41	0.26	0.28	0.34*	0.36*
Greater Welfare Context						
Monthly TANF benefit	0.00	0.00	0.00	0.00	0.00	0.00
Neighboring state policy	−0.12	0.04	0.20	−0.16	−0.58**	−0.43**
Constant	2.00*	0.01	1.72	0.81	0.28	−0.97
N	976	976	976	976	976	976

Note: Year dummy variables not shown; standard errors are clustered by state.

* p < 0.05, ** p < 0.01, *** p < 0.001

NOTES

CHAPTER 1. THE UNDESERVING POOR

1 Donald J. Trump. 2020. "Remarks at a White House Coronavirus Task Force Press Briefing." *American Presidency Project*. www.presidency.ucsb.edu.

2 Michael Gelman and Melvin Stephens Jr. 2022. "Lessons Learned from Economic Impact Payments during COVID-19." In *Recession Remedies: Lessons Learned from the U.S. Economic Policy Response to COVID-19*, ed. Wendy Edelberg, Louise Sheiner, and David Weissel. Hamilton Project. www.hamiltonproject.org.

3 Pew Research Center. 2020. "Positive Economic Views Plummet; Support for Government Aid Crosses Party Lines." April 21. www.pewresearch.org.

4 William J. Clinton. 1992. "Address Accepting the Presidential Nomination at the Democratic National Convention in New York." *American Presidency Project*. www.presidency.ucsb.edu.

5 Congressional Research Service. 2023. "The Temporary Assistance for Needy Families (TANF) Block Grant: A Legislative History." https://crsreports.congress.gov.

6 Dan Balz. 1994. "GOP 'Contract' Pledges 10 Tough Acts to Follow." *Washington Post*. November 20. www.washingtonpost.com.

7 Pamela Winston. 2002. *Welfare Policymaking in the States: The Devil in Devolution*. Washington, DC: Georgetown University Press.

8 Congressional Research Service, "The Temporary Assistance for Needy Families (TANF) Block Grant."

9 As quoted in Mary Hawkesworth. 2003. "Congressional Enactments of Race-Gender: Toward a Theory of Raced-Gendered Institutions." *American Political Science Review* 97 (4): 529–550, 540.

10 As quoted in Hawkesworth, "Congressional Enactments of Race-Gender," 541.

11 Gwendolyn Mink. 1998. *Welfare's End*. Ithaca, NY: Cornell University Press.

12 Winston, *Welfare Policymaking in the States*.

13 Congressional Research Service, "The Temporary Assistance for Needy Families (TANF) Block Grant."

14 CBPP. 2023. "State Fact Sheets: How States Spend Funds under the TANF Block Grant." *Center on Budget and Policy Priorities*. www.cbpp.org.

15 Congressional Research Service, "The Temporary Assistance for Needy Families (TANF) Block Grant."

16 CBPP. 2022. "Policy Basics: Temporary Assistance for Needy Families." *Center on Budget and Policy Priorities*. March 1. www.cbpp.org.

17 Donald J. Trump. 2019. "Press Release—Pro-Growth Economic Policies Benefit Previously Left Behind Americans the Most." *American Presidency Project.* www.presidency.ucsb.edu.

18 Republican Party. 2016. Republican Party Platform. *American Presidency Project.* www.presidency.ucsb.edu.

19 Michael Davern, Rene Bautista, Jeremy Freese, Stephen L. Morgan, and Tom W. Smith. 2021. "General Social Surveys, 1972–2021 Cross-Section" (machine-readable data file; 68,846 cases). Michael Davern, principal investigator; Rene Bautista, Jeremy Freese, Stephen L. Morgan, and Tom W. Smith, co-principal investigators; sponsored by National Science Foundation. Chicago: NORC at the University of Chicago.

20 Ronald Reagan. [1981] 2003. "Address before a Joint Session of Congress on the Program for Economic Recovery." In *Welfare: A Documentary History of U.S. Policy and Politics*, ed. Gwendolyn Mink and Rickie Solinger, 457–458. New York: New York University Press.

21 On the value of individualism, see Thomas Halper. 1973. "The Poor as Pawns: The New 'Deserving Poor' & the Old." *Polity* 6 (1): 71–86; and Theda Skocpol. 1992. *Protecting Mothers and Soldiers: The Political Origins of Social Policy in the United States.* Cambridge, MA: Belknap Press of Harvard University Press. On the family ethic, see Mimi Abramovitz. 1996. *Regulating the Lives of Women: Social Welfare Policy from Colonial Times to the Present.* Boston: South End Press; and Dorothy C. Miller. 1990. *Women and Social Welfare: A Feminist Analysis.* New York: Praeger.

22 Halper, "Poor as Pawns"; Michael B. Katz. 2013. *The Undeserving Poor: America's Enduring Confrontation with Poverty.* 2nd ed. New York: Oxford University Press.

23 Martin Gilens. 1999. *Why Americans Hate Welfare: Race, Media, and the Politics of Antipoverty Policy.* Chicago: University of Chicago Press, 35.

24 Abramovitz, *Regulating the Lives of Women*, 78.

25 As quoted in Gilens, *Why Americans Hate Welfare*, 33.

26 Halper, "Poor as Pawns," 73.

27 Katz, *Undeserving Poor*, 8.

28 Skocpol, *Protecting Mothers and Soldiers*, 531.

29 Ibid., 532.

30 Gallup Organization. Gallup Poll (AIPO), Aug, 1937. USGALLUP.37-94.Q03. Gallup Organization. Cornell University, Ithaca, NY: Roper Center for Public Opinion Research, iPOLL.

31 Pew Research Center. 2019. "Little Public Support for Reductions in Federal Spending." April 11. www.pewresearch.org.

32 From 1976 to 1982, respondents were asked to identify a total of three areas in which they favored either increasing or decreasing spending. The graphs show the percentage of respondents who named the category as their first response. From 1983 to 1989, respondents were asked to name only one category.

33 Skocpol, *Protecting Mothers and Soldiers*, 217.

34 Ibid., 213.

35 Abramovitz, *Regulating the Lives of Women*, 245.

36 As quoted in ibid., 248.

37 Miller, *Women and Social Welfare*, 117.

38 Davern et al., General Social Surveys.

39 Gilens, *Why Americans Hate Welfare*.

40 Patricia Ventura. 2012. *Neoliberal Culture: Living with American Neoliberalism.* Abingdon: Ashgate Publishing Group.

41 Katz, *Undeserving Poor*; Virginia Sapiro. 1990. "The Gender Basis of American Social Policy." In *Women, the State, and Welfare*, ed. Linda Gordon, 36–54. Madison: University of Wisconsin Press.

42 Abramovitz, *Regulating the Lives of Women*; Miller, *Women and Social Welfare*; Sapiro, "Gender Basis."

43 Abramovitz, *Regulating the Lives of Women*, 38.

44 Miller, *Women and Social Welfare*, 23.

45 Suzanne Mettler. 1998. *Dividing Citizens: Gender and Federalism in New Deal Public Policy.* Ithaca, NY: Cornell University Press.

46 Abramovitz, *Regulating the Lives of Women*, 84–86.

47 Sapiro, "Gender Basis."

48 Abramovitz, *Regulating the Lives of Women*, 262.

49 Mettler, *Dividing Citizens*; Miller, *Women and Social Welfare*.

50 United States Department of Labor. 1931. "Mothers' Aid, 1931." *Bureau Publication No. 220.* www.mchlibrary.org.

51 Abramovitz 1996, *Regulating the Lives of Women*; Sapiro, "Gender Basis"; United States Department of Labor, "Mothers' Aid."

52 Mark H. Leff. 1973. "Consensus for Reform: The Mothers'-Pension Movement in the Progressive Era." *Social Service Review* 47 (3): 397–417.

53 As quoted in Gwendolyn Mink. 1990. "The Lady and the Tramp." In *Women, the State, and Welfare*, ed. Linda Gordon, 92–122. Madison: University of Wisconsin Press, 109.

54 As quoted in Leff, "Consensus for Reform," 398.

55 Abramovitz, *Regulating the Lives of Women*, 200.

56 United States Department of Labor, "Mothers' Aid," 1.

57 Ibid., 13.

58 Miller, *Women and Social Welfare*, 32.

59 Skocpol, *Protecting Mothers and Soldiers*, 467.

60 Miller, *Women and Social Welfare*, 31.

61 Leff, "Consensus for Reform," 407.

62 Skocpol, *Protecting Mothers and Soldiers*; Barbara J. Nelson. 1990. "The Origins of the Two-Channel Welfare State: Workmen's Compensation and Mothers' Aid." In *Women, the State, and Welfare*, ed. Linda Gordon, 123–151.

63 Leff, "Consensus for Reform," 409.

64 As quoted in Skocpol, *Protecting Mothers and Soldiers*, 451.

65 Skocpol, *Protecting Mothers and Soldiers*.

66 Gilens, *Why Americans Hate Welfare*.

67 Mettler, *Dividing Citizens*.

68 Ibid.

69 Miller, *Women and Social Welfare*, 33.

70 Mettler, *Dividing Citizens*.

71 Neil Gilbert. 2009. "US Welfare Reform: Rewriting the Social Contract." *Journal of Social Policy* 38 (3): 383–399.

72 Jeffrey A. Will. 1993. "The Dimensions of Poverty: Public Perceptions of the Deserving Poor." *Social Science Research* 22: 312–332.

73 Ibid.

74 Teresa L. Amott. 1990. "Black Women and AFDC: Making Entitlement Out of Necessity." In *Women, the State, and Welfare*, ed. Linda Gordon, 280–298. Madison: University of Wisconsin Press, 290.

75 Lisbeth B. Schorr. 2019. "Piecing Together the Real Woman behind Reagan's 'Welfare Queen.'" *Washington Post*. May 31. www.washingtonpost.com.

76 Rickie Solinger. 2001. *Beggars and Choosers: How the Politics of Choice Shapes Adoption, Abortion, and Welfare in the United States*. New York: Hill & Wang.

77 Carly Hayden Foster. 2008. "The Welfare Queen: Race, Gender, Class, and Public Opinion." *Race, Gender & Class* 15 (3/4): 162–179; Dorothy Roberts. 2017. *Killing the Black Body: Race, Reproduction, and the Meaning of Liberty*. New York: Vintage Books.

78 Hancock, *Politics of Disgust*, 77.

79 Gilens, *Why Americans Hate Welfare*.

80 Ibid.

81 Miller, *Women and Social Welfare*, 3.

82 Scott W. Allard. 2007. "The Changing Face of Welfare during the Bush Administration." *Publius* 37 (3): 304–332; Sharon Hays. 2003. *Flat Broke with Children: Women in the Age of Welfare Reform*. New York: Oxford University Press.

83 Kimberly Kelly and Linda Grant. 2007. "State Abortion and Nonmarital Birthrates in the Post–Welfare Reform Era: The Impact of Economic Incentives on Reproductive Behaviors of Teenage and Adult Women." *Gender and Society* 21 (6): 878–904.

84 Mimi Abramovitz. 2006. "Welfare Reform in the United States: Gender, Race, and Class Matter." *Critical Social Policy* 26 (2): 336–364.

85 Gene Falk and Jill Tauber. 2001. "Welfare Reform: TANF Provisions Related to Marriage and Two-Parent Families." *CRS Report for Congress*.

86 Allard, "Changing Face of Welfare," 305.

87 Holloway Sparks. 2003. "Queens, Teends, and Model Mothers: Race, Gender, and the Discourse of Welfare Reform." In *Race and the Politics of Welfare Reform*, ed. Sanford F. Schram, Joe Soss, and Richard C. Fording, 171–195. Ann Arbor: University of Michigan Press, 172.

88 Regina S. Baker. 2022. "The Historical Racial Regime and Racial Inequality in Poverty in the American South." *American Journal of Sociology* 127 (6): 1721–1781.

89 Melvin L. Oliver and Thomas M. Shapiro. 2006. *Black Wealth/White Wealth: A New Perspective on Racial Inequality*. New York: Routledge.

90 Nelson, "Two-Channel Welfare State," 139.

91 Brown. *Race, Money, and the American Welfare State*; Mettler, *Dividing Citizens*.

92 Jill Quadagno. 1990. "Race, Class, and Gender in the U.S. Welfare State: Nixon's Failed Family Assistance Plan." *American Sociological Review* 55 (1): 11–28.

93 Jill Quadagno. 1994. *The Color of Welfare: How Racism Undermined the War on Poverty*. New York: Oxford University Press.

94 Frances Fox Piven and Richard A. Cloward. 1993. *Regulating the Poor: The Functions of Public Welfare*. New York: Vintage Books.

95 Quadagno, "Race, Class, and Gender."

96 Baker, "Historical Racial Regime."

97 Harrell R. Rodgers, Jr., and Kent L. Tedin. 2006. "State TANF Spending: Predictors of State Tax Effort to Support Welfare Reform." *Review of Policy Research* 23 (3): 745–759. See also Robert R. Preuhs. 2007. "Descriptive Representation as a Mechanism to Mitigate Policy Backlash: Latino Incorporation and Welfare Policy in the American States." *Political Research Quarterly* 60 (2): 277–292.

98 Matthew C. Fellowes and Gretchen Rowe. 2004. "Politics and the New American Welfare States." *American Journal of Political Science* 48 (2): 362–373. See also Beth Reingold and Adrienne R. Smith. 2012. "Welfare Policymaking and Intersections of Race, Ethnicity, and Gender in U.S. State Legislatures." *American Journal of Political Science* 56 (1): 131–147.

99 James M. Avery and Mark Peffley. 2005. "Voter Registration Requirements, Voter Turnout, and Welfare Eligibility Policy: Class Bias Matters." *State Politics & Policy Quarterly* 5 (1): 47–67.

    On the relationship between race and sanction severity, see also Byungkyu Kim and Richard C. Fording. 2010. "Second-Order Devolution and the Implementation of TANF in the U.S. States." *State Politics & Policy Quarterly* 10 (4): 341–367.

    On the relationship between race and time limits, see also Christopher Ojeda, Anne M. Whitesell, Michael B. Berkman, and Eric Plutzer. 2019. "Federalism and the Racialization of Welfare Policy." *State Politics & Policy Quarterly* 19 (4): 474–501.

100 Piven and Cloward, *Regulating the Poor*, 185.

101 As quoted in Katz, *Undeserving Poor*, 13.

102 Kenneth J. Neubeck and Noel A. Cazenave. 2001. *Welfare Racism: Playing the Race Card against America's Poor*. New York: Routledge, 153.

103 Patricia Hill Collins. 2000. *Black Feminist Thought: Knowledge, Consciousness, and the Politics of Empowerment*. 2nd ed. New York: Routledge.

104 Collins, *Black Feminist Thought*, 78; see also Neubeck and Cazenave, *Welfare Racism*. Other scholars, most notably Piven and Cloward, argue that attempts to regulate the sexuality of welfare recipients are just another mechanism to control the labor market.

105 Miller, *Women and Social Welfare*; Gilbert, "US Welfare Reform"; Ange-Marie Hancock. 2004. *The Politics of Disgust: The Public Identity of the Welfare Queen*. New York: New York University Press; Cathy Marie Johnson, Georgia Duerst-Lahti, and Noelle H. Norton. 2007. *Creating Gender: The Sexual Politics of Welfare Policy*. Boulder, CO: Lynne Rienner Publishers.

106 Hancock, *Politics of Disgust*, 38.

107 Skocpol, *Protecting Mothers and Soldiers*; Mink, "Lady and the Tramp."

108 Mary E. Triece. 2013. *Tell It Like It Is: Women in the National Welfare Rights Movement*. Columbia: University of South Carolina Press; Guida West. 1981. *The National Welfare Rights Movement: The Social Protest of Poor Women*. New York: Praeger.

109 Triece, *Tell It Like It Is*.

110 As quoted in ibid., 74.

111 Ian Haney López. 2014. *Dog Whistle Politics: How Coded Racial Appeals Have Reinvented Racism & Wrecked the Middle Class*. New York: Oxford University Press, 31.

112 Gilbert, "US Welfare Reform."

113 Amott, "Black Women and AFDC," 281.

114 Gilens, *Why Americans Hate Welfare*; Neuback and Cazenave, *Welfare Racism*.

115 Catherine A. Luther, Deseriee A. Kennedy, and Terri Combs-Orme. 2005. "Intertwining of Poverty, Gender, and Race: A Critical Analysis of Welfare News Coverage from 1993–2000." *Race, Class, & Gender* 12 (2): 10–33.

116 Katz, *Undeserving Poor*, 238.

117 Skocpol, *Protecting Mothers and Soldiers*, 469.

118 Ann C. Foster and Arcenis Rojas. 2018. "Program Participation and Spending Patterns of Families Receiving Government Means-Tested Assistance." *U.S. Bureau of Labor Statistics*. www.bls.gov.

119 Suzanne Mettler. 2011. *The Submerged State: How Invisible Government Policies Undermine American Democracy*. Chicago: University of Chicago Press; Philip Rucker. 2009. "Sen. DeMint of S.C. Is Voice of Opposition to Health-Care Reform." *Washington Post*. July 28. www.washingtonpost.com.

120 Christopher Faricy. 2015. *Welfare for the Wealthy: Parties, Social Spending, and Inequality in the U.S.* New York: Cambridge University Press.

121 Ibid.

122 Tax Policy Center. 2020. "Briefing Book." *Urban Institute and Brookings Institution*. www.taxpolicycenter.org.

123 Faricy, *Welfare for the Wealthy*.

124 Christopher Ellis and Christopher Faricy. 2020. "Race, 'Deservingness,' and Social Spending Attitudes: The Role of Policy Delivery Mechanism." *Political Behavior* 42: 819–843.

125 Spencer Piston. 2018. *Class Attitudes in America: Sympathy for the Poor, Resentment of the Rich, and Political Implications*. New York: Cambridge University Press.

126 Franklin Delano Roosevelt. [1938] 2003. "A Social Security Program Must Include All Those Who Need Its Protection." In *Welfare: A Documentary History of U.S. Policy and Politics*, ed. Gwendolyn Mink and Rickie Solinger, 77–80. New York: New York University Press.

127 Will, "Dimensions of Poverty"; Jeffrey A. Will and John K. Cochran. 1995. "God Helps Those Who Help Themselves? The Effects of Religious Affiliation, Religiosity, and Deservedness on Generosity toward the Poor." *Sociology of Religion* 56 (3): 327–338.

128 Christopher D. DeSante. 2013. "Working Twice as Hard to Get Half as Far: Race, Work Ethic, and America's Deserving Poor." *American Journal of Political Science* 57 (2): 342–356.

CHAPTER 2. REPRESENTING THE NEEDY

1 While AFDC/TANF is technically only one of many welfare programs available in the United States, throughout this chapter, and in future chapters, I will use "TANF" and "welfare" interchangeably. References to "AFDC" or "TANF recipients" are equivalent to those to "welfare recipients."

2 Audre Lorde. 1984. "Age, Race, Class, and Sex: Women Redefining Difference." In *Sister Outsider*. Trumansburg, NY: Crossing Press, 116.

3 Collins, *Black Feminist Thought*, 70.

4 Isabel Wilkerson. 2020. *Caste: The Origin of Our Discontents*. New York: Penguin Random House, 17.

5 bell hooks. 2000. *Feminist Theory: From Margin to Center*. Cambridge, MA: South End Press, 43.

6 Kimberlé Crenshaw. 1989. "Demarginalizing the Intersection of Race and Sex: A Black Feminist Critique of Antidiscrimination Doctrine, Feminist Theory, and Antiracist Politics." *University of Chicago Legal Forum* 140: 139–167, 140.

7 Lorde, "Age, Race, Class, and Sex," 117.

8 hooks, *Feminist Theory*, 5.

9 Hancock, *Politics of Disgust*, 23.

10 Ibid., chapter 2.

11 Helen Ingram and Anne Schneider. 1991. "The Choice of Target Population." *Administration & Society* 23 (3): 333–356, 334.

12 Anne Schneider and Helen Ingram. 1993. "Social Construction of Target Populations: Implications for Politics and Policy." *American Political Science Review* 87 (2): 334–347, 335.

13 Schneider and Ingram, "Social Construction of Target Populations."

14 Joe Soss, Richard C. Fording, and Sanford F. Schram. 2008. "The Color of Devolution: Race, Federalism, and the Politics of Social Control." *American Journal of Political Science* 52 (3): 536–553, 539.

15 Ibid., 540.

16 For other research on the racialized effects of welfare sanctions, see Shannon Monnat. 2010. "The Color of Welfare Sanctioning: Exploring the Individual and

Contextual Roles of Race on TANF Case Closures and Benefit Reductions." *Socio-logical Quarterly* 51 (4): 678–707; Christopher Ojeda, Anne M. Whitesell, Michael B. Berkman, and Eric Plutzer. 2019. "Federalism and the Racialization of Welfare Policy." *State Politics & Policy Quarterly* 19 (4): 474–501.

17 Matthew J. Uttermark, Kenneth R. Mackie, and Carol S. Weissert. 2023. "The Color of Discretion: Race and Ethnicity Biases in School Suspension." *Polity* 55 (2): 302–331; Huriya Jabbar, Eupha Jeanne Daramola, Julie A. Marsh, Taylor Enoch-Stevens, Jacob Aloson, and Taylor N. Allbright. 2022. "Social Construc-tion Is Racial Construction: Examining the Target Populations in School-Choice Policies." *American Journal of Education* 128 (3): 487–518; Brian An, Morris Levy, and Rodney Hero. 2018. "It's Not Just Welfare: Racial Inequality and the Local Provision of Public Goods in the United States." *Urban Affairs Review* 54 (5): 833–865.

18 Katelyn E. Stauffer and Bernard L. Fraga. 2022. "Contextualizing the Gender Gap in Voter Turnout." *Politics, Groups, and Identities* 10 (2): 334–341.

19 Ibid.; see also Celeste Montoya. 2020. "Intersectionality and Voting Rights." *PS: Political Science & Politics* 53(3): 484–489.

20 Sidney Verba, Nancy Burns, and Kay Lehman Schlozman. 1997. "Knowing and Caring about Politics: Gender and Political Engagement." *Journal of Politics* 59 (4): 1051–1072.

21 Hilde Coffé and Catherine Bolzendahl. 2010. "Same Games, Different Rules? Gen-der Differences in Political Participation." *Sex Roles* 62: 318–333; Kathleen Dolan. 2011. "Do Women and Men Know Different Things? Measuring Gender Differ-ences in Political Knowledge." *Journal of Politics* 73 (1): 97–107.

22 E. E. Schattschneider. 1960. *The Semisovereign People: A Realist's View of Democ-racy in America*. New York: Holt, Rinehart and Winston; Kay Lehman Schloz-man and John T. Tierney. 1986. *Organized Interests and American Democracy*. New York: Harper & Row; Kay Lehman Schlozman, Sidney Verba, and Henry E. Brady. 2012. *Unheavenly Chorus: Unequal Political Voice and the Broken Promise of American Democracy*. Princeton, NJ: Princeton University Press.

23 Schlozman et al., *Unheavenly Chorus*.

24 Hannah Hartig, Andrew Daniller, Scott Keeter, and Ted Van Green. 2023. "Repub-lic Gains in 2022 Midterms Driven Mostly by Turnout Advantage." *Pew Research Center*. July 12. www.pewresearch.org.

25 Montoya, "Intersectionality and Voting Rights."

26 Henry E. Brady, Sidney Verba, and Kay Lehman Schlozman. 1995. "Beyond SES: A Resource Model of Political Participation." *American Political Science Review* 89 (2): 271–294.

27 Benjamin I. Page, Larry M. Bartels, and Jason Seawright. 2013. "Democracy and the Policy Preferences of Wealthy Americans." *Perspective on Politics* 11 (1): 51–73, 54.

28 Page et al., "Democracy and Wealthy Americans."

29 Skocpol, *Protecting Mothers and Soldiers*, 478.

30 Katherine Tate. 1993. *From Protest to Politics: The New Black Voters in American Elections*. New York: Russell Sage Foundation, 93.

31 Brady et al., "Beyond SES," 284.

32 American National Election Studies. 2021. "ANES 2020 Time Series Study Full Release" (dataset and documentation). July 19, 2021 version. www.electionstudies .org.

33 Schneider and Ingram, "Social Construction," 344.

34 Ibid.

35 Jane Mansbridge. 1999. "Should Blacks Represent Blacks and Women Represent Women? A Contingent 'Yes.'" *Journal of Politics* 61 (3): 628–657.

36 Elizabeth Rigby and Gerald C. Wright. 2013. "Political Parties and Representation of the Poor in the American States." *American Journal of Political Science* 57 (3): 552–565.

37 Martin Gilens. 2012. *Affluence and Influence: Economic Inequality and Political Power in America*. Princeton, NJ: Princeton University Press.

38 Hannah Pitkin. 1967. *The Concept of Representation*. Berkeley: University of California Press, 80.

39 Ibid., 81.

40 Mansbridge, "Should Blacks Represent Blacks."

41 Claudine Gay. 2002. "Spirals of Trust? The Effect of Descriptive Representation on the Relationship between Citizens and Their Government." *American Journal of Political Science* 46 (4): 717–732.

42 Ibid.

43 Beth Reingold and Adrienne R. Smith. 2012. "Welfare Policymaking and Intersections of Race, Ethnicity, and Gender in U.S. State Legislatures." *American Journal of Political Science* 56 (1): 131–147.

44 Debra L. Dodson. 2006. *The Impact of Women in Congress*. New York: Oxford University Press.

45 Edith Barrett. 1997. "Gender and Race in the State House: The Legislative Experience." *The Social Science Journal* 34 (2): 131–144.

46 Kathleen A. Bratton and L. Haynie Kerry. 1999. "Agenda Setting and Legislative Success in State Legislatures: The Effects of Gender and Race." *Journal of Politics* 61 (3): 658–679; Michele L. Swers. 2002. *The Difference Women Make: The Policy Impact of Women in Congress*. Chicago: University of Chicago Press.

47 Tiffany D. Barnes, Victoria D. Beall, and Mirya R. Holman. 2021. "Pink-Collar Representation and Budgetary Outcomes in US States." *Legislative Studies Quarterly* 46 (1): 119–154.

48 Lisa A. Bryant and Julia Marin Hellwege. 2019. "Working Mothers Represent: How Children Affect the Legislative Agenda of Women in Congress." *American Politics Research* 47 (3): 447–470.

49 Kathleen A. Bratton, Kerry L. Haynie, and Beth Reingold. 2006. "Agenda Setting and African American Women in State Legislatures." *Journal of Women, Politics & Policy* 28 (3/4): 71–96.

50 Kimberly Cowell-Meyers and Laura Langbein. 2009. "Linking Women's Descriptive and Substantive Representation in the United States." *Politics & Gender* 5 (4): 491–518, 508.

51 Ibid., 511.

52 David E. Broockman. 2013. "Black Politicians Are More Intrinsically Motivated to Advance Blacks' Interests: A Field Experiment Manipulating Political Incentives." *American Journal of Political Science* 57 (3): 521–536.

53 Andy Baker and Corey Cook. 2005. "Representing Black Intests and Promoting Black Culture: The Importance of African American Descriptive Representation in the U.S. House." *Du Bois Review* 2 (2): 227–246.

54 Tyson King-Meadows and Thomas F. Schaller. 2006. *Devolution and Black State Legislators: Challenges and Choices in the Twenty-First Century*. Albany: State University of New York Press, 149.

55 Ibid., 148.

56 Bratton and Haynie, "Agenda Setting," 670.

57 Chris T. Owens. 2005. "Black Substantive Representation in State Legislators from 1971–1994." *Social Science Quarterly* 86 (4): 779–791.

58 Robert Preuhs. 2006. "The Conditional Effects of Minority Descriptive Representation: Black Legislators and Policy Influence in the American States." *Journal of Politics* 68 (3): 585–599.

59 Reingold and Smith, "Welfare Policymaking and Intersections," 132.

60 Gilens, *Why Americans Hate Welfare*, 70.

61 Kristina C. Miler. 2018. *Poor Representation: Congress and the Politics of Poverty in the United States*. New York: Cambridge University Press, 144–145.

62 Bratton et al., "Agenda Setting," 87. See also Beth Reingold, Kerry L. Haynie, and Kirsten Widner. 2021. *Race, Gender, and Political Representation: Toward a More Intersectional Approach*. New York: Oxford University Press.

63 Reingold and Smith, "Welfare Policymaking and Intersections."

64 Ibid., 142.

65 Michael D. Minta and Nadia E. Brown. 2014. "Intersecting Interests: Gender, Race, and Congressional Attention to Women's Issues." *Du Bois Review* 11 (2): 253–272.

66 Zoltan L. Hajnal and Taeku Lee. 2011. *Why Americans Don't Join the Party: Race, Immigration, and the Failure (of Political Parties) to Engage the Electorate*. Princeton, NJ: Princeton University Press.

67 Tracy L. Osborn. 2012. *How Women Represent Women: Political Parties, Gender, and Representation in State Legislatures*. New York: Oxford University Press.

68 Gilens, *Affluence and Influence*, 184.

69 Schlozman et al., *Unheavenly Chorus*, 248.

70 Gwendolyn Mink. 1998. *Welfare's End*. Ithaca, NY: Cornell University Press.

71 V. O. Key. 1949. *Southern Politics in State and Nation*. New York: Alfred A. Knopf, 299.

72 Ibid., 301.

73 Ibid., 303–304.
74 Robert D. Brown. 1995. "Party Cleavages and Welfare Effort in the American States." *American Political Science Review* 89 (1): 23–33, 25.
75 Ibid., 27.
76 Ibid.
77 Paul Frymer. 1999. *Uneasy Alliances: Race and Party Competition in America.* Princeton, NJ: Princeton University Press.
78 Ibid., 10.
79 Ibid., 8; Tate, *From Protest to Politics.*
80 Frymer, *Uneasy Alliances,* 28.
81 Tate, *From Protest to Politics,* 50.
82 Andrew Gelman, David Park, Boris Shor, and Jeronimo Cortina. 2010. *Red State, Blue State, Rich State, Poor State: Why Americans Vote the Way They Do.* Princton, NJ: Princeton University Press, 46.
83 Gilens, *Affluence and Influence,* 167.
84 Brown, "Party Cleavages," 30.
85 Rigby and Wright, "Political Parties and Representation."
86 Ibid., 560.
87 Ibid., 562.
88 Charles Barrilleaux, Thomas Holbrook, and Laura Langer. 2002. "Electoral Competition, Legislative Balance, and American State Welfare Policy." *American Journal of Political Science* 46 (2): 415–427.
89 Schlozman et al., *Unheavenly Chorus.*
90 Gilens, *Affluence and Influence,* 171–173.
91 Ibid., 178.
92 David Truman. 1951. *The Governmental Process: Political Interests and Public Opinion.* New York: Alfred Knopf.
93 Tate, *From Protest to Politics.*
94 Alexander A. Schuessler. 2000. *A Logic of Expressive Choice.* Princeton, NJ: Princeton University Press.
95 John D. McCarthy and Mayer N. Zald. 1977. "Resource Mobilization and Social Movements: A Partial Theory." *American Journal of Sociology* 82 (6): 1212–1241. These conscience adherents may even be so moved as to provide resources to the cause; McCarthy and Zald refer to these individuals as "conscience constituents."
96 Daniel M. Cress and David A. Snow. 1996. "Mobilization at the Margins: Resources, Benefactors, and the Viability of Homeless Social Movement Organizations." *American Sociological Review* 61 (6): 1089–1109.
97 Premila Nadasen. 2005. *Welfare Warriors: The Welfare Rights Movement in the United States.* New York: Routledge, 11.
98 Guida West. 1981. *The National Welfare Rights Movement: The Social Protest of Poor Women.* New York: Praeger, 15.
99 Neubeck and Cazenave, *Welfare Racism,* 126.
100 Triece, *Tell It Like It Is.*

101 Nadasen, *Welfare Warriors*.

102 Ibid., 136.

103 West, *National Welfare Rights Movement*, 178.

104 Lawrence Neils Bailis. *Bread or Justice: Grassroots Organizing in the Welfare Rights Movement*. Lexington, KY: Lexington Books, 79.

105 McCarthy and Zald, "Resource Mobilization and Social Movements."

106 Schlozman et al., *Unheavenly Chorus*.

107 Dara Strolovitch. 2007. *Affirmative Advocacy: Race, Class, and Gender in Interest Group Politics*. Chicago: University of Chicago Press.

108 Ibid., 83.

109 Ibid., 48.

110 Ibid., 55.

111 West, *National Welfare Rights Movement*.

112 Hancock, *Politics of Disgust*, 43.

113 West, *National Welfare Rights Movement*.

114 R. Allen Hays. 2001. *Who Speaks for the Poor? National Interest Groups and Social Policy*. New York: Routledge.

115 Ibid., 66.

116 Schlozman et al., *Unheavenly Chorus*, 386.

117 Ibid., 388.

118 Ibid., 392.

119 Mark A. Smith. 2000. *American Business and Political Power: Public Opinion, Elections, and Democracy*. Chicago: University of Chicago Press.

120 Carl Klarner, Xiaotong Mao, and Stan Buchanan. 2007. "Business Interest Group Power and Temporary Assistance to Needy Families." *Social Science Quarterly* 88 (1): 104–119.

121 Ibid., 113.

122 Virginia Gray and David Lowery. 1996. *The Population Ecology of Interest Representation: Lobbying Communities in the American States*. Ann Arbor: University of Michigan Press.

123 Ibid.

124 Schattschneider, *Semisovereign People*; Schlozman and Tierney, *Organized Interests*.

125 David Lowery. 2013. "Lobbying Influence: Meaning, Measurement and Missing." *Interest Groups and Advocacy* 2 (1): 1–26.

126 Ibid., 7.

127 Ann R. Tickamyer and Debra A. Henderson. 2010. "Devolution, Social Exclusion, and Spatial Inequality in U.S. Welfare Provision." In *Welfare Reform in Rural Places: Comparative Perspectives*, ed. Paul Milbourne and Terry Marsden. Bingley: Emerald Group Publishing Limited.

128 Lowery, "Lobbying Influence," 6.

129 Throughout the expectations section, I discuss the expectations in terms of whether I would expect an interest group to promote a more lenient or stringent

policy. All of these expectations can be rephrased to discuss how the density of an interest group affects the leniency of a policy.

130 West, *National Welfare Rights Movement*, 210.

131 Catherine M. Paden. 2008. "Disentangling Race and Poverty: The Civil Rights Response to Antipoverty Policy." *Du Bois Review* 5 (2): 339–368.

132 West, *National Welfare Rights Movement*, 227.

133 As quoted in ibid., 228.

134 Paden, "Disentangling Race and Poverty."

135 West, *National Welfare Rights Movement*, 213.

136 Ibid., 214.

137 Ibid., 215.

138 Ibid., 218.

139 Ibid.

140 Ibid., 219.

141 Michael Camasso. 2007. *Family Caps, Abortion and Women of Color: Research Connection and Political Rejection*. New York: Oxford University Press, 16–17.

142 Paden, "Disentangling Race and Poverty"; Michael K. Brown. 1999. *Race, Money, and the American Welfare State*. Ithaca, NY: Cornell University Press.

143 Kaaryn Gustafson. 2009. "The Criminalization of Poverty." *Journal of Criminal Law and Criminology* 99 (3): 643–716, 643.

144 Michael Leo Owens and Adrienne Smith. 2012. "'Deviants' and Democracy: Punitive Policy Designs and the Social Rights of Felons as Citizens." *American Politics Research* 40 (3): 531–567.

145 Reese, *Backlash against Welfare Mothers*, 204.

146 Susan Lloyd. 1997. "The Effects of Domestic Violence on Women's Employment." *Law & Policy* 19 (2): 139–167, 153.

147 Mink, *Welfare's End*; Smith, *Welfare Reform and Sexual Regulation*.

148 Allard, "Changing Face of Welfare"; Sandra K. Danziger and Kristin S. Seefeldt. 2002. "Barriers to Employment and the 'Hard to Serve': Implication for Services, Sanctions and Time Limits." *Social Policy & Society* 2 (2): 151–160; Judy L. Postmus. 2004. "Battered and on Welfare: The Experiences of Women with the Family Violence Option." *Journal of Sociology and Social Welfare* 31 (2): 113–123.

149 Naomi Stern. 2003. "Battered by the System: How Advocates against Domestic Violence Have Improved Victims' Access to Child Support and TANF." *Hastings Women's Law Journal* 14 (1): 47–69.

150 Anne Whitesell. 2019. "Who Represents the Needs of Domestic Violence Survivors in State Welfare Policy?" *Politics & Gender* 15 (3): 514–546.

151 Pamela Loprest and Elaine Maag. 2009. "Disabilities among TANF Recipients: Evidence from the NHIS." *U.S. Department of Health and Human Services, Office of the Assistant Secretary for Planning and Evaluation*.

152 David C. Stapleton, David C. Wittenburg, Michael E. Fishman, and Gina A. Livermore. 2002. "Transitions from AFDC to SSI Before Welfare Reform." *Social Security Bulletin* 64 (1): 84–114.

153 Center on Budget and Policy Priorities. 2022. "Policy Basics: Supplemental Security Income." *Center on Budget and Policy Priorities*. March 2. www.cbpp.org.

154 Gilens, *Affluence and Influence*, 158.

155 Ibid.

156 Ashley English. 2019. "She Who Shall Not Be Named: The Women That Women's Organizations Do (and Do Not) Represent in the Rulemaking Process." *Politics & Gender* 15: 572–598.

157 Hays, *Who Speaks for the Poor*, 93.

158 Ibid., 133.

159 Gilbert, "US Welfare Reform."

160 Jae Yeon Kim. 2022. "How Other Minorities Gained Access: The War on Poverty and Asian American and Latino Community Organizing." *Political Research Quarterly* 75 (1): 89–102.

161 Doris Ng. 2002. "From War on Poverty to War on Welfare: The Impact of Welfare Reform on the Lives of Immigrant Women." In *Work, Welfare, and Politics*, ed. Frances Fox Piven, Joan Acker, Margaret Hallock, and Sandra Morgen. Eugene: University of Oregon Press.

162 María Josefa Canino-Arroyo. 2003. "Reflections on Latino Advocacy and Welfare Reform in New Jersey." *Centro Journal* 15 (1): 177–195.

163 Alexandra Filindra. 2012. "Immigrant Social Policy in the American States: Race Politics and State TANF and Medicaid Eligibility Rules for Legal Permanent Residents." *State Politics & Policy Quarterly* 13 (1): 26–48, 40.

164 Anne Marie Cammisa and Paul Christopher Manuel. 2016. "Religious Groups as Interest Groups: The United States Catholic Bishops in the Welfare Reform Debate of 1995–1996 and the Health Care Reform Debate of 2009–2010." *Religions* 7 (16): 1–28, 5.

165 Allard, "Changing Face of Welfare," 317.

166 Pamela Winston. 2002. *Welfare Policymaking in the States: The Devil in Devolution*. Washington, DC: Georgetown University Press, 134.

167 Cammisa and Manuel, "Religious Groups as Interest Groups," 15.

168 Ibid., 14.

169 Cynthia G. Whitney, Fangjun Zhou, James Singleton, and Anne Schuchat. 2014. "Benefits from Immunization during the Vaccines for Children Program Era— United States, 1994–2013." *Morbidity and Mortality Weekly Report* 63 (16): 352–355. www.cdc.gov.

170 Winston, *Welfare Policymaking in the States*, 92.

171 Daguerre, "Second Phase of US Welfare Reform," 370.

172 Heather Hahn, David Kassabian, Lina Breslav, and Yvette Lamb. 2015. "A Descriptive Study of County- Versus State-Administered Temporary Assistance for Needy Families Programs." *Urban Institute*. OPRE Report 2015–42. www .urban.org.

173 Gilens, *Affluence and Influence*, 159.

174 Sharon Parrott. 1998. "Welfare Recipients Who Find Jobs: What Do We Know about Their Employment and Earnings?" *Center on Budget and Policy Priorities*, 1. www.cbpp.org.

175 Ibid., 33.

176 Parrott, "Welfare Recipients Who Find Jobs," 40.

177 Richard C. Fording. 2003. "'Laboratories of Democracy' or Symbolic Politics? The Racial Origins of Welfare Reform." In *Race and the Politics of Welfare Reform*, ed. Sanford F. Schram, Joe Soss, and Richard C. Fording, 72–97. Ann Arbor: University of Michigan Press, 89.

178 Elizabeth Wiener. 2021. "Getting a High Heel in the Door: An Experiment on State Legislator Responsiveness to Women's Issue Lobbying." *Political Research Quarterly* 74 (3): 729–743.

179 Gilens, *Why Americans Hate Welfare*.

180 Neubeck and Cazenave, *Welfare Racism*, 4.

181 Hancock, *Politics of Disgust*.

CHAPTER 3. MORALITY AND MOTHERHOOD

1 Marco Rubio. 2014. "Reclaiming the Land of Opportunity: Conservative Reforms for Combatting Poverty." January 8. www.rubio.senate.gov.

2 Joshua Gillin. 2015. "Jeb Bush Did Say Women Should 'Find a Husband' to Get Off Welfare—in 1994." *Politifact*. June 25. www.politifact.com.

3 Krissy Clark. 2016. "'Oh My God—We're on Welfare?'" *Slate*. June 2. www.slate .com.

4 Susan Tebben. 2021. "Federal Funding for Low-Income Families Stayed in State Coffers amid Pandemic." *Ohio Capital Journal*. April 12. https://ohiocapitaljournal .com .

5 Bureau of the Census. 1940. "Families in the United States by Type and Size: 1930." www2.census.gov.

6 "Table FM-1. Families by Presence of Own Children under Age 18: 1950 to Present." Current Population Survey, U.S. Census Bureau, last modified November 2022. www2.census.gov.

7 Michael Davern, Rene Bautista, Jeremy Freese, Stephen L. Morgan, and Tom W. Smith. 2021. General Social Surveys, 1972–2021 Cross-section. Chicago: NORC at the University of Chicago.

8 Roberts, *Killing the Black Body*.

9 Gilbert, "US Welfare Reform," 391.

10 Hancock, *Politics of Disgust*, 25.

11 Ibid., 31.

12 Collins, *Black Feminist Thought*, 79.

13 Roberts, *Killing the Black Body*.

14 Mink, *Welfare's End*, 22.

15 Mettler, *Divided Citizens*, 170.

16 Gilbert, "US Welfare Reform."

17 Ibid.; Hancock, *Politics of Disgust.*

18 Robert C. Lieberman. 1998. *Shifting the Color Line: Race and the American Welfare State.* Cambridge, MA: Harvard University Press, 122.

19 Smith, *Welfare Reform and Sexual Regulation,* 5.

20 Neubeck and Cazenave, *Welfare Racism,* 72.

21 Rickie Solinger. 2001. *Beggars and Choosers: How the Politics of Choice Shapes Adoption, Abortion, and Welfare in the United States.* New York: Hill & Wang, 148.

22 Jill Quadagno. 1994. *The Color of Welfare: How Racism Undermined the War on Poverty.* New York: Oxford University Press.

23 Daniel Patrick Moynihan. 1965. *The Negro Family: The Case for National Action.* United States Department of Labor, 12.

24 Collins, *Black Feminist Thought,* 76.

25 Quadagno, *Color of Welfare*; Roberts, *Killing the Black Body.*

26 Moynihan, *Negro Family.*

27 Collins, *Black Feminist Thought,* 75.

28 Moynihan, *Negro Family.*

29 Ibid.

30 "About Us." *National Responsible Fatherhood Clearinghouse.* www.fatherhood.gov.

31 Barack Obama. 2008. "Remarks at the Apostolic Church of God in Chicago." *American Presidency Project.* www.presidency.ucsb.edu.

32 Ta-Nehisi Coates. 2017. "My President Was Black." *The Atlantic.* January/February. www.theatlantic.com.

33 Frederick C. Harris. 2015. "The Challenges of My Brother's Keeper." *Brookings Institution.* October 29. www.brookings.edu.

34 Quadagno, *Color of Welfare,* 176.

35 Gilbert, "US Welfare Reform."

36 Hancock, *Politics of Disgust,* 72.

37 Lawrence M. Mead, ed. 1997. *The New Paternalism: Supervisory Approaches to Poverty.* Washington, DC: Brookings Institution Press.

38 Smith, *Welfare Reform and Sexual Regulation,* 174–175.

39 Joel F. Handler and Yeheskel Hasenfeld. 2007. *Blame Welfare, Ignore Poverty and Inequality.* New York: Cambridge University Press, 285.

40 Annie E. Casey Foundation. 2023. "Child Well-Being in Single-Parent Families." *Annie E. Casey Foundation.* June 23. www.aecf.org.

41 Ann Cammett. 2014. "Deadbeat Dads & Welfare Queens: How Metaphor Shapes Poverty Law." *Boston College Journal of Law and Social Justice* 34 (2): 233–266.

42 As quoted in Sparks, "Queens, Teens, and Model Mothers," 179.

43 Roberts, *Killing the Black Body*; Sparks, "Queens, Teens, and Model Mothers."

44 Sparks, "Queens, Teens, and Model Mothers."

45 Rebecca A. Maynard. 1997. "Paternalism, Teenage Pregnancy Prevention, and Teenage Parent Services." In *The New Paternalism: Supervisory Approaches to Poverty,* ed. Lawrence M. Mead. Washington, DC: Brookings Institution Press.

46 David Campbell and Joan Wright. 2005. "Rethinking Welfare School-Attendance Policies." *Social Science Service Review* 79 (1): 2–28.

47 Ibid., 2.

48 Frances Fox Piven and Richard A. Cloward. 1993. *Regulating the Poor: The Functions of Public Welfare*. New York: Vintage Books, 162.

49 Smith, *Welfare Reform and Sexual Regulation*, 99.

50 Ronald M. Mincy and Hillard Pouncy. 1997. "Paternalism, Child Support Enforcement, and Fragile Families." In *The New Paternalism: Supervisory Approaches to Poverty*, ed. Lawrence M. Mead. Washington, DC: Brookings Institution Press.

51 New Jersey Senate Judiciary Committee. January 6, 1998.

52 Smith, *Welfare Reform and Sexual Regulation*, 97.

53 Daniel L. Hatcher. 2012. "Don't Forget Dad: Addressing Women's Poverty by Rethinking Forced and Outdated Child Support Policies." *Journal of Gender, Social Policy & the Law* 20 (4): 775–796, 782.

54 Smith, *Welfare Reform and Sexual Regulation*, 101.

55 Johnson et al., *Creating Gender*, 154.

56 Mink, *Welfare's End*; Smith, *Welfare Reform and Sexual Regulation*.

57 Camasso, *Family Caps*.

58 Joe Soss, Sanford F. Schram, Thomas P. Vartanian, and Erin O'Brien. 2001. "Setting the Terms of Relief: Explaining State Policy Choices in the Devolution Revolution." *American Journal of Political Science* 45 (2): 378–395; Smith, *Welfare Reform and Sexual Regulation*.

59 Jeff Grogger and Stephen G. Bronars. 2001. "The Effect of Welfare Payments on the Marriage and Fertility Behavior of Unwed Mothers: Results from a Twins Experiment." *Journal of Political Economy* 109 (3): 529–545; Leonard M. Lopoo and Kerri M. Raissian. 2012. "Natalist Policies in the United States." *Journal of Policy Analysis and Management* 31 (4): 905–946.

60 One exception to the operationalization of the family cap as a dichotomous variable is found in Reingold, Haynie, and Widner, *Race, Gender, and Political Representation*.

61 Hancock, *Politics of Disgust*, 41.

62 R. Kent Weaver. 2000. *Ending Welfare as We Know It*. Washington, DC: Brookings Institution Press.

63 Ibid.

64 Ibid.

65 For a discussion of what constitutes "women's interests," see Dodson, *Impact of Women*; Swers, *Difference Women Make*; Christina Wolbrecht. 2000. *The Politics of Women's Rights: Parties, Positions, and Change*. Princeton, NJ: Princeton University Press.

66 Gilens, *Why Americans Hate Welfare*; Fellowes and Rowe, "New American Welfare States"; Filindra, "Immigrant Social Policy"; Kim and Fording, "Second-Order Devolution."

67 Due to its nonpartisan legislature, Nebraska is dropped from the models.

68 Hawaii and Alaska are dropped from the models because these states are missing neighboring state policy data.

69 Richard E. Dawson and James A. Robinson. 1963. "Inter-party Competition, Economic Variables, and Welfare Policies in the American States." *Journal of Politics* 25 (2): 265–289; Bailey and Rom, "A Wider Race?"; William D. Berry, Richard C. Fording, and Russell L. Hanson. 2003. "Reassessing the 'Race to the Bottom' in State Welfare Policy." *Journal of Politics* 65 (2): 327–349; Reingold and Smith, "Welfare Policymaking"; Craig Volden. 2002. "The Politics of Competitive Federalism: A Race to the Bottom in Welfare Benefits?" *American Journal of Political Science* 46 (2): 352–363.

70 Dimiter Toshkov, David Lowery, Brendan Carroll, and Joost Berkhout. 2013. "Timing Is Everything? Organized Interests and the Timing of Legislative Activity." *Interest Groups & Advocacy* 2 (1): 48–70.

71 Alaska State Legislature House Health and Social Services Standing Committee. March 12, 2013.

72 Ibid.

73 Letter to Members of Wisconsin Assembly Committee on Public Benefits Reform. April 30, 2015.

74 Wisconsin State Legislature Public Hearing Committee Records, Committee on Children and Families. November 17, 2005.

75 Ibid.

76 Ibid.

77 Nebraska Health and Human Services Committee. March 10, 2011.

78 Email from David Marshall to Representative Shelley Hughes. February 6, 2013.

79 Texas Health and Human Services Committee. March 26, 2013.

80 ACLU. 2008. "Drug Testing of Public Assistance Recipients as a Condition of Eligibility." April 8. www.aclu.org.

81 Nebraska Health and Human Services Committee. March 10, 2011.

82 Email from Jeffrey Mittman to Representatives Pete Higgins and Wes Keller. February 12, 2013.

83 Wisconsin State Legislature Public Hearing Committee Records, Committee on Children and Families. November 17, 2005. Quotations come from Pamela Fendt (UW Milwaukee Center for Economic Development) and Mary Thomas (Child Abuse Prevention Network Public Policy Committee), respectively.

84 Nebraska Committee on Health and Human Services. January 25, 2006.

85 Ibid.

86 Connecticut Human Services Committee. February 19, 2015.

87 Ibid.

88 Ibid.

89 Roberts, *Killing the Black Body*.

90 Katie Shantz, Ilham Dehry, Sarah Knowles, Sarah Minton, and Linda Giannarelli. 2020. Welfare Rules Databook: State TANF Policies as of July 2019, OPRE Report

2020–141, Washington, DC: Office of Planning, Research, and Evaluation, Administration for Children and Families, US Department of Health and Human Services.

91 Hatcher, "Don't Forget Dad," 77.

92 Nebraska Judiciary Committee. February 3, 2011.

93 New Jersey Senate Judiciary Committee. January 6, 1998.

94 Ibid.

CHAPTER 4. WORKING FOR THE MAN

1 Brent Hill. 2015. "Guest Column: The Work We Achieve." *Idaho Falls Post Register*. September 8.

2 Benjamin Franklin. n.d. "Poor Richard Improved, 1758." Founders Online. https://founders.archives.gov.

3 bell hooks. 2000. *Feminist Theory: From Margin to Center*. 2nd ed. Cambridge, MA: South End Press.

4 Public Law 104–193, Part A, Sec. 401. (a)(2).

5 Christopher Ojeda, Anne M. Whitesell, Michael B. Berkman, and Eric Plutzer. 2019. "Federalism and the Racialization of Welfare." *State Politics & Policy Quarterly* 19 (4): 474–501.

6 Gilens, *Why Americans Hate Welfare*.

7 Mead, *New Paternalism*.

8 Mettler, *Divided Citizens*, 172.

9 Piven and Cloward, *Regulating the Poor*, 131.

10 Mettler, *Divided Citizens*, 174.

11 Collins, *Black Feminist Thought*; Johnson et al., *Creating Gender*; Smith, *Welfare Reform and Sexual Regulation*.

12 Ange-Marie Hancock. 2003. "Contemporary Welfare Reform and the Public Identity of the 'Welfare Queen.'" *Race, Gender & Class* 10 (1): 31–59.

13 Karen Seccombe, Delores James, and Kimberly Battle-Walters. 1998. "'They Think You Ain't Much of Nothing': The Social Construction of the Welfare Mother." *Journal of Marriage and the Family* 60 (4): 849–865.

14 Ibid., 855.

15 Gilens, *Why Americans Hate Welfare*, 62.

16 Ibid., 62.

17 Piven and Cloward, *Regulating the Poor*, 133.

18 Triece, *Tell It Like It Is*.

19 Ibid., 76.

20 Gilens, *Why Americans Hate Welfare*, 68.

21 Heather E. Bullock, Karen Fraser Wyche, and Wendy R. Williams. 2001. "Media Images of the Poor." *Journal of Social Issues* 57 (2): 229–246.

22 Mead, *New Paternalism*.

23 Gilbert, "US Welfare Reform."

24 Ibid.

25 Allard, "Changing Face of Welfare," 306.

26 It is worth noting that the definition of elderly, ill or incapacitated, and young child vary across states. For instance, some states grant exemptions if the youngest child is under forty-eight months; in other states the child must be less than three months old.

27 Kim and Fording, "Second-Order Devolution"; Joe Soss, Richard C. Fording, and Sanford F. Schram. 2011. *Disciplining the Poor: Neoliberal Paternalism and the Persistent Power of Race*. Chicago: University of Chicago Press; Reingold and Smith, "Welfare Policymaking."

28 Fellowes and Rowe, "New American Welfare States," 371.

29 Peggy Kahn and Valerie Polakow. 2002. "Struggling to Live and to Learn: Single Mothers, Welfare Policy and Post-secondary Education in Michigan." In *Work, Welfare, and Politics: Confronting Poverty in the Wake of Welfare Reform*, ed. Frances Fox Piven, Joan Acker, Margaret Hallock, and Sandra Morgen. Eugene: University of Oregon Press.

30 Mink, *Welfare's End*.

31 Linda Giannarelli, Christine Heffernan, Sarah Minton, Megan Thompson, and Kathryn Stevens. 2017. Welfare Rules Databook: State TANF Policies as of July 2016, OPRE Report 2017–82. Washington, DC: Office of Planning, Research and Evaluation, Administration for Children and Families, US Department of Health and Human Services.

32 Anna C. Kortweg. 2003. "Welfare Reform and the Subject of the Working Mother: 'Get a Job, a Better Job, Then a Career.'" *Theory and Society* 32: 445–480.

33 Nebraska Health and Human Services Committee. February 15, 2012.

34 Hays, *Flat Broke with Children*.

35 Harry J. Holzer. 2002. "Can Work Experience Programs Work for Welfare Recipients?" *Welfare Reform & Beyond*. Policy Brief No. 24. Washington, DC: Brookings Institution. www.brookings.edu.

36 Noah Zatz. 2006. "What Welfare Requires from Work." *UCLA School of Law Public Law & Legal Theory Research Paper Series*. Research Paper No. 06–33, 425.

37 Gilens, *Why Americans Hate Welfare*, 186.

38 Ibid.

39 Nadasen, *Welfare Warriors*, 32.

40 Mink, *Welfare's End*, 24.

41 NOW. 2015. "Action Alert: Urge Your Representative to Co-sponsor the Social Security Caregiver Credit Act, a NOW Priority." August 19. http://now.org.

42 Mink, *Welfare's End*.

43 Winston, "Welfare Policymaking."

44 Soss, Fording, and Schram, *Disciplining the Poor*.

45 Piven and Cloward, *Regulating the Poor*, 125.

46 Reese, *Backlash against Welfare Mothers*.

47 Ibid., 167.

48 Michael Becher and Daniel Stegmueller. 2021. "Reducing Unequal Representation: The Impact of Labor Unions on Legislative Responsiveness in the U.S. Congress." *Perspectives on Politics* 19 (1): 92–109.

49 Piven and Cloward, *Regulating the Poor*, 370.

50 The eight states used as case studies are identified on the graph as points of reference.

51 Even in this case, opponents have questioned why caring for one's own children is not considered "work," but looking after someone else's children is considered work. Could there be a racial undertone to this policy—when the majority of welfare recipients were white women, staying at home with children was sufficient reason to receive aid, but minority women have historically cared for other (white) people's children?

52 Christina Walker and Stephanie Schmit. 2016. "A Closer Look at Latino Access to Child Care Subsidies." *CLASP*. www.clasp.org.

53 New Jersey Assembly Advisory Council on Women. "Discussion of General Issues of Day Care and Testimony Concerning Specific Efforts to Promote Regulatory Flexibility." May 6, 1997.

54 Wisconsin Assembly on Children and Families. November 17, 2005.

55 Alaska Senate Health and Social Services Committee. February 15, 2019.

56 Wisconsin Assembly Committee on Public Benefit Reform and Senate Committee Public Benefits, Licensing and State-Federal Relations. January 31, 2018.

57 Ibid.

58 "Issues Surrounding the 'Prevention of Domestic Violence Act of 1991.'" May 16, 1996.

59 Connecticut Human Services Committee. March 9, 1999, 62.

60 Connecticut Human Services Committee. February 14, 2013.

61 New Jersey Assembly Labor Committee. May 22, 2000.

62 Connecticut Human Services Committee. February 18, 1997.

63 Connecticut Human Services Committee. February 25, 1997.

64 Letter to Judith B. Robson from Jane Crisler. April 7, 1999.

65 South Dakota Senate Appropriations Subcommittee #2. February 17, 1998.

66 Nebraska Health and Human Services Committee. February 15, 2012.

67 Ibid.

68 New Jersey Assembly Labor Committee, "To provide representatives of business and labor and members of the general public an opportunity to express their concerns and objectives to the committee, relating to issues which may be addressed during the 2000–2001 session." January 24, 2000.

69 AFSCME, "Preserving and Strengthening Temporary Assistance for Needy Families (TANF) and the Workforce Investment Act (WIA)," Resolution No. 62, 35th International Convention, 2002. www.afscme.org.

70 AFSCME, "The Pitfalls of a Privatized Safety Net," Resolution No. 14, 41st International Convention, 2014. www.afscme.org.

71 New Jersey Assembly Labor Committee. January 24, 2000.

72 Ibid.

CHAPTER 5. TIME'S UP

1   Connecticut Human Services Committee. February 18, 1997.

2   Sapiro, "Gender Basis."

3   Skocpol, *Protecting Mothers and Soldiers*; Ethan G. Sribnick. 2011. "The Origins of Modern Child Welfare: Liberalism, Interest Groups, and the Transformation of Public Policy in the 1970s." *Journal of Policy History* 23 (2): 150–176.

4   Gilbert, "US Welfare Reform"

5   Sapiro, "Gender Basis."

6   Cynthia Edmonds-Cady. 2009. "Mobilizing Motherhood: Race, Class, and the Uses of Maternalism in the Welfare Rights Movement." *Women's Studies Quarterly* 37 (3/4): 206–222.

7   Joya Misra, Stephanie Moller, and Marina Karides. 2003. "Envisioning Dependency: Changing Media Depictions of Welfare in the 20th Century." *Social Problems* 50 (4): 482–504.

8   As quoted in Roberts, *Killing the Black Body*, 219.

9   Weaver, *Ending Welfare*.

10 Bullock et al., "Media Images of the Poor."

11 Ibid.; Gilens, *Why Americans Hate Welfare*.

12 Gilens, *Why Americans Hate Welfare*, 37.

13 Robin Dennis, Jill Braunstein, and Heidi Hartmann. 1995. "Welfare to Work: The Job Opportunities of AFDC Recipients." *Institute for Women's Policy Research*.

14 Mary Jo Bane and David T. Ellwood. 1994. *Welfare Realities: From Rhetoric to Reform*. Cambridge, MA: Harvard University Press, 29.

15 Ibid., 38.

16 Christopher Mazzeo, Sara Rab, and Susan Eachus. 2003. "Work-First or Work-Only: Welfare Reform, State Policy, and Access to Postsecondary Education." *Annals of the American Academy of Political and Social Science* 586: 144–171.

17 Korteweg, "Welfare Reform."

18 Similar to the activity requirements, however, states can exempt up to 20 percent of their caseload from the time limit in any given month.

19 Idaho Senate Health and Welfare Committee. January 12, 2005.

20 Liz Schott. 1998. "State Choices on Time Limit Policies in TANF-Funded Programs." *Center for Budget and Policy Priorities*. September 1. www.cbpp.org.

21 See figures B.3a–j/A5.1a–j in the second appendix for graphs showing the change in the number of states allowing time limit exemptions and extensions over time.

22 Gilens, *Why Americans Hate Welfare*, 190.

23 Ibid.

24 Cammissa and Manuel, "Religious Groups as Interest Groups."

25 Mazzeo et al., "Work-First or Work-Only."

26 Klarner et al., "Business Interest Group Power," 114.

27 Parrott, "Welfare Recipients Who Find Jobs," 1.

28 Weaver, *Ending Welfare*, 212.

29 Roberts, *Killing the Black Body*, 219.

30 Winston, *Welfare Policymaking*, 42.

31 Cohen et al., *Welfare Rules Databook*.

32 Nebraska Health and Human Services Committee. January 25, 2007.

33 Ibid.

34 Ojeda et al., "Federalism and Racialization."

35 Alaska Senate Finance Committee. March 12, 2015.

36 Wisconsin State Legislature Senate Committee on Public Benefits, Licensing and State-Federal Relations. January 31, 2018.

37 These results remain the same when the interest group variables are lagged by five years.

38 Wisconsin State Legislature Assembly Committee on Children and Families. May 13, 2002.

39 Leila Schochet. 2019. "The Child Care Crisis Is Keeping Women Out of the Workforce." *Center for American Progress*. March 28. www.americanprogress.org.

40 New Jersey Assembly Advisory Council on Women, "Discussion of General Issues of Day Care," 1.

41 Ibid., 6.

42 Ibid., 46.

43 Connecticut Human Services Committee. February 25, 1997.

44 *Bureau of Economic Analysis*. Table CA1: "Personal Income Summary: Personal Income, Population, Per Capita Income." www.bea.gov.

45 Connecticut Human Services Committee. February 18, 1997.

46 Ibid.

47 Marisa Osorio Colon. 1997. "Welfare Recipients Look to Cordero for Leadership and Passion." *Hartford Courant*. July 1. http://articles.courant.com.

48 Connecticut Human Services Committee. February 18, 1997.

49 Ibid.

50 Connecticut Human Services Committee. February 22, 2001.

51 Ibid.

52 Connecticut Human Services Committee. March 7, 2006.

53 Connecticut Human Services Committee. February 18, 1997.

54 Ibid.

55 Ibid.

CHAPTER 6. BENEFIT BOUNDARIES

1 Lou Dobbs, Wendell Goler, and Walid Phares. "Syria and Chemical Weapons; Interview with Former Fed Vice Chair Alan Blinder; Illegal Immigrants and Welfare." *Lou Dobbs Tonight (CNN)*. Accessed May 17, 2023.

2 Donald J. Trump, "Remarks on Immigration at the Phoenix Convention Center in Phoenix, Arizona." *American Presidency Project*. www.presidency.ucsb.edu.

3 Ted Cruz repeated this line, or something very similar, at primary debates in January, February, and March 2016. See Presidential Candidate Debates, Republican Candidates Debate in Des Moines, Iowa. *American Presidency Project*. www .presidency.ucsb.edu; Presidential Candidate Debates, Republican Candidates Debate in Manchester, New Hampshire. *American Presidency Project*. www .presidency.ucsb.edu; Presidential Candidate Debates, Republican Candidates Debate in Miami, Florida. *American Presidency Project*. www.presidency.ucsb.edu.

4 Presidential Candidate Debates, Republican Candidates Debate in Des Moines, Iowa. *American Presidency Project*. www.presidency.ucsb.edu.

5 Presidential Candidate Debates, Republican Candidates Debate in Greenville, South Carolina. *American Presidency Project*. www.presidency.ucsb.edu.

6 Ron Haskins. 2009. "Limiting Welfare Benefits for Non-citizens: Emergence of Compromises." In *Immigrants and Welfare: The Impact of Welfare Reform on America's Newcomers*, ed. Michael E. Fix. New York: Russell Sage Foundation, 39–68, 44.

7 Jane Addams. 1911. *Twenty Years at Hull House*. Monee, IL: Pantianos Classics.

8 Mink, *Welfare's End*; Deborah E. Ward. 2005. *The White Welfare State: The Racialization of U.S. Welfare Policy*. Ann Arbor: University of Michigan Press, 70.

9 Thomas J. Espenshade, Jessica L. Baraka, and Gregory A. Huber. 1997. "Implications of the 1996 Welfare and Immigration Reform Acts for US Immigration." *Population and Development Review* 23 (4): 769–801.

10 Michael B. Katz. 2008. *The Price of Citizenship: Redefining the American Welfare State*. Philadelphia: University of Pennsylvania Press, 327.

11 Leo R. Chavez. 2008. *The Latino Threat: Constructing Immigrants, Citizens, and the Nation*. Stanford, CA: Stanford University Press, 25.

12 Katz, *Price of Citizenship*.

13 Neubeck and Cazenave, *Welfare Racism*, 148.

14 Ibid., 149.

15 George J. Borjas. 1995. "The Economic Benefits from Immigration." *The Journal of Economic Perspectives* 9 (2): 3–22.

16 Filindra, "Immigrant Social Policy," 39.

17 Laura S. Hussey and Shanna Pearson-Merkowitz. 2011. "The Changing Role of Race in Social Welfare Attitude Formation: Partisan Divides over Undocumented Immigrants and Social Welfare Policy." *Political Research Quarterly* 66 (3): 572–584.

18 Hana E. Brown. 2013. "Race, Legality, and the Social Policy Consequences of Anti-Immigration Mobilization." *American Sociological Review* 78 (2): 290–314.

19 George J. Borjas. 1999. "Immigration and Welfare Magnets." *Journal of Labor Economics* 17 (4): 607–637.

20 Jennifer Van Hook and Frank D. Bean. 2009. "Explaining Mexican-Immigrant Welfare Behaviors: The Importance of Employment-Related Cultural Repertoires." *American Sociological Review* 74 (3): 423–444.

21 Randy Capps, Michael E. Fix, and Everett Henderson. 2009. "Trends in Immigrants' Use of Public Assistance after Welfare Reform." In *Immigrants and Welfare: The Impact of Welfare Reform on America's Newcomers*, ed. Michael E. Fix. New York: Russell Sage Foundation, 123–152.

22 Bailey and Rom, "Wider Race"; Berry, Fording, and Hanson, "Reassessing the 'Race to the Bottom.'"

23 Berry, Fording, and Hanson, "Reassessing the 'Race to the Bottom.'"

24 Bailey and Rom, "Wider Race."

25 Philip Kretsedemas and Ana Aparicio, eds. 2004. *Immigrants, Welfare Reform, and the Poverty of Policy*. Westport, CT: Praeger Publishers, 5.

26 Barbara Franz. 2007. "Guest Workers and Immigration Reform: The Rise of a New Feudalism in America?" *New Political Science* 29 (3): 349–368.

27 Michael E. Fix, ed. 2009. *Immigrants and Welfare: The Impact of Welfare Reform on America's Newcomers*. New York: Russell Sage Foundation.

28 Ibid.

29 Wendy Zimmerman and Karen C. Tumlin. 1999. "Patchwork Policies: State Assistance for Immigrants under Welfare Reform." *Urban Institute*. www.urban.org.

30 Parolees are noncitizens who are permitted entry into the United States because of emergency or overriding public interest.

31 Ruth Ellen Wasem. 2004. "Non-citizen Eligibility for Major Federal Public Assistance Programs: Policies and Legislation." *Congressional Research Service*.

32 Maurice Goldman. 1999. "The Violence Against Women Act: Meeting Its Goals in Protecting Battered Immigrant Women?" *Family and Conciliation Courts Review* 37 (3): 375–392.

33 GAO. 2009. "Sponsored Noncitizens and Public Benefits: More Clarity in Federal Guidance and Better Access to Federal Information Could Improve Implementation of Income Eligibility Rules." GAO-09-375.

34 Zimmerman and Tumlin, "Patchwork Policies."

35 Richard Speiglman, Rosa-Maria Castaneda, Hana Brown, and Randy Capps. 2013. "Welfare Reform's Ineligible Immigrant Parents: Program Reach and Enrollment Barriers." *Journal of Children and Poverty* 19 (2): 91–106, 92.

36 Filindra, "Immigrant Social Policy," 40.

37 Carolyn Wong. 2006. *Lobbying for Inclusion: Rights Politics and the Making of Immigration Policy*. Stanford, CA: Stanford University Press, 39,

38 Winston, *Welfare Policymaking*, 134; Julie Stewart and Kenneth P. Jameson. 2012. "Interests Aren't Everything: An Exploration of Economic Explanations of Immigration Policy in a New Destination." *International Migration* 51 (4): 33–52.

39 Paula D. McClain. 1993. "The Changing Dynamics of Urban Politics: Black and Hispanic Municipal Employment—Is There Competition?" *Journal of Politics* 55 (2): 399–414.

40 Jason P. Casellas. 2011. *Latino Representation in State Houses and Congress*. New York: Cambridge University Press.

41 Jason P. Casellas. 2009. "Coalitions in the House? The Election of Minorities to State Legislatures and Congress." *Political Research Quarterly* 62 (1): 120–131; Karen M. Kaufmann 2003. "Cracks in the Rainbow: Group Commonality as a Basis for Latino and African-American Political Coalitions." *Political Research Quarterly* 56 (2): 199–210.

42 Filindra, "Immigrant Social Policy."

43 Justin Allen Berg. 2015. "Explaining Attitudes towards Immigrants and Immigration Policy: A Review of the Theoretical Literature." *Sociology Compass* 9 (1): 23–34, 25.

44 Jeffrey S. Passel and D'Vera Cohn. 2016. "Size of U.S. Unauthorized Immigrant Workforce Stable after the Great Recession." *Pew Research Center*. www .pewhispanic.org.

45 Wong, *Lobbying for Inclusion*, 29.

46 Amy L. Fairchild. 2004. "Policies of Inclusion: Immigrants, Disease, Dependency, and American Immigration Policy at the Dawn and Dusk of the 20th Century." *American Journal of Public Health* 94 (4): 528–539.

47 Graefe et al., "Immigrants' TANF Eligibility."

48 Preuhs, "Descriptive Representation."

49 Graefe et al., "Immigrants' TANF Eligibility."

50 Hero and Preuhs, "Immigration and the Evolving American Welfare State," 507–508.

51 Vickie D. Ybarra, Lisa M. Sanchez, and Gabriel R. Sanchez. 2016. "Anti-immigrant Anxieties in State Policy: The Great Recession and Punitive Immigration Policy in the American States, 2005–2012." *State Politics & Policy Quarterly* 16 (3): 313–339.

52 Graefe et al., "Immigrants' TANF Eligibility."

53 Ibid., 116.

54 Filindra, "Immigrant Social Policy."

55 Kretsedemas and Aparicio, *Immigrants, Welfare Reform*, 6.

56 Una Newton and Brian E. Adams. 2009. "State Immigration Policies: Innovation, Cooperation or Conflict?" *Publius* 39 (3): 408–431.

57 Walter Clark Wilson. 2010. "Descriptive Representation and Latino Interest Bill Sponsorship in Congress." *Social Science Quarterly* 91 (4): 1043–1062.

58 Sophia J. Wallace. 2014. "Representing Latinos: Examining Descriptive and Substantive Representation in Congress." *Political Research Quarterly* 67 (4): 917–929.

59 William Curtis Ellis and Walter Clark Wilson. 2013. "Minority Chairs and Congressional Attention to Minority Issues: The Effect of Descriptive Representation in Positions of Institutional Power." *Social Science Quarterly* 94 (5): 1207–1221.

60 Preuhs, "Descriptive Representation."

61 There could be noncitizens eligible for assistance, but they are not in the categories that I am including in the analysis here. For instance, they could be noncitizens that arrived prior to PRWORA, or those who have been in the country for less than five years.

62 Pew Research Center. 2018. "Shifting Public Views on Legal Immigration into the U.S." *Pew Research Center.* June 28. www.pewresearch.org.

63 Connecticut Human Services Committee. February 24, 2004.

64 Alaska House Health, Education, and Social Services Committee. April 1, 1997.

65 Connecticut Human Services Committee. February 24, 2004.

66 Brown, "Race Legality, and the Social Policy Consequences."

67 Nebraska Judiciary Committee. March 2, 2017.

68 Ibid.

69 Connecticut Human Services Committee. February 24, 2004.

70 Nebraska Judiciary Committee. March 2, 2017.

71 Alaska House Health, Education and Social Services Committee. April 1, 1997.

72 Ibid.

73 Cammisa and Manuel, "Religious Groups as Interest Groups."

74 Strolovitch, *Affirmative Advocacy.*

75 Texas Human Services Committee witness list for hearing on March 26, 2001. www.capitol.state.tx.us.

76 New Jersey Public Hearing before Assembly Task Force on Domestic Violence. March 6, 1998; Task Force Meeting of Assembly Task Force on Domestic Violence. March 20, 1998.

77 Texas Human Services Committee. March 26, 2001.

CHAPTER 7. EXPANDING THE SOCIAL SAFETY NET

1 Robert Samuels. 2018. "Wisconsin Is the GOP Model for 'Welfare Reform.' But as Work Requirements Grow, So Does One Family's Desperation." *Washington Post.* April 22. www.washingtonpost.com; Reid Wilson. 2018. "Wisconsin Welfare Reform Could Be Model for GOP." *The Hill.* February 21. https://thehill.com; J. B. Wagan. 2018. "Wisconsin's Unprecedented Welfare Reform Could Inspire Conservative Changes Elsewhere." *Governing.* February 22. www.governing.com.

2 National Conference of State Legislatures. 2017. "Drug Testing for Welfare Recipients and Public Assistance." March 24. *National Conference of State Legislatures.* www.ncsl.org.

3 Wisconsin Senate Committee on Public Benefits, Licensing and State-Federal Relations, and Assembly Committee on Public Benefit Reform. January 31, 2018.

4 South Dakota House Health and Human Services Committee. February 7, 2012.

5 Ibid.

6 Alaska House, "An Act relating to disqualification from the food stamp program for refusal to cooperate with the child support services agency or for past due child support payments; relating to the duties of the Department of Health and Social Services; and relating to the duties of the child support services agency." HB 167, introduced in House May 14, 2019.

7 Wisconsin Assembly Committee on Public Benefit Reform. April 11, 2017.

8   Letter to Members of the Senate Committee on Public Benefits, Licensing and State-Federal Relations and Members of the Assembly Committee on Public Benefit Reform. January 31, 2018.

9   Wisconsin Council of Churches. Letter to Assembly Committee on Public Benefit Reform and Senate Committee on Public Benefits, Licensing, and State-Federal Relations. January 31, 2018; Jon Peacock, research director of Kids Forward. Letter to Joint Committee on Public Benefit Reform. January 31, 2018.

10 Letter to Committee on Assembly Organization. January 31, 2018.

11 Seema Verma. 2017. Remarks at the National Association of Medicaid Directors (NAMD) 2017 Fall Conference. www.cms.gov.

12 KFF. 2023. "Medicaid Waiver Tracker: Approved and Pending Section 1115 Waivers by State." *Kaiser Family Foundation.* June 5. www.kff.org.

13 Idaho House Health and Welfare Committee. February 7, 2018.

14 Ibid.

15 Ibid.

16 Ibid.

17 Alaska Senate Finance Committee. April 12, 2018.

18 Ibid.

19 Alaska Senate Health and Social Services Committee. February 15, 2019.

20 Idaho House Health and Welfare Committee. February 7, 2018.

21 Center on Budget and Policy Priorities. 2022. "A Quick Guide to SNAP Eligibility and Benefits." *Center on Budget and Policy Priorities.* January 6. www.cbpp.org.

22 Laura Wheaton, Tracy Vericker, Jonathan Schwabish, Theresa Anderson, Kevin Baier, Joseph Gasper, Nathan Sick, and Kevin Werner. 2021. "The Impact of SNAP Able-Bodied Adults Without Dependents (ABAWD) Time Limit Reinstatement in Nine States." *Urban Institute.* June 22. www.urban.org.

23 Ed Bolen and Stacy Dean. 2018. "Waivers Add Key State Flexibility to SNAP's Three-Month Time Limit." *Center on Budget and Policy Priorities.* February 6. www.cbpp.org.

24 New Jersey Senate Legislative Oversight Committee. January 28, 2016.

25 Ibid.

26 Food and Nutrition Service. 2020. "Supplemental Nutrition Assistance Program (SNAP)—Families First Coronavirus Response Act and Impact on Time Limit for Able-Bodied Without Dependents (ABAWDs)." *United States Department of Agriculture.* March 20. www.fns.usda.gov.

27 Pew Research Center. 2020. "Positive Economic Views Plummet; Support for Government Aid Crosses Party Lines." *Pew Research Center.* April 21. www.pewresearch.org.

28 Ibid.

29 Sarah D. Asebedo, Yi Liu, Blake Gray, and Taufiq Hasan Quadria. 2020. "How Americans Used Their COVID-19 Economic Impact Payments." *Financial Planning Review* 3 (4).

30 Center on Budget and Policy Priorities. 2022. "Robust COVID Relief Achieved Historic Gains against Poverty and Hardship, Bolstered Economy." *Center on Budget and Policy Priorities*. February 24. www.cbpp.org.

31 Michael Karpman and Gregory Acs. 2020. "Unemployment Insurance and Economic Impact Payments Associated with Reduced Hardship following CARES Act." *Urban Institute*. June. www.urban.org.

32 Ibid., 7.

33 See, for instance, Kate Davidson, 2020. "Is $600 a Week in Extra Unemployment Aid Deterring People from Seeking Work?" *Wall Street Journal*. July 29. www.wsj.com.

34 AP. 2021. "Chamber of Commerce Seeks End to Enhanced US Jobless Aid." *AP News*. May 7. https://apnews.com.

35 Center on Budget and Policy Priorities, "Robust COVID Relief."

36 Ashley Burnside. 2021. "Key Findings from National Child Tax Credit Survey: CTC Monthly Payments Are Helping Improve Family Well-Being." *CLASP*. November 17. www.clasp.org.

37 Rachel Scott and Benjamin Siegel. 2021. "Sen. Joe Manchin Suggests Child Tax Credit Payments Would Be Used to Buy Drugs." *ABC News*. December 20. https://abcnews.go.com.

38 Ben Casselman. 2022. "Child Tax Credit's Extra Help Ends, Just as Covid Surges Anew." *New York Times*. January 2. www.nytimes.com.

39 Samuel Hammond and Robert Orr. 2021. "The Conservative Case for a Child Allowance." *Niskanen Center*. February 4. www.niskanencenter.org.

40 "Romney Offers Path to Provide Greater Financial Security for American Families." 2021. *Mitt Romney: U.S. Senator for Utah*. February 4. www.romney.senate.gov.

41 Teaganne Finn and Phil McCausland. 2022. "Romney's Push to Revive Child Tax Credit Hinges on Work Requirements." *NBC News*. February 21. www.nbcnews.com.

42 Sheelah Kolhatkar. 2021. "Biden's Stimulus Plan Contains an Experiment in Universal Basic Income." *New Yorker*. March 15. www.newyorker.com.

43 GAO. 2012. "Temporary Assistance for Needy Families: More Accountability Needed to Reflect Breadth of Block Grant Services." GAO-13-33. Washington, DC. www.gao.gov.

44 Vincent A. Fusaro. 2021. "State Politics, Race, and 'Welfare' as a Funding Stream: Cash Assistance Spending under Temporary Assistance for Needy Families." *Policy Studies Journal* 49 (3): 811–834.

45 Skocpol, *Protecting Mothers and Soldiers*.

46 Steven Mufson and Tracy Jan. 2017. "If You're a Poor Person in America, Trump's Budget Is Not for You." *Washington Post*. March 16. www.washingtonpost.com; Erica Werner and Alan Fram. 2017. "House to Vote on Health Care Bill Thursday." *Chicago Tribune*. May 3. www.chicagotribune.com.

APPENDIX A

1 For work that uses the Welfare Rules Database, see Gordon F. De Jong, Deborah Roempke, Shelley K. Irving, and Tanja St. Pierre. 2006. "Measuring State TANF Policy Variations and Changes After Reform." *Social Science Quarterly* 87 (4): 755–781; Matthew C. Fellowes and Gretchen Rowe. 2004. "Politics and the New American Welfare States." *American Journal of Political Science* 48 (2): 362–373; Signe-Mary McKernan, Jen Bernstein, and Lynne Fender. 2012. "Taming the Beast: Categorizing State Welfare Policies: A Typology of Welfare Policies Affecting Recipient Job Entry." *Journal of Policy Analysis and Management* 24 (2): 443–460; Reingold and Smith, "Welfare Policymaking,"; Soss, Fording, and Schram, "Color of Devolution."

2 Michael A. Bailey and Mark Carl Rom. 2004. "A Wider Race? Interstate Competition across Health and Welfare Programs." *Journal of Politics* 66 (2): 326–347; Rodney E. Hero and Robert R. Preuhs. 2007. "Immigration and the Evolving American Welfare State: Examining Policies in the U.S. States." *American Journal of Political Science* 51 (3): 498–517; Owens and Reingold, "'Deviants' and Democracy"; Robert R. Preuhs. 2007. "Descriptive Representation as a Mechanism to Mitigate Policy Backlash: Latino Incorporation and Welfare Policy in the American States." *Political Research Quarterly* 60 (2): 277–292.

3 For research that replicates the Fellowes and Rowe scales, see Byungkyu Kim and Richard C. Fording. 2010. "Second-Order Devolution and the Implementation of TANF in the U.S. States." *State Politics & Policy Quarterly* 10 (4): 341–367; Soss, Fording, and Schram, *Disciplining the Poor*; and Reingold and Smith, "Welfare Policymaking."

4 DeJong et al., "Measuring State TANF."

5 Fellowes and Rowe, "New American Welfare States"; Soss et al., "Setting the Terms of Relief."

6 Schneider and Ingram, "Social Construction of Target Populations."

7 Justin Allen Berg. 2015. "Explaining Attitudes toward Immigrants and Immigration Policy: A Review of the Theoretical Literature." *Sociology Compass* 9 (1): 23–34.

8 Elissa Cohen, Sarah Minton, Megan Thompson, Elizabeth Crowe, and Linda Giannarelli. 2016. *Welfare Rules Databook: State TANF Policies as of July 2015.* OPRE Report 2016–67. Washington, DC: Office of Planning, Research, and Evaluation, Administration for Children and Families, US Department of Health and Human Services.

9 Ellen Reese. 2005. *Backlash against Welfare Mothers: Past and Present.* Berkeley: University of California Press.

10 Cowell-Meyers and Langbein, "Linking Women's Descriptive."

11 Preuhs, "Conditional Effects"; Reingold and Smith, "Welfare Policymaking"; Klarner et al., "Business Interest Group Power"; Fellowes and Rowe, "New American Welfare States."

12 Winston, *Welfare Policymaking.*

13 No information could be found for Alabama, Delaware, Florida, Georgia, Indiana, Louisiana, Mississippi, North Carolina, Rhode Island, South Carolina, Washington, West Virginia, or Wyoming. Material beginning in 2010 or later was available for Arkansas, Colorado, the District of Columbia, Kentucky, Maine, Michigan, North Dakota, and Oklahoma.

14 Deborah Roempke Graefe, Gordon F. De Jong, Matthew Hall, Samuel Sturgeon, and Julie VanEerden. 2008. "Immigrants' TANF Eligibility, 1996–2003: What Explains the New Across-State Inequalities?" *International Migration Review* 42 (1): 89–133; Hero and Preuhs, "Immigration and the Evolving American Welfare State."

15 Soss, Fording, and Schram, "Color of Devolution."

16 Richard C. Fording, Joe Soss, and Sanford F. Schram. 2007. "Devolution, Discretion, and the Effect of Local Political Values on TANF Sanctioning." *Social Sciences Review* 81 (2):285–316; Soss et al., "Setting the Terms of Relief."

17 Notably, some of these states were pioneers in their policies: Wisconsin was one of the first states to implement strict work requirements, and New Jersey was the first state to adopt a family cap.

18 Baumgartner et al. 2009. *Lobbying and Policy Change: Who Wins, Who Loses, and Why.* Chicago: University of Chicago Press.

19 Bryce Covert. 2015. "An 'Ugly Policy' Systematically Devalues Poor Children. One State Is Ready to Stop It." *Think Progress*, July 15. http://thinkprogress.org.

BIBLIOGRAPHY

Abramovitz, Mimi. 1996. *Regulating the Lives of Women: Social Welfare Policy from Colonial Times to the Present*. Boston, MA: South End Press.

———. 2006. "Welfare Reform in the United States: Gender, Race, and Class Matter." *Critical Social Policy* 26 (2): 336–364.

ACLU. 2008. "Drug Testing of Public Assistance Recipients as a Condition of Eligibility." *American Civil Liberties Union*. April 8. www.aclu.org.

Addams, Jane. 1911. *Twenty Years at Hull House*. Monee, IL: Pantianos Classics.

AFSCME. 2002. "Preserving and Strengthening Temporary Assistance for Needy Families (TANF) and the Workforce Investment Act (WIA)." *Resolution No. 62, 35th International Convention*. www.afscme.org.

———. 2014. "The Pitfalls of a Privatized Safety Net." *Resolution N. 14, 41st International Convention*. www.afscme.org.

Allard, Scott W. 2007. "The Changing Face of Welfare during the Bush Administration." *Publius* 37 (3): 304–332.

American National Election Studies. 2021. "ANES 2020 Times Series Study Full Release" (dataset and documentation). July 19. www.electionstudies.org.

Amott, Teresa L. 1990. "Black Women and AFDC: Making Entitlement Out of Necessity." In *Women, the State, and Welfare*, edited by Linda Gordon, 280–298. Madison: University of Wisconsin Press.

An, Brian, Morris Levy, and Rodney Hero. 2018. "It's Not Just Welfare: Racial Inequality and the Local Provision of Public Goods in the United States." *Urban Affairs Review* 54 (5): 833–865.

Annie E. Casey Foundation. 2023. "Child Well-Being in Single-Parent Families." *Annie E. Casey Foundation*. June 23. www.aecf.org.

AP. 2021. "Chamber of Commerce Seeks End to Enhanced US Jobless Aid." *AP News*. May 7. https://apnews.com.

Asebedo, Sarah D., Yi Liu, Blake Gray, and Taufiq Hasan Quadria. 2020. "How Americans Used Their COVID-19 Economic Impact Payments." *Financial Planning Review* 3 (4).

Avery, James M., and Mark Peffley. 2005. "Voter Registration Requirements, Voter Turnout, and Welfare Eligibility Policy: Class Bias Matters." *State Politics & Policy Quarterly* 5 (1): 47–67.

Bailey, Michael A., and Mark Carl Rom. 2004. "A Wider Race? Interstate Competition across Health and Welfare Programs." *Journal of Politics* 66 (2): 326–347.

Bailis, Lawrence Neil. 1974. *Bread or Justice: Grassroots Organizing in the Welfare Rights Movement.* Lexington, MA: Lexington Books.

Baker, Andy, and Corey Cook. 2005. "Representing Black Intests and Promoting Black Culture: The Importance of African American Descriptive Representation in the U.S. House." *Du Bois Review* 2 (2): 227–246.

Baker, Regina S. 2022. "The Historical Racial Regime and Racial Inequality in Poverty in the American South." *American Journal of Sociology* 127 (6): 1721–1781.

Balz, Dan. 1994. "GOP 'Contract' Pledges 10 Tough Acts to Follow." *Washington Post.* November 20. www.washingtonpost.com.

Bane, Mary Jo, and David T. Ellwood. 1994. *Welfare Realities: From Rhetoric to Reform.* Cambridge, MA: Harvard University Press.

Barnes, Tiffany D., Victoria D. Beall, and Mirya R. Holman. 2021. "Pink-Collar Representation and Budgetary Outcomes in US States." *Legislative Studies Quarterly* 46 (1): 119–154.

Barrett, Edith. 1997. "Gender and Race in the State House: The Legislative Experience." *Social Science Journal* 34 (2): 131–144.

Barrilleaux, Charles, Thomas Holbrook, and Laura Langer. 2002. "Electoral Competition, Legislative Balance, and American State Welfare Policy." *American Journal of Political Science* 46 (2): 415–427.

Baumgartner, Frank R., Jeffrey M. Berry, Marie Hojnacki, David C. Kimball, and Beth L. Leech. 2009. *Lobbying and Policy Change: Who Wins, Who Loses, and Why.* Chicago: University of Chicago Press.

Becher, Michael, and Daniel Stegmueller. 2021. "Reducing Unequal Representation: The Impact of Labor Unions on Legislative Responsiveness in the U.S. Congress." *Perspectives on Politics* 19 (1): 92–109.

Berg, Justin Allen. 2015. "Explaining Attitudes toward Immigrants and Immigration Policy: A Review of the Theoretical Literature." *Sociology Compass* 9 (1): 23–34.

Berry, William D., Richard C. Fording, and Russell L. Hanson. 2003. "Reassessing the 'Race to the Bottom' in State Welfare Policy." *Journal of Politics* 65 (2): 327–349.

Berry, William D., Evan J. Rinquist, Richard C. Fording, and Russell L. Hanson. 1998. "Measuring Citizen Ideology and Government Ideology in the American States, 1960–93." *American Journal of Political Science* 42 (1): 327–348.

Bolen, Ed, and Stacy Dean. 2018. "Waivers Add Key State Flexibility to SNAP's Three-Month Time Limit." *Center on Budget and Policy Priorities.* February 6. www.cbpp.org.

Borjas, George J. 1995. "The Economic Benefits from Immigration." *Journal of Economic Perspectives* 9 (2): 3–22.

———. 1999. "Immigration and Welfare Magnets." *Journal of Labor Economics* 17 (4): 607–637.

Brady, Henry E., Sidney Verba, and Kay Lehman Schlozman. 1995. "Beyond SES: A Resource Model of Political Participation." *American Political Science Review* 89 (2): 271–294.

Bratton, Kathleen A., and Kerry L. Haynie. 1999. "Agenda Setting and Legislative Success in State Legislatures: The Effects of Gender and Race." *Journal of Politics* 61 (3): 658–679.

Bratton, Kathleen A., Kerry L. Haynie, and Beth Reingold. 2006. "Agenda Setting and African American Women in State Legislatures." *Journal of Women, Politics & Policy* 28 (3/4): 71–96.

Broockman, David E. 2013. "Black Politicians Are More Intrinsically Motivated to Advance Blacks' Interests: A Field Experiment Manipulating Political Incentives." *American Journal of Political Science* 57 (3): 521–536.

Brown, Hana E. 2013. "Race, Legality, and the Social Policy Consequences of Anti-Immigration Mobilization." *American Sociological Review* 78 (2): 290–314.

Brown, Michael K. 1999. *Race, Money, and the American Welfare State*. Ithaca, NY: Cornell University Press.

Brown, Robert D. 1995. "Party Cleavages and Welfare Effort in the American States." *American Political Science Review* 89 (1): 23–33.

Bryant, Lisa A., and Julia Marin Hellwege. 2019. "Working Mothers Represent: How Children Affect the Legislative Agenda of Women in Congress." *American Politics Research* 47 (3): 447–470.

Bullock, Heather E., Karen Fraser Wyche, and Wendy R. Williams. 2001. "Media Images of the Poor." *Journal of Social Issues* 57 (2): 229–246.

Bureau of the Census. 1940. "Families in the United States by Type and Size: 1930." *U.S. Census*. www2.census.gov.

Burnside, Ashley. 2021. "Key Findings from National Child Tax Credit Survey: CTC Monthly Payments Are Helping Improve Family Well-Being." *CLASP*. November 17. www.clasp.org.

Camasso, Michael. 2007. *Family Caps, Abortion and Women of Color: Research Connection and Political Rejection*. New York: Oxford University Press.

Cammett, Ann. 2014. "Deadbeat Dads & Welfare Queens: How Metaphor Shapes Poverty Law." *Boston College Journal of Law and Social Justice* 34 (2): 233–266.

Cammisa, Anne Marie, and Paul Christopher Manuel. 2016. "Religious Groups as Interest Groups: The United States Catholic Bishops in the Welfare Reform Debate of 1995–1996 and the Health Care Reform Debate of 2009–2010." *Religions* 7 (16): 1–28.

Campbell, David, and Joan Wright. 2005. "Rethinking Welfare School-Attendance Policies." *Social Science Service Review* 79 (1): 2–28.

Canino-Arroyo, María Josefa. 2003. "Reflections on Latino Advocacy and Welfare Reform in New Jersey." *Centro Journal* 15 (1): 177–195.

Capps, Randy, Michael E. Fix, and Everett Henderson. 2009. "Trends in Immigrants' Use of Public Assistance after Welfare Reform." In *Immigrants and Welfare: The Impact of Welfare Reform on America's Newcomers*, edited by Michael E. Fix, 123–152. New York: Russell Sage Foundation.

Casellas, Jason P. 2009. "Coalitions in the House? The Election of Minorities to State Legislatures and Congress." *Political Research Quarterly* 62 (1): 120–131.

———. 2011. *Latino Representation in State Houses and Congress*. New York: Cambridge University Press.

Casselman, Ben. 2022. "Child Tax Credit's Extra Help Ends, Just as Covid Surges Anew." *New York Times*. January 2. www.nytimes.com.

Center on Budget and Policy Priorities. 2022. "A Quick Guide to SNAP Eligibility and Benefits." *Center on Budget and Policy Priorities*. January 6. www.cbpp.org.

———. 2022. "Robust COVID Relief Achieved Historic Gains against Poverty and Hardship, Bolstered Economy." *Center on Budget and Policy Priorities*. February 24. www.cbpp.org.

———. 2022. "Policy Basics: Temporary Assistance for Needy Families." *Center on Budget and Policy Priorities*. March 1. www.cbpp.org.

———. 2022. "Policy Basics: Supplemental Security Income." *Center on Budget and Policy Priorities*. March 2. www.cbpp.org.

———. 2023. "State Fact Sheets: How States Spend Funds under the TANF Block Grant." *Center on Budget and Policy Priorities*. www.cbpp.org.

Chavez, Leo R. 2008. *The Latino Threat: Constructing Immigrants, Citizens, and the Nation*. Stanford, CA: Stanford University Press.

Clark, Krissy. 2016. "'Oh My God—We're on Welfare?'" *Slate*. June 2. www.slate.com.

Clinton, William J. 1992. "Address Accepting the Presidential Nomination at the Democratic National Convention in New York." *American Presidency Project*. www.presidency.ucsb.edu.

Coates, Ta-Nehisi. 2017. "My President Was Black." *The Atlantic*. January/February. www.theatlantic.com.

Coffé, Hilde, and Catherine Bolzendahl. 2010. "Same Game, Different Rules: Gender Differences in Political Participation." *Sex Roles* (62): 318–333.

Cohen, Elissa, Sarah Minton, Megan Thompson, Elizabeth Crowe, and Linda Giannarelli. 2016. *Welfare Rules Databook: State TANF Policies as of July 2015*. OPRE Report 2016–67, Washington, DC: Office of Planning, Research, and Evaluation, Administration for Children and Families, US Department of Health and Human Services.

Collins, Patricia Hill. 2000. *Black Feminist Thought: Knowledge, Consciousness, and the Politics of Empowerment*. 2nd ed. New York: Routledge.

Colon, Marisa Osorio. 1997. "Welfare Recipients Look to Cordero for Leadership and Passion." *Hartford Courant*. July 1. http://articles.courant.com.

Congressional Research Service. 2023. *The Temporary Assistance for Needy Families (TANF) Block Grant: A Legislative History*. https://crsreports.congress.gov.

Covert, Bryce. 2015. "An 'Ugly Policy' Systematically Devalues Poor Children. One State Is Ready to Stop It." *Think Progress*. July 15. http://thinkprogress.org.

Cowell-Meyers, Kimberly, and Laura Langbein. 2009. "Linking Women's Descriptive and Substantive Representation in the United States." *Politics & Gender* 5 (4): 491–518.

Crenshaw, Kimberlé. 1989. "Demarginalizing the Intersection of Race and Sex: A Black Feminist Critique of Antidiscrimination Doctrine, Feminist Theory, and Antiracist Politics." *University of Chicago Legal Forum* 140: 139–167.

Cress, Daniel M., and David A. Snow. 1996. "Mobilization at the Margins: Resources, Benefactors, and the Viability of Homeless Social Movement Organizations." *American Sociological Review* 61 (6): 1089–1109.

Daguerre, Anne. 2008. "The Second Phase of US Welfare Reform, 2000–2006: Blaming the Poor Again?" *Social Policy & Administration* 42 (4): 362–378.

Danziger, Sandra K., and Kristin S. Seefeldt. 2002. "Barriers to Employment and the 'Hard to Serve': Implications for Service, Sanctions, and Time Limits." *Social Policy & Society* 2 (2): 151–160.

Davern, Michael, Rene Bautista, Jeremy Freese, Stephen L. Morgan, and Tom W. Smith. 2021. "General Social Surveys, 1972–2021 Cross-Section." Chicago: NORC at the University of Chicago.

Davidson, Kate. 2020. "Is $600 a Week in Extra Unemployment Aid Deterring People from Seeking Work?" *Wall Street Journal.* July 29. www.wsj.com.

Dawson, Richard E., and James A. Robinson. 1963. "Inter-party Competition, Economic Variables, and Welfare Policies in the American States." *Journal of Politics* 25 (2): 265–289.

De Jong, Gordon F., Deborah Roempke, Shelley K. Irving, and Tanja St. Pierre. 2006. "Measuring State TANF Policy Variations and Changes after Reform." *Social Science Quarterly* 87 (4): 755–781.

Dennis, Robin, Jill Braunstein, and Heidi Hartmann. 1995. *Welfare to Work: The Job Opportunities of AFDC Recipients.* Institute for Women's Policy Research.

DeSante, Christopher D. 2013. "Working Twice as Hard to Get Half as Far: Race, Work Ethic, and America's Deserving Poor." *American Journal of Political Science* 57 (2): 342–356.

Dodson, Debra L. 2006. *The Impact of Women in Congress.* New York: Oxford University Press.

Dolan, Kathleen. 2011. "Do Women and Men Know Different Things? Measuring Gender Differences in Political Knowledge." *Journal of Politics* 73 (1): 97–107.

Edmonds-Cady, Cynthia. 2009. "Mobilizing Motherhood: Race, Class, and the Uses of Maternalism in the Welfare Rights Movement." *Women's Studies Quarterly* 37 (3/4): 206–222.

Ellis, Christopher, and Christopher Faricy. 2020. "Race, 'Deservingness,' and Social Spending Attitudes: The Role of Policy Delivery Mechanism." *Political Behavior* 42: 819–843.

Ellis, William Curtis, and Walter Clark Wilson. 2013. "Minority Chairs and Congressional Attention to Minority Issues: The Effect of Descriptive Representation in Positions of Institutional Power." *Social Science Quarterly* 94 (5): 1207–1221.

English, Ashley. 2019. "She Who Shall Not Be Named: The Women That Women's Organizations Do (and Do Not) Represent in the Rulemaking Process." *Politics & Gender* 15: 572–598.

Espenshade, Thomas J., Jessica L. Baraka, and Gregory A. Huber. 1997. "Implications of the 1996 Welfare and Immigration Reform Acts for US Immigration." *Population and Development Review* 23 (4): 769–801.

Fairchild, Amy L. 2004. "Policies of Inclusion: Immigrants, Disease, Dependency, and American Immigration Policy at the Dawn and Dusk of the 20th Century." *American Journal of Public Health* 94 (4): 528–539.

Falk, Gene, and Jill Tauber. 2001. *Welfare Reform: TANF Provisions Related to Marriage and Two-Parent Families.* CRS Report for Congress.

Faricy, Christopher. 2015. *Welfare for the Wealthy: Parties, Social Spending, and Inequality in the U.S.* New York: Cambridge University Press.

Fellowes, Matthew C., and Gretchen Rowe. 2004. "Politics and the New American Welfare States." *American Journal of Political Science* 48 (2): 362–373.

Filindra, Alexandra. 2012. "Immigrant Social Policy in the American States: Race Politics and State TANF and Medicaid Eligibility Rules for Legal Permanent Residents." *State Politics & Policy Quarterly* 13 (1): 26–48.

Finn, Teaganne, and Phil McClausland. 2022. "Romney's Push to Revive Child Tax Credit Hinges on Work Requirements." *NBC News.* February 21. www.nbcnews.com.

Fix, Michael E., ed. 2009. *Immigrants and Welfare: The Impact of Welfare Reform on America's Newcomers.* New York: Russell Sage Foundation.

Food and Nutrition Service. 2020. "SNAP—Families First Coronavirus Response Act and Impact on Time Limit for Able-Bodied Adults without Dependents (ABAWDs)." *United States Department of Agriculture.* March 20. www.fns.usda.gov.

Fording, Richard C. 2003. "'Laboratories of Democracy' or Symbolic Politics? The Racial Origins of Welfare Reform." In *Race and the Politics of Welfare Reform,* edited by Sanford F. Schram, Joe Soss, and Richard C. Fording, 72–97. Ann Arbor: University of Michigan Press.

Fording, Richard C., Joe Soss, and Sanford F. Schram. 2007. "Devolution, Discretion, and the Effect of Local Political Values on TANF Sanctioning." *Social Sciences Review* 81 (2): 285–316.

Foster, Ann C., and Arcenis Rojas. 2018. "Program Participation and Spending Patterns of Families Receiving Government Means-Tested Assistance." *U.S. Bureau of Labor Statistics.* www.bls.gov.

Foster, Carly Hayden. 2008. "The Welfare Queen: Race, Gender, Class, and Public Opinion." *Race, Gender & Class* 15 (3/4): 162–179.

Franklin, Benjamin. n.d. "Poor Richard Improved, 1758." *Founders Online.* https://founders.archives.gov.

Franz, Barbara. 2007. "Guest Workers and Immigration Reform: The Rise of a New Feudalism in America?" *New Political Science* 29 (3): 349–368.

Frymer, Paul. 1999. *Uneasy Alliances: Race and Party Competition in America.* Princeton, NJ: Princeton University Press.

Fusaro, Vincent A. 2021. "State Politics, Race, and 'Welfare' as a Funding Stream: Cash Assistance Spending under Temporary Assistance for Needy Families." *Policy Studies Journal* 49 (3): 811–834.

GAO. 2009. "Sponsored Noncitizens and Public Benefits: More Clarity in Federal Guidance and Better Access to Federal Information Could Improve Implementation of Income Eligibility Rules." GAO-09-375, Washington, DC.

———. 2012. "Temporary Assistance for Needy Families: More Accountability Needed to Reflect Breadth of Block Grant Services." GAO-13-33, Washington, DC. www.gao.gov.

Gay, Claudine. 2002. "Spirals of Trust? The Effect of Descriptive Representation on the Relationship between Citizens and Their Government." *American Journal of Political Science* 46 (4): 717–732.

Gelman, Andrew, David Park, Boris Shor, and Jeronimo Cortina. 2010. *Red State, Blue State, Rich State, Poor State: Why Americans Vote the Way They Do.* Princton, NJ: Princeton University Press.

Gelman, Michael, and Melvin Stephens. 2022. "Lessons Learned from Economic Impact Payments during COVID-19." In *Recession Remedies: Lessons Learned from the U.S. Economic Policy Response to COVID-19,* edited by Wendy Edelberg, Louise Sheiner, and David Weissel. Hamilton Project. www.hamiltonproject.org.

Giannarelli, Linda, Christine Heffernan, Sarah Minton, Megan Thompson, and Kathryn Stevens. 2017. *Welfare Rules Databook: State TANF Policies as of July 2016.* OPRE Report 2017-82, Washington, DC: Office of Planning, Research, and Evaluation, Administration for Children and Families, US Department of Health and Human Services.

Gilbert, Neil. 2009. "US Welfare Reform: Rewriting the Social Contract." *Journal of Social Policy* 38 (3): 383–399.

Gilens, Martin. 1999. *Why Americans Hate Welfare: Race, Media, and the Politics of Antipoverty Policy.* Chicago: University of Chicago Press.

———. 2012. *Affluence and Influence: Economic Inequality and Political Power in America.* Princeton, NJ: Princeton University Press.

Gillin, Joshua. 2015. "Jeb Bush Did Say Women Should 'Find a Husband' to Get Off Welfare—in 1994." *Politifact.* June 15. www.politifact.com.

Goldman, Maurice. 1999. "The Violence Against Women Act: Meeting Its Goals in Protecting Battered Immigrant Women?" *Family and Conciliation Courts Review* 37 (3): 375–392.

Graefe, Deborah Roempke, Gordon F. De Jong, Matthew Hall, Samuel Sturgeon, and Julie VanEerden. 2008. "Immigrants' TANF Eligibility, 1996–2003: What Explains the New Across-State Inequalities?" *International Migration Review* 42 (1): 89–133.

Gray, Virginia, and David Lowery. 1996. *The Population Ecology of Interest Representation: Lobbying Communities in the American States.* Ann Arbor: University of Michigan Press.

Grogger, Jeff, and Stephen G. Bronars. 2001. "The Effect of Welfare Payments on the Marriage and Fertility Behavior of Unwed Mothers: Results from a Twins Experiment." *Journal of Political Economy* 109 (3): 529–545.

Gustafson, Kaaryn. 2009. "The Criminalization of Poverty." *Journal of Criminal Law and Criminology* 99 (3): 643–716.

Hahn, Heather, David Kassabian, Lina Breslav, and Yvette Lamb. 2015. "A Descriptive Study of County- versus State-Administered Temporary Assistance for Needy Programs." *Urban Institute.* www.urban.org.

Hajnal, Zoltan L., and Taeku Lee. 2011. *Why Americans Don't Join the Party: Race, Immigration, and the Failure (of Political Parties) to Engage the Electorate*. Princeton, NJ: Princeton University Press.

Halper, Thomas. 1973. "The Poor as Pawns: The New 'Deserving Poor' & the Old." *Polity* 6 (1): 71–86.

Hammond, Samuel, and Robert Orr. 2021. "The Conservative Case for a Child Allowance." *Niskanen Center*. February 4. www.niskanencenter.org.

Hancock, Ange-Marie. 2003. "Contemporary Welfare Reform and the Public Identity of the 'Welfare Queen.'" *Race, Gender & Class* 10 (1): 31–59.

———. 2004. *The Politics of Disgust: The Public Identity of the Welfare Queen*. New York: New York University Press.

Handler, Joel F., and Yeheskel Hasenfeld. 2007. *Blame Welfare, Ignore Poverty and Inequality*. New York: Cambridge University Press.

Harris, Frederick C. 2015. *The Challenges of My Brother's Keeper*. Washington, DC: Brookings Institution.

Hartig, Hannah, Andrew Daniller, Scott Keeter, and Ted Van Green. 2023. "Republican Gains in 2022 Midterms Driven Mostly by Turnout Advantage." *Pew Research Center*. July 12. www.pewresearch.org.

Haskins, Ron. 2009. "Limiting Welfare Benefits for Noncitizens: Emergence of Compromises." In *Immigrants and Welfare: The Impact of Welfare Reform on America's Newcomers*, edited by Michael E. Fix, 39–68. New York: Russell Sage Foundation.

Hatcher, Daniel L. 2012. "Don't Forget Dad: Addressing Women's Poverty by Rethinking Forced and Outdated Child Support Policies." *Journal of Gender, Social Policy & the Law* 775–796.

Hawkesworth, Mary. 2003. "Congressional Enactments of Race-Genders: Toward a Theory of Raced-Gendered Institutions." *American Political Science Review* 97 (4): 529–550.

Hays, R. Allen. 2001. *Who Speaks for the Poor? National Interest Groups and Social Policy*. New York: Routledge.

Hays, Sharon. 2003. *Flat Broke with Children: Women in the Age of Welfare Reform*. New York: Oxford University Press.

Hero, Rodney E., and Robert R. Preuhs. 2007. "Immigration and the Evolving American Welfare State: Examining Policies in the U.S. States." *American Journal of Political Science* 51 (3): 498–517.

Hill, Brent. 2015. "Guest Column: The Work We Achieve." *Idaho Falls Post Register*, September 8.

Holzer, Harry J. 2002. "Can Work Experience Programs Work for Welfare Recipients?" *Welfare Reform & Beyond*. Brookings Institution. www.brookings.edu.

hooks, bell. 2000. *Feminist Theory: From Margin to Center*. 2nd ed. Cambridge, MA: South End Press.

Hussey, Laura S., and Shanna Pearson-Merkowitz. 2011. "The Changing Role of Race in Social Welfare Attitude Formation: Partisan Divides over Undocumented Immigrants and Social Welfare Policy." *Political Research Quarterly* 66 (3): 572–584.

Ingram, Helen, and Anne Schneider. 1991. "The Choice of Target Population." *Administration & Society* 23 (3): 333–356.

Jabbar, Huriya, Eupha Jeanne Daramola, Julie A. Marsh, Taylor Enoch-Stevens, Jacob Aloson, and Taylor N. Allbright. 2022. "Social Construction Is Racial Construction: Examining the Target Populations in School-Choice Politics." *American Journal of Education* 487–518.

Johnson, Cathy Marie, Georgia Duerst-Lahti, and Noelle H. Norton. 2007. *Creating Gender: The Sexual Politics of Welfare Policy*. Boulder, CO: Lynne Rienner Publishers.

Kahn, Peggy, and Valerie Polakow. 2002. "Struggling to Live and to Learn: Single Mothers, Welfare Policy and Post-secondary Education in Michigan." In *Work, Welfare and Politics: Confronting Poverty in the Wake of Welfare Reform*, edited by Frances Fox Piven, Joan Acker, Margaret Hallock, and Sandra Morgen, 157–174. Eugene: University of Oregon Press.

Karpman, Michael, and Gregory Acs. 2020. "Unemployment Insurance and Economic Impact Payments Associated with Reduced Hardship following CARES Act." *Urban Institute*. June. www.urban.org.

Katz, Michael B. 2008. *The Price of Citizenship: Redefining the American Welfare State*. Philadelphia: University of Pennsylvania Press.

———. 2013. *The Undeserving Poor: America's Enduring Confrontation with Poverty*. 2nd ed. New York: Oxford University Press.

Kaufmann, Karen M. 2003. "Cracks in the Rainbow: Group Commonality as a Basis for Latino and African-American Political Coalitions." *Political Research Quarterly* 56 (2): 199–210.

Kelly, Kimberly, and Linda Grant. 2007. "State Abortion and Nonmarital Birthrates in the Post–Welfare Reform Era: The Impact of Economic Incentives on Reproductive Behaviors of Teenage and Adult Women." *Gender and Society* 21 (6): 878–904.

Key, V. O. 1949. *Southern Politics in State and Nation*. New York: Alfred A. Knopf.

KFF. 2023. "Medicaid Waiver Tracker: Approved and Pending Section 1115 Waivers by State." *Kaiser Family Foundation*. June 5. www.kff.org.

Kim, Byungkyu, and Richard C. Fording. 2010. "Second-Order Devolution and the Implementation of TANF in the U.S. States." *State Politics & Policy Quarterly* 10 (4): 341–367.

Kim, Jae Yeon. 2022. "How Other Minorities Gained Access: The War on Poverty and Asian American and Latino Community Organizing." *Political Research Quarterly* 75 (1): 89–102.

King-Meadows, Tyson, and Thomas F. Schaller. 2006. *Devolution and Black State Legislators: Challenges and Choices in the Twenty-First Century*. Albany: State University of New York Press.

Klarner, Carl, Xiaotong Mao, and Stan Buchanan. 2007. "Business Interest Group Power and Temporary Assistance to Needy Families." *Social Science Quarterly* 88 (1): 104–119.

Kolhatkar, Sheelah. 2021. "Biden's Stimulus Plan Contains an Experiment in Universal Basic Income." *New Yorker*. March 15. www.newyorker.com.

Kortweg, Anna C. 2003. "Welfare Reform and the Subject of the Working Mother: 'Get a Job, a Better Job, Then a Career.'" *Theory and Society* 32: 445–480.

Kretsedemas, Philip, and Ana Aparacio, eds. 2004. *Immigrants, Welfare Reform, and the Poverty of Policy*. Westport, CT: Praeger Publications.

Leff, Mark H. 1973. "Consensus for Reform: The Mothers'-Pension Movement in the Progressive Era." *Social Service Review* 47 (3): 397–417.

Lieberman, Robert C. 1998. *Shifting the Color Line: Race and the American Welfare State*. Cambridge, MA: Harvard University Press.

Lloyd, Susan. 1997. "The Effects of Domestic Violence on Women's Employment." *Law & Policy* 19 (2): 139–167.

Lopoo, Leonard M., and Kerri M. Raissian. 2012. "Natalist Policies in the United States." *Journal of Policy Analysis and Management* 31 (4): 905–946.

Loprest, Pamela, and Elaine Maag. 2009. *Disabilities among TANF Recipients: Evidence from the NHIS*. US Department of Health and Human Services, Office of the Assistant Secretary for Planning and Evaluation.

Lowery, David. 2013. "Lobbying Influence: Meaning, Measurement and Missing." *Interest Groups and Advocacy* 2 (1): 1–26.

López, Ian Haney. 2014. *Dog Whistle Politics: How Coded Racial Appeals Have Reinvented Racism & Wrecked the Middle Class*. New York: Oxford University Press.

Luther, Catherine A., Deseriee A. Kennedy, and Terri Combs-Orne. 2005. "Intertwining of Poverty, Gender, and Race: A Critical Analysis of Welfare News Coverage from 1993–2000." *Race, Class, & Gender* 12 (2): 10–33.

Mansbridge, Jane. 1999. "Should Blacks Represent Blacks and Women Represent Women? A Contingent 'Yes.'" *Journal of Politics* 61 (3): 628–657.

Maynard, Rebecca A. 1997. "Paternalism, Teenage Pregnancy Prevention, and Teenage Parent Services." In *The New Paternalism: Supervisory Approaches to Poverty*, edited by Lawrence M. Mead. Washington, DC: Brookings Institution Press.

Mazzeo, Christopher, Sara Rab, and Susan Eachus. 2003. "Work-First or Work-Only: Welfare Reform, State Policy, and Access to Postsecondary Education." *Annals of the American Academy of Political and Social Science* (586): 144–171.

McCarthy, John D., and Mayer N. Zald. 1977. "Resource Mobilization and Social Movements: A Partial Theory." *American Journal of Sociology* 82 (6): 1212–1241.

McClain, Paula D. 1993. "The Changing Dynamics of Urban Politics: Black and Hispanic Municipal Employment—Is There Competition?" *Journal of Politics* 55 (2): 399–414.

McKernan, Signe-Mary, Jen Bernstein, and Lynne Fender. 2012. "Taming the Beast: Categorizing State Welfare Policies: A Typology of Welfare Policies Affecting Recipient Job Entry." *Journal of Policy Analysis and Management* 24 (2): 443–460.

Mead, Lawrence M. 1997. *The New Paternalism: Supervisory Approaches to Poverty*. Washington, DC: Brookings Institution Press.

Mettler, Suzanne. 1998. *Dividing Citizens: Gender and Federalism in New Deal Public Policy*. Ithaca, NY: Cornell University Press.

———. 2011. *The Submerged State: How Invisible Government Policies Undermine American Democracy*. Chicago: University of Chicago Press.

Miller, Dorothy C. 1990. *Women and Social Welfare: A Feminist Analysis*. New York: Praeger.

Miler, Kristina C. 2018. *Poor Representation: Congress and the Politics of Poverty in the United States*. New York: Cambridge University Press.

Mincy, Ronald M., and Hillard Pouncy. 1997. "Paternalism, Child Support Enforcement, and Fragile Families." In *The New Paternalism: Supervisory Approaches to Poverty*, edited by Lawrence M. Mead. Washington, DC: Brookings Institution Press.

Mink, Gwendolyn. 1990. "The Lady and the Tramp." In *Women, the State, and Welfare*, edited by Linda Gordon, 92–122. Madison: University of Wisconsin Press.

———. 1998. *Welfare's End*. Ithaca, NY: Cornell University Press.

Minta, Michael D., and Nadia E. Brown. 2014. "Intersecting Interests: Gender, Race, and Congressional Attention to Women's Issues." *Du Bois Review* 11 (2): 253–272.

Misra, Joy, Stephanie Moller, and Marina Karides. 2003. "Envisioning Dependency: Changing Media Depictions of Welfare in the 20th Century." *Social Problems* 50 (4): 482–504.

Monnat, Shannon. 2010. "The Color of Welfare Sanctioning: Exploring the Individual and Contextual Roles of Race on TANF Case Closures and Benefit Reductions." *Sociological Quarterly* 51 (4): 678–707.

Montoya, Celeste. 2020. "Intersectionality and Voting Rights." *PS: Political Science & Politics* 53 (3): 484–489.

Moynihan, Daniel Patrick. 1965. *The Negro Family: The Case for National Action*. United States Department of Labor.

Mufson, Steven, and Tracy Jan. 2017. "If You're a Poor Person in America, Trump's Budget Is Not for You." *Washington Post*. March 16. www.washingtonpost.com.

Nadasen, Premilla. 2005. *Welfare Warriors: The Welfare Rights Movement in the United States*. New York: Routledge.

National Conference of State Legislatures. 2017. "Drug Testing for Welfare Recipients and Public Assistance." *National Conference of State Legislatures*. March 24. www.ncsl.org.

National Responsible Fatherhood Clearinghouse. n.d. "About Us." www.fatherhood.gov.

Nelson, Barbara J. 1990. "The Origins of the Two-Channel Welfare State: Workmen's Compensation and Mothers' Aid." In *Women, the State, and Welfare*, edited by Linda Gordon, 123–151. Madison: University of Wisconsin Press.

Neubeck, Kenneth J., and Noel A. Cazenave. 2001. *Welfare Racism: Playing the Race Card against America's Poor*. New York: Routledge.

Newton, Una, and Brian E. Adams. 2009. "State Immigration Policies: Innovation, Cooperation or Conflict." *Publius* 39 (3): 408–431.

Ng, Doris. 2002. "From War on Poverty to War on Welfare: The Impact of Welfare Reform on the Lives of Immigrant Women." In *Work, Welfare and Politics: Confronting Poverty in the Wake of Welfare Reform*, edited by Frances Fox Piven, Joan Acker, Margaret Hallock, and Sandra Morgen, 277–288. Eugene: University of Oregon Press.

NOW. 2015. "Action Alert: Urge Your Representative to Co-sponsor the Social Security Caregiver Credit Act, A NOW Priority." August 19. http://now.org.

Ojeda, Christopher, Anne M. Whitesell, Michael B. Berkman, and Eric Plutzer. 2019. "Federalism and the Racialization of Welfare Policy." *State Politics & Policy Quarterly* 19 (4): 474–501.

Oliver, Melvin L., and Thomas M. Shapiro. 2006. *Black Wealth/White Wealth: A New Perspective on Racial Inequality*. New York: Routledge.

Olson, Mancur. 1965. *The Logic of Collective Action: Public Goods and Theory of Groups*. Cambridge, MA: Harvard University Press.

Osborn, Tracy L. 2012. *How Women Represent Women: Political Parties, Gender, and Representation in State Legislatures*. New York: Oxford University Press.

Owens, Chris T. 2005. "Black Substantive Representation in State Legislators from 1971–1994." *Social Science Quarterly* 86 (4): 779–791.

Owens, Michael Leo, and Adrienne Smith. 2012. "'Deviants' and Democracy: Punitive Policy Designs and the Social Rights of Felons as Citizens." *American Politics Research* 40 (3): 531–567.

Paden, Catherine M. 2008. "Disentangling Race and Poverty: The Civil Rights Response to Antipoverty Policy." *Du Bois Review* 5 (2): 339–368.

Page, Benjamin I., Larry M. Bartels, and Jason Seawright. 2013. "Democracy and the Policy Preferences of Wealthy Americans." *Perspective on Politics* 11 (1): 51–73.

Parrott, Sharon. 1998. "Welfare Recipients Who Find Jobs: What Do We Know about Their Employment and Earnings?" *Center on Budget and Policy Priorities*. www.cbpp.org.

Passel, Jeffrey S., and D'Vera Cohn. 2016. "Size of U.S. Unauthorized Immigrant Workforce Stable after the Great Recession." *Pew Research Center*. www.pewhispanic.org.

Pew Research Center. 2018. "Shifting Public Views on Legal Immigration Into the U.S." *Pew Research Center*. June 28. www.pewresearch.org.

———. 2019. "Little Public Support for Reductions in Federal Spending." *Pew Research Center*. April 11. www.pewresearch.org.

———. 2020. "Positive Economic Views Plummet; Support for Government Aid Crosses Party Lines." *Pew Research Center*. April 21. www.pewresearch.org.

Piston, Spencer. 2018. *Class Attitudes in America: Sympathy for the Poor, Resentment of the Rich, and Political Implications*. New York: Cambridge University Press.

Pitkin, Hannah. 1967. *The Concept of Representation*. Berkeley: University of California Press.

Piven, Frances Fox, and Richard A. Cloward. 1993. *Regulating the Poor: The Functions of Public Welfare*. New York: Vintage Books.

Postmus, Judy L. 2004. "Battered and on Welfare: The Experiences of Women with the Family Violence Option." *Journal of Sociology and Social Welfare* 31 (2): 113–123.

Preuhs, Robert. 2006. "The Conditional Effects of Minority Descriptive Representation: Black Legislators and Policy Influence in the American States." *Journal of Politics* 68 (3): 585–599.

———. 2007. "Descriptive Representation as a Mechanism to Mitigate Policy Backlash: Latino Incorporation and Welfare Policy in the American States." *Political Research Quarterly* 60 (2): 277–292.

Quadagno, Jill. 1990. "Race, Class, and Gender in the U.S. Welfare State: Nixon's Failed Family Assistance Plan." *American Sociological Review* 55 (1): 11–28.

———. 1994. *The Color of Welfare: How Racism Undermined the War on Poverty.* New York: Oxford University Press.

Reagan, Ronald. [1981] 2003. "Address before a Joint Session of Congress on the Program for Economic Recovery." In *Welfare: A Documentary History of U.S. Policy and Politics*, edited by Gwendolyn Mink and Rickie Solinger, 457–458. New York: New York University Press.

Reese, Ellen. 2005. *Backlash against Welfare Mothers: Past and Present.* Berkeley: University of California Press.

Reingold, Beth, Kerry L. Haynie, and Kirsten Widner. 2021. *Race, Gender, and Political Representation: Toward a More Intersectional Approach.* New York: Oxford University Press.

Reingold, Beth, and Adrienne R. Smith. 2012. "Welfare Policymaking and Intersections of Race, Ethnicity, and Gender in U.S. State Legislatures." *American Journal of Political Science* 56 (1): 131–147.

Republican Party. 2016. "2016 Republican Party Platform Online." *American Presidency Project.* www.presidency.ucsb.edu.

Rigby, Elizabeth, and Gerald C. Wright. 2013. "Political Parties and Representation of the Poor in the American States." *American Journal of Political Science* 57 (3): 552–565.

Roberts, Dorothy. 2017. *Killing the Black Body: Race, Reproduction, and the Meaning of Liberty.* New York: Vintage Books.

Rodgers, Harrell R., and Kent L. Tedin. 2006. "State TANF Spending: Predictors of State Tax Effort to Support Welfare Reform." *Review of Policy Research* 23 (3): 745–759.

Romney, Mitt. 2021. "Romney Offers Path to Provide Greater Financial Security for American Families." *Mitt Romney: U.S. Senator for Utah.* February 4. www.romney.senate.gov.

Roosevelt, Franklin Delano. [1938] 2003. "A Social Security Program Must Include All Those Who Need Its Protection." In *Welfare: A Documentary History of U.S. Policy and Politics*, edited by Gwendolyn Mink and Rickie Solinger, 77–80. New York: New York University Press.

Rubio, Marco. 2014. "Reclaiming the Land of Opportunity: Conservative Reforms for Combatting Poverty." January 8. www.rubio.senate.gov.

Rucker, Philip. 2009. *Sen. DeMint of S.C. Is Voice of Opposition to Health-Care Reform.* July 28. www.washingtonpost.com.

Samuels, Robert. 2018. "Wisconsin Is the GOP Model for 'Welfare Reform.' But as Work Requirements Grow, So Does One Family's Desperation." *Washington Post*. April 22. www.washingtonpost.com.

Sapiro, Virginia. 1990. "The Gender Basis of American Social Policy." In *Women, the State, and Welfare*, edited by Linda Gordon, 36–54. Madison: University of Wisconsin Press.

Schattschneider, E. E. 1960. *The Semisovereign People: A Realist's View of Democracy in America*. New York: Holt, Rinehart and Winston.

Schlozman, Kay Lehman, and John T. Tierney. 1986. *Organized Interests and American Democracy*. New York: Harper & Row.

Schlozman, Kay Lehman, Sidney Verba, and Henry E. Brady. 2012. *Unheavenly Chorus: Unequal Political Voice and the Broken Promise of American Democracy*. Princeton, NJ: Princeton University Press.

Schneider, Anne, and Helen Ingram. 1993. "Social Construction of Target Populations: Implications for Politics and Policy." *American Political Science Review* 87 (2): 334–347.

Schochet, Leila. 2019. "The Child Care Crisis Is Keeping Women Out of the Workforce." *Center for American Progress*. March 28. www.americanprogress.org.

Schorr, Lisbeth B. 2019. "Piecing Together the Real Woman behind Reagan's 'Welfare Queen.'" May 31. www.washingtonpost.com.

Schott, Liz. 1998. "State Choices on Time Limit Policies on TANF-Funded Programs." *Center for Budget and Policy Priorities*. September 1. www.cbpp.org.

Schuessler, Alexander A. 2000. *A Logic of Expressive Choice*. Princeton, NJ: Princeton University Press.

Scott, Rachel, and Benjamin Siegel. 2021. "Sen. Joe Manchin Suggests Child Tax Credit Would Used to Buy Drugs." *ABC News*. December 20. https://abcnews.go.com.

Seccombe, Karen, Delores James, and Kimberly Battle-Walters. 1998. "'They Think You Ain't Much of Nothing': The Social Construction of the Welfare Mother." *Journal of Marriage and the Family* 60 (4): 849–865.

Shantz, Katie, Ilham Dehry, Sarah Knowles, Sarah Minton, and Linda Giannarelli. 2020. *Welfare Rules Databook: State TANF Policies as of July 2019*. OPRE Report 2020–141, Washington, DC: Office of Planning, Research, and Evaluation, Administration for Children and Families, US Department of Health and Human Services.

Skocpol, Theda. 1992. *Protecting Mothers and Soldiers: The Political Origins of Social Policy in the United States*. Cambridge, MA: Belknap Press of Harvard University Press.

Smith, Anna Marie. 2007. *Welfare Reform and Sexual Regulation*. New York: Cambridge University Press.

Smith, Mark A. 2000. *American Business and Political Power: Public Opinion, Elections, and Democracy*. Chicago: University of Chicago Press.

Solinger, Rickie. 2001. *Beggars and Choosers: How the Politics of Choice Shapes Adoption, Abortion, and Welfare in the United States*. New York: Hill & Wang.

Soss, Joe, Richard C. Fording, and Sanford F. Schram. 2008. "The Color of Devolution: Race, Federalism, and the Politics of Social Control." *American Journal of Political Science* 52 (3): 536–553.

———. 2011. *Disciplining the Poor: Neoliberal Paternalism and the Persistent Power of Race*. Chicago: University of Chicago Press.

Soss, Joe, Sanford F. Schram, Thomas P. Vartanian, and Erin O'Brien. 2001. "Setting the Terms of Relief: Explaining State Policy Choices in the Devolution Revolution." *American Journal of Political Science* 45 (2): 378–395.

Sparks, Holloway. 2003. "Queens, Teens, and Model Mothers: Race, Gender, and the Discourse of Welfare Reform." In *Race and the Politics of Welfare Reform*, edited by Sanford F. Schram, Joe Soss, and Richard C. Fording, 171–195. Ann Arbor: University of Michigan Press.

Speiglman, Richard, Rosa-Maria Castaneda, Hana Brown, and Randy Capps. 2013. "Welfare Reform's Ineligible Immigrant Parents: Program Reach and Enrollment Barriers." *Journal of Children and Poverty* 19 (2): 91–106.

Sribnick, Ethan G. 2011. "The Origins of Modern Child Welfare: Liberalism, Interest Groups, and the Transformation of Public Policy in the 1970s." *Journal of Policy History* 23 (2): 150–176.

Stapleton, David C., David C. Wittenburg, Michael E. Fishman, and Gina A. Livermore. 2002. "Transitions from AFDC to SSI before Welfare Reform." *Social Security Bulletin* 64 (1): 84–114.

Stauffer, Katelyn E., and Bernard L. Fraga. 2022. "Contextualizing the Gender Gap in Voter Turnout." *Politics, Groups, and Identities* 10 (2): 334–341.

Stern, Naomi. 2003. "Battered by the System: How Advocates against Domestic Violence Have Improved Victims' Access to Child Support and TANF." *Hastings Women's Law Journal* 14 (1): 47–69.

Stewart, Julie, and Kenneth P. Jameson. 2012. "Interests Aren't Everything: An Exploration of Economic Explanations of Immigration Policy in a New Destination." *International Migration* 51 (4): 33–52.

Strolovitch, Dara. 2007. *Affirmative Advocacy: Race, Class, and Gender in Interest Group Politics*. Chicago: University of Chicago Press.

Swers, Michele L. 2002. *The Difference Women Make: The Policy Impact of Women in Congress*. Chicago: University of Chicago Press.

Tate, Katherine. 1993. *From Protest to Politics: The New Black Voters in American Elections*. New York: Russell Sage Foundation.

Tax Policy Center. 2020. "Briefing Book." *Urban Institute and Brookings Institution*. www.taxpolicycenter.org.

Tebben, Susan. 2021. "Federal Funding for Low-Income Families Stayed in State Coffers amid Pandemic." *Ohio Capital Journal*. April 12. https://ohiocapitaljournal .com.

Tickamyer, Ann R., and Debra A. Henderson. 2010. "Devolution, Social Exclusion, and Spatial Inequality in U.S. Welfare Provision." In *Welfare Reform in Rural Places:*

Comparative Perspectives, edited by Paul Milbourne and Terry Marsden. Bingley: Emerald Group Publishing Limited.

Toshkov, Dimiter, David Lowery, Brendan Carroll, and Joost Berkhout. 2013. "Timing Is Everything? Organized Interests and the Timing of Legislative Activity." *Interest Groups & Advocacy* 48–70.

Triece, Mary E. 2013. *Tell It Like It Is: Women in the National Welfare Rights Movement.* Columbia: University of South Carolina Press.

Truman, David. 1951. *The Governmental Process: Political Interests and Public Opinion.* New York: Alfred Knopf.

Trump, Donald J. 2019. "Press Release—Pro-growth Economic Policies Benefit Previously Left Behind Americans the Most." *American Presidency Project.* www .presidency.ucsb.edu.

———. 2020. "Remarks at a White House Coronavirus Task Force Press Briefing." *American Presidency Project.* www.presidency.ucsb.edu.

United States Department of Labor. 1931. "Mothers' Aid, 1931." *Bureau Publication No. 220.* www.mchlibrary.org.

Uttermark, Matthew J., Kenneth R. Mackie, and Carol S. Weissert. 2023. "The Color of Discretion: Race and Ethnicity Biases in School Suspension." *Polity* 55 (2): 302–331.

Van Hook, Jennifer, and Frank D. Bean. 2009. "Explaining Mexican-Immigrant Welfare Behaviors: The Importance of Employment-Related Cultural Repertoires." *American Sociological Review* 74 (3): 423–444.

Ventura, Patricia. 2012. *Neoliberal Culture: Living with American Neoliberalism.* Abingdon: Ashgate Publishing Group.

Verba, Sidney, Nancy Burns, and Kay Lehman Schlozman. 1997. "Knowing and Caring about Politics: Gender and Political Engagement." *Journal of Politics* 59 (4): 1051–1072.

Verma, Seema. 2017. "Remarks at the National Association of Medicaid Directors (NAMD) 2017 Fall Conference." www.cms.gov.

Volden, Craig. 2002. "The Politics of Competitive Federalism: A Race to the Bottom in Welfare Benefits?" *American Journal of Political Science* 46 (2): 352–363.

Wagan, J. B. 2018. "Wisconsin's Unprecedented Welfare Reform Could Inspire Conservative Changes Elsewhere." *Governing.* February 22. www.governing.com.

Walker, Christina, and Stephanie Schmit. 2016. "A Closer Look at Latino Access to Child Care Subsidies." *CLASP.* www.clasp.org.

Wallace, Sophia J. 2014. "Representing Latinos: Examining Descriptive and Substantive Representation in Congress." *Political Research Quarterly* 67 (4): 917–929.

Ward, Deborah E. 2005. *The White Welfare State: The Racialization of U.S. Welfare Policy.* Ann Arbor: University of Michigan Press.

Wasem, Ruth Ellen. 2004. *Noncitizen Eligibility for Major Federal Public Assistance Programs: Policies and Legislation.* Congressional Research Service.

Weaver, R. Kent. 2000. *Ending Welfare as We Know It.* Washington, DC: Brookings Institution Press.

Werner, Erica, and Alan Fram. 2017. "House to Vote on Health Care Bill Thursday." *Chicago Tribune.* May 3. www.chicagotribune.com.

West, Guida. 1981. *The National Welfare Rights Movement: The Social Protest of Poor Women*. New York: Praeger.

Wheaton, Laura, Tracy Vericker, Jonathan Schwabish, Theresa Anderson, Kevin Baier, Joseph Gasper, Nathan Sick, and Kevin Werner. 2021. "The Impact of SNAP Able Bodied Adults Without Dependents (ABAWD) Time Limit Reinstatement in Nine States." *Urban Institute*. June 22. www.urban.org.

Whitesell, Anne. 2019. "Who Represents the Needs of Domestic Violence Survivors in State Welfare Policy?" *Politics & Gender* 15 (3): 514–546.

Whitney, Cynthia G., Fangjun Zhou, James Singleton, and Anne Schuchat. 2014. "Benefits from Immunization during the Vaccines for Children Program Era—United States, 1994–2013." *Morbidity and Mortality Weekly Report* 63 (16): 352–355. www.cdc.gov.

Wiener, Elizabeth. 2021. "Getting a High Heel in the Door: An Experiment on State Legislator Responsiveness to Women's Issue Lobbying." *Political Research Quarterly* 74 (3): 729–743.

Will, Jeffrey A. 1993. "The Dimensions of Poverty: Public Perceptions of the Deserving Poor." *Social Science Research* 22: 312–332.

Will, Jeffrey A., and John K. Cochran. 1995. "God Helps Those Who Help Themselves? The Effects of Religious Affiliation, Religiosity, and Deservedness on Generosity toward the Poor." *Sociology of Religion* 56 (3): 327–338.

Wilson, Reid. 2018. "Wisconsin Welfare Reform Could Be Model for GOP." *The Hill*. February 21. https://thehill.com.

Wilson, Walter Clark. 2010. "Descriptive Representation and Latino Interest Bill Sponsorship in Congress." *Social Science Quarterly* 91 (4): 1043–1062.

Winston, Pamela. 2002. *Welfare Policymaking in the States: The Devil in Devolution*. Washington, DC: Georgetown University Press.

Wolbrecht, Christina. 2000. *The Politics of Women's Rights: Parties, Positions, and Change*. Princeton, NJ: Princeton University Press.

Wong, Carolyn. 2006. *Lobbying for Inclusion: Rights Politics and the Making of Immigration Policy*. Stanford, CA: Stanford University Press.

Ybarra, Vickie D., Lisa M. Sanchez, and Gabriel R. Sanchez. 2016. "Anti-immigrant Anxieties in State Policy: The Great Recession and Punitive Immigration Policy in the American States, 2005–2012." *State Politics & Policy Quarterly* 16 (3): 313–339.

Zatz, Noah. 2006. *What Welfare Requires from Work*. Research Paper No. 06 33, UCLA School of Law Public Law & Legal Theory Research Paper Series.

Zimmerman, Wendy, and Karen C. Tumlin. 1999. "Patchwork Policies: State Assistance for Immigrants under Welfare Reform." *Urban Institute*. https://webarchive.urban.org.

ABOUT THE AUTHOR

ANNE M. WHITESELL is Assistant Professor of Political Science at Miami University. Her research on the intersection of representation and public policy has been published in *Politics & Gender*, *State Politics & Policy Quarterly*, and *Policy Studies Journal*. She received her PhD in Political Science and Women's, Gender, and Sexuality Studies from the Pennsylvania State University in 2017.

www.ingramcontent.com/pod-product-compliance
Lightning Source LLC
Chambersburg PA
CBHW031141020426
42333CB00013B/473